Perspectives on Development:
The Euro-Mediterranean Partnership

T0320499

Books of Related Interest

The Euro-Mediterranean Partnership
Political and Economic Perspectives

Richard Gillespie, University of Portsmouth (ed.)

Southern European Welfare States
Between Crisis and Reform

Martin Rhodes, European University Institute, Florence (ed.)

The Regions and the European Community
The Regional Response to the Single Market in the Underdeveloped Areas

Robert Leonardi, London School of Economics (ed.)

The Political Economy of Regionalism

Michael Keating, University of Western Ontario and John Loughlin,
University of Wales, Cardiff (eds.)

Perspectives on Development:
The Euro-Mediterranean Partnership

Edited by George Joffé

FRANK CASS
LONDON • PORTLAND, OR

First published in 1999 in Great Britain by
FRANK CASS PUBLISHERS
Newbury House, 900 Eastern Avenue
London IG2 7HH

and in the United States of America by
FRANK CASS PUBLISHERS
c/o ISBS
5804 N.E. Hassalo Street
Portland, Oregon 97213-3644

Website: http://www.frankcass.com

British Library Cataloguing in Publication Data
Perspectives on development : the Euro-Mediterranean
partnership
1. Mediterranean Region – Economic policy. 2. Mediterranean
Region – Economic conditions 3. Mediterranean Region –
Commerce – European Union countries 4. European Union
countries – Commerce – Mediterranean Region
I. Joffé, E. G. H. (E. George H.)
382.9'4'01822

ISBN 0 7146 4939 2
ISBN 0 7146 4499 4

Library of Congress Cataloging-in-Publication Data
Perspectives on development : the Euro-mediterranean partnership /
edited by George Joffé.
    p. cm.
Includes bibliographical references and index.
ISBN 0-7146-4939-2. – ISBN 0-7146-4499-4 (pbk.)
    1. Free trade–Mediterranean Region. 2. European Union
countries–Foreign economic relations–Mediterranean Region–
3. Mediterranean Region–Foreign economic relations–European
countries–Congresses. 4. European Union–Mediterranean Region
–Congresses. 5. Economic development–Congresses.
I. Joffé, E. G. H. (E. George H.)
HF2290.7.P47   1998
337.40182'2–dc21   98–42274
                                                CIP

This group of studies first appeared in a Special Issue on 'Perspectives
on Development: the Euro-Mediterranean Partnership' of
Journal of North African Studies (ISSN 1362-9387) 3/2 (Summer 1998).

Contents

Introduction

The Euro-Mediterranean Partnership Initiative (EMPI) formally unveiled at the Barcelona conference on 27–28 November 1995, sought to create a 'zone of peace and prosperity' in the Mediterranean Basin by the year 2010. This was to be achieved, in the economic sphere at least, by the institution of a series of bilateral free trade agreements between the European Union and the individual countries of the South Mediterranean rim.

The European Union had long sought to influence economic development in the region through a series of Association and Cooperation Agreements that go back to 1969. The new agreements were novel, however, in that they provided for mutual removals of tariff barriers to free trade in industrial goods. Europe had removed its barriers for industrial goods from the Mediterranean region long before, but for the Mediterranean states themselves this was a major step to take. It was hoped that the removal of tariff barriers and the resulting free competition with European industry would provide the stimulus necessary to create self-sustainable economic development in Mediterranean partner countries.

In order to investigate the EMPI proposals and the likelihood of their success, the Middle East Programme at the Royal Institute of International Affairs embarked on an 18-month project from September 1996 to March 1998. This project was designed to test the various assumptions that had been built into the European Union's initiative. Beyond that, it was intended to compare developmental experiences in other parts of the world and examine the extent to which the European Union's assumptions corresponded with past experience. Its ultimate objective was to assess the likely outcome of the Initiative and to determine what additional initiatives might be required to allow it to succeed.

In order to achieve these objectives, a group of researchers was brought together to engage in a series of seminars which would investigate different aspects of the initiative itself. They included development and trade economists, regional specialists and experts on Latin America and South-East Asia. In view of the fact that the Euro-Mediterranean Partnership also included social, cultural, political and security provisions, commentators were brought in to cover these areas as well. The researcher for the project defined the actual research agenda and laid out the terms of reference for a series of six research workshops and for the papers that were presented at them. Each workshop consisted of three sessions, each of which addressed a specific topic through a presenter and a discussant, followed by general discussion.

This special edition of the *Journal of North African Studies* contains most of the papers presented in the six workshops (listed below). The complete findings of the project will be published in a book by George Joffé in 1999.

Workshop One, Taroudant, Morocco, 8/9 December 1996,
The Euro-Mediterranean Partnership Programme (Papers 1–4).
Workshop Two, London, 5 March 1997,
The EU-Med Initiative in Context: the New Global Economic Order (Papers 5–7).
Workshop Three, Tozeur, Tunisia, 17/18 May 1997,
Cultural Outlook and Economic Behaviour (Papers 8–10).
Workshop Four, London, 24 July 1997,
Development Models for North Africa? Comparisons and Contrasts (Papers 11–13).
Workshop Five, Casablanca, 11/12 October 1997,
The Security Agenda (Paper 14).
Workshop Six, London, 9 January 1998,
Overall Review, Scenarios and Evaluation (Papers 15–16).

The Royal Institute of International Affairs would like to thank the Leverhulme Trust, the European Commission and the United States Institute of Peace for their generous finding of this project.

The Editor would like to thank Valerie Grove for her tireless work in organising and administering both the seminars and this book. He would also like to express his gratitude to Dr Rosemary Hollis, Head of the Middle East Programme, for her support and encouragement.

Euro-Med Free Trade Area for 2010: Whom Will it Benefit?

EBERHARD RHEIN

Introduction

Never before have so many countries with such different levels of development, the richest disposing of some 20 times the per capita revenue of the poorest, attempted to establish free trade among themselves. This policy declaration therefore constitutes an extraordinarily ambitious political blueprint which made policy makers wary of fixing a single legal mould for all 27 signatories of the Barcelona Declaration. What has been established is one basic model of agreement to be further negotiated between the EU and the 12 Mediterranean countries. Implementation of the overall objective of realising Euro-Mediterranean free trade by 2010 will be done in stages, and each of the 12 countries will be free to decide how they would like to establish free trade amongst themselves, parallel to the creation of their free trade area with the EU. They are also free to decide on the form of their future trade relations with Eastern Europe.

The foreign ministers of the 15 EU states insisted that the free trade area be fully compatible with the provisions of the WTO, particularly with regard to coverage of products, but could not agree to include agricultural trade fully in their scheme, despite objections from the Mediterranean partner countries. The EU was only prepared to accept a progressive liberalisation 'through reciprocal preferential access among the parties'.

There were few ministers or even high officials who had proceeded with substantive debate on the underlying assumptions and pre-conditions required to assure a successful outcome of the enterprise. Rather politicians went ahead having accepted the basic aims, leaving more thorough scrutiny of the actual policies necessary to those charged with implementation. However, implementation of the overall Euro-Mediterranean policy concept is actually more advanced than most people are aware. Indeed, at the end of 1997 almost half of the EU's overall trade with Mediterranean countries was

Dr. Eberhard Rhein is former Director for the Mediterranean, Near and Middle East at the Commission of the European Communities.

already taking place under conditions of free trade:

(i) with the Union's two major trading partners in the Mediterranean,
Turkey and Israel (free trade was actually achieved with these two
countries by 1996), and with Cyprus and Malta. Initial agreements
were negotiated with all of these countries between 1964 and 1978;

(ii) with Morocco, Tunisia, Palestine and Jordan, all of which signed free
trade agreements between 1995 and 1997;

(iii) with Algeria, Egypt, Syria and Lebanon, all of which have ongoing
negotiations.

Considering that these developments are already underway, there are good
reasons to believe that the establishment of progressive free trade within the
Euro-Mediterranean area will be realised, if not in time for the target date of
2010, then by no later than 2015. Significantly, Israel and Turkey signed the
first free trade agreement *between* Mediterranean countries in 1997.

The Meaning of Euro-Mediterranean Free Trade

The idea of Euro-Mediterranean free trade was born in the wake of the EU's
free trade reach towards Central and Eastern Europe in the early 1990s, after
the fall of the Berlin Wall. Back in the 1970s, however, long before these
crucial developments, the Mediterranean had become involved in unilateral
free trade with the European Community. For almost 20 years the countries
of the Maghrib and the Mashrik enjoyed essentially free access to most of
the European market, without any reciprocity on their part.

The results of that unilateral free trade have not been impressive with
only two countries, Morocco and Tunisia, having really benefited. The
growth of their garment industry and intensive sub-contracting in that sector
would not have been conceivable without the advantageous conditions of
access that Europe offered as of 1978, with the entry into force of co-
operation agreements. However, industrial development and trade in
manufactured products remained essentially limited to this one major sector.
The impact of the unilateral trade regime on the other countries of the
region, Algeria, Egypt, Lebanon, Syria and Jordan, was almost nil. There
was no development of manufactured exports to Europe, nor was industrial
development encouraged, except locally. The countries remained largely
closed to the rest of the world, not only Europe but even Asia and America.

This deplorable lack of a positive response from entrepreneurs, either in
the Mediterranean countries or in Europe, to selling without any
impediment in the world's most affluent market can be essentially explained
by three factors:

- throughout the 1970s and 1980s all Mediterranean countries had tried to develop their economies by import substitution and high protective barriers, so none of them was prepared to compete outside: most of their manufactured products were geared to internal consumption and were not competitive in terms of either price or quality;
- by the mid-1970s the entrepreneurial class in the Mediterranean countries was not strong and not keen on investing in manufacturing;
- the overall regulatory environment with excessive government intervention in the economy was not conducive to attracting European investors to the Mediterranean: they were much more likely to go to East Asia and Latin America, both of which appeared more promising.

When the idea of reciprocal free trade resurfaced for the Mediterranean at the beginning of the 1990s, the international framework had dramatically changed from the mid-1970s when Europe had concluded the first generation of asymmetrical free trade agreements with the Maghrib and the Mashrik. Trade liberalisation had become the accepted paradigm throughout the world and the doctrine of industrialisation through import substitution had been thrown overboard, essentially under the impact of impressive export-led growth in East Asia. Free trade areas had become more popular than ever with a great number of projects under discussion or negotiation, and, most significantly, the value of a competitive environment for economic development was rated more highly.

From the European perspective, it was not so much the progressive abolition of all import barriers or the free and preferential access that European business would obtain in the Mediterranean markets that mattered, but the reform process and enhancement of competitiveness that were expected to go along with the establishment of free trade. Free trade was seen as a catalyst that would bring about urgently necessary but difficult reforms in the overall business environment.

The individual free trade agreements to be concluded between the EU and Mediterranean countries were therefore seen as part of a strategy to create a Euro-Mediterranean area whose members would not only abolish all trade obstacles but also adopt a whole range of common rules and procedures for doing trade and business among themselves (customs, competition, subsidies, intellectual property, standards, convertibility of currencies, free movement of capital, rules of origin, etc.). Thus the EU strongly encouraged similar arrangements to be negotiated among the Mediterranean countries themselves as the EU considered intra-Mediterranean free trade as a precondition for cumulation of rules of origin to be really effective.

From the Mediterranean point of view, the EU concept of Euro-

Mediterranean free trade had one major flaw: it did not include (or inadequately included) trade in agricultural products. The European side was unable to fully include agricultural products in this system as had also been the case in previous agreements with the EFTA countries and with the Central and Eastern European countries. The EU simply could not afford to put its agriculture at risk by exposing it, even in the long-term, to competition from neighbouring countries. Furthermore, the inclusion of agriculture into the free trade scheme was not integral to WTO terms, given that agriculture amounts to less than 10 per cent of total EU-Mediterranean trade (except for Israel and Morocco) and that most of that trade is not subject to import duties on the part of the EU.

From a short-term political and economic point of view, this may have been justified. Indeed, sectoral and regional interests within the Union were so strong that it proved impossible to envisage any generous offer to the Mediterranean partners for open access to their fruit and vegetable production. Objectively, however, this is proving to be short-sighted both from an overall economic perspective and even from an agricultural one: economically it is quite clear that at least in the short term there are some, albeit limited, export possibilities for the Mediterranean countries in this sector which would have helped to partially offset the soaring trade deficit with the EU. From a longer-term agricultural perspective, it is quite evident that essentially all of the Mediterranean countries are bound to become, sooner or later, net importers of agricultural products like grains, dairy products and meat, for which Europe will possess durable export capabilities.

Nevertheless, and whatever the reasoning, agricultural free trade between Europe and the Mediterranean countries will not be on the cards for another 10-15 years, until the EU realises that agriculture is just an ordinary economic sector, like industry or services, that will have to be subject to the same basic rules of competition, including prohibition of subsidies. However, it is clear that it is not trade in agricultural products that will be the most dynamic element in future Euro-Mediterranean trade relations. Overall, the emphasis had to be more on industry than on agriculture as it is in that sector where prospects for employing growing numbers of people appear to be the most favourable and where the need for catching up with worldwide competition, especially from Asia, is greatest.

Euro-Mediterranean free trade is, therefore, essentially industrial, although in the longer term it is quite possible that the free trade area might evolve into a more comprehensive Euro-Mediterranean Economic Area, as did the EU relationship with the EFTA countries in the late 1980s. Nobody should be under any illusion, however, that such a development is likely for at least another decade and certainly not until industrial free trade has passed the difficult tests ahead and Europe and its Mediterranean neighbours have grown much more closely interwoven than they are today.

Prerequisites for Euro-Mediterranean Free Trade

The prospect of dismantling all trade obstacles between Europe and its Mediterranean neighbours not only raises concerns but also raises hopes on the part of governments and business. Concerns about whether the free trade area can actually function rest on whether European industry will crush the small and mostly inefficient industries on the other side of the Mediterranean and whether Mediterranean business has the stamina to defend itself and make inroads into the vast European market. The hope that European (or Asian and American) investors will finally flood into the Maghrib and Mashrik to build manufacturing capacities for the global market is also questioned.

Such apprehensions are understandable, but what is particular in this case is the fact that the apprehensions are all concentrated on the Mediterranean side–European business has hardly taken note of the grand Euro-Mediterranean design launched in Barcelona because in its overall global strategies the Mediterranean neighbourhood does not loom large. Nor have European unions expressed any exaggerated fears about jobs being lost in favour of additional investments in the Mediterranean.

This situation contrasts significantly with the one in North America during the very heated debates that took place on the creation of NAFTA in the early 1990s. Here, US business and unions expressed many fears about massive outflow of jobs and inflow of Mexican-produced cheap consumer goods flooding the American market. However, different assessments of similar policy prospects in Europe on the one hand, and in the USA on the other, reflect the considerable differences in the objective situations on both sides:

- When Europe launched the idea of reciprocal free trade with the Mediterranean it had already completely opened its market to manufactures from those countries. It had suffered adjustments in the textile and clothing sector during the late 1970s and early 1980s, but that process had been completed;
- Europe had been traditionally running a considerable export surplus with its Mediterranean neighbours, while the opposite was true for the USA and Mexico, reflecting differences of relative industrial strength and competitiveness.

Therefore, when asking about the prerequisites for Euro-Mediterranean free trade we find that at the European end not much remains to be done on the trade related aspects. European industry will not have to face another painful adjustment process and whatever additional competition may appear from the Mediterranean in time, it is not perceived as a great danger. By the turn of the century European industry will be confronted by far bigger challenges resulting from other advanced countries when it comes to high-tech industries, and from Asian countries as far as traditional manufactures are concerned. Still, Europe has a part to play in making Euro-Mediterranean free trade work smoothly:

- It is up to the European Union to help its Mediterranean partners in defining and implementing the accompanying policies without which free trade is unlikely to work successfully. This requires a constant, informal policy dialogue between the two sides. It is not for the EU to interfere in the internal policies of its partners but the EU does have considerable experience in devising and implementing appropriate policies for encouraging economic and technological change which it can share with those Mediterranean partners interested.
- The European Union is also under a political obligation to assist its partners financially, as it has amply done in Eastern Europe. Very few people, on either side, are fully aware of the gulf that separates Europe from the Mediterranean when it comes to levels of education, infrastructure and industrial efficiency. Without this performance gap being narrowed, it will prove difficult for most Mediterranean countries to fully avail themselves of the opportunities that free trade with Europe offers. It would indeed be fatal for the health of the free trade area if it were to be perceived as serving predominantly European interests when a balance of advantage remains of critical importance. It is all the more necessary to bear these basic facts in mind as future EU enlargement towards the East drains Europe's overall financial resources.
- Ultimately, the success of Euro-Mediterranean free trade will depend on the extent to which European business will get actively involved in establishing partnerships and joint ventures with Mediterranean counterparts. Indeed, it is at this level that the most important information is available, not in public administrations.

European business, however, is globally active and the extent to which it will become more active around the Mediterranean will much depend on whether the overall political and economic environment compares advantageously with other parts of the world. The changes that have to be encouraged and the role governments should play in the adjustment process need examination but there is no doubt that business itself must be the primary mover. Without an adequate and constructive response from the business community, free trade risks the kind of failure which destroys the existing structures of tiny workshops and manufacturing geared to the local or, at best, the national markets. These concerns work with outmoded tools of management and technology and produce goods which rarely reach the quality standards of the European or the world market. It is this fact that presents the real conundrum of successfully implementing free trade between such unequal partners.

Conventional wisdom in Europe and other parts of the developed world tells us that social groups, if exposed to the right competitive pressure, will develop positively corresponding reactions, and there is no reason that this should not also apply to the business community around the Mediterranean. However, the process of adjustment will only be facilitated if the external environment is favourable to economic and social change and this environment needs to be stimulated. Tunisia and Morocco, following the Portuguese example, have been leading the way in this regard. Both are embarking on a process of 'upgrading' or 'mise à niveau' as the basic strategy to be followed by the business community. Business associations have become fully involved in this and it is up to them to assist their members by offering advice, management courses and possibilities for exploring external markets etc. However, much remains to be done through more intensive co-operation between European and Mediterranean chambers of commerce, industry and other commercial associations.

It is inevitable that some entrepreneurs will do better than others in this process of adapting to a totally new competitive environment but, again, it is up to the more successful to help the less talented to find their way by teaching them some of the basic lessons of their success. Indeed, much of the success of the free trade approach will depend on small numbers of businessmen with medium-size and flourishing export-oriented companies who have demonstrated the capacity to work even under unfavourable conditions. It is up to these companies to develop small business groups in various sectors and thereby improve the overall business environment for the smaller and less resourceful handicraft and trading companies. Turkey sets an example in this respect: much of its impressive industrial development would have been inconceivable without the gifted leadership of a relatively small number of creative entrepreneurs. In Morocco, Tunisia and Egypt we find encouraging signs of similar trends.

Industrial development depends on a viable financial system that is able and willing to help finance industrial expansion and modernisation, either through long-term loans or through participation in the companies' capital. The absence of a strong, innovative banking sector has been a stumbling block for industrial and economic development in most Mediterranean countries and continues to be so in at least two of them (Algeria and Syria). In others, remarkable progress has been made towards a more diversified banking sector, including investment banking, so it is no longer possible to attribute the shortcomings of industrial development in most of the Mediterranean countries to the weaknesses of their banking sectors.

That said, however, progressive privatisation of the banking sector remains a decisive step to be taken by all the countries, if only to attract more international banks into the region and thereby enhance the competitiveness of banking within the Mediterranean. This should take place through appropriate regulatory authorities as everywhere else in the world, and in order to encourage a smooth transition to free trade without excessive economic or social havoc, governments should avoid too much *laisser-faire* or too much interventionism in the process. Indeed, there is no reason for governments to maintain control of borrowing and lending through ownership in the banking sector.

It will not be possible for the governments of Mediterranean countries simply to declare the progressive dismantling of external protections (against the EU) and sit back as business goes ahead with the job of adjusting. However, neither should government bureaucracies intervene directly into the way the adjustment process takes place. They should not attempt to make decisions on behalf of entrepreneurs about what is produced, where it is produced, with what technology or with which foreign partner. The role of governments in this process is actually much more fundamental. First of all, they have to explain to their constituencies the rationale behind Euro-Mediterranean free trade. This means promoting a wide-ranging debate within society aimed at giving everyone a sufficient grasp of basic economic notions to understand what the process is about, even if they may not fully approve of it. In Tunisia, Morocco, Egypt and Jordan such a debate has been effectively taking place for a few years now, beyond what is required to get the agreements ratified by parliaments. This debate has been instrumental in changing mentalities and making policy makers, bureaucrats and above all the business community, aware of the changing external conditions and of the need to adjust and to plunge into the global economy whatever the future of Euro-Mediterranean links.

Secondly, governments are responsible for putting into place a regulatory framework that is conducive to performance, efficiency and competitiveness. Behind this notion are a host of measures that each of the participating countries need to define and deliver as a medium-term programme of legislative reforms. This is indeed the heart of the matter–without far-reaching reforms of the overall economic and political environment the risks of the whole approach are magnified. Among the reforms accompanying successful free trade the following ought to be especially mentioned:

- *Full respect for the rule of law*
  Laws, both penal and civil, have to be applied without regard for the person. This requires that laws are non-discriminatory, universally applicable and accessible to everybody. Equally important is a functioning judiciary–cases must not remain pending and thus unresolved for many years, nor must there be any doubt about the impartiality and independence of the judges. In this respect, most of the Mediterranean countries have a major backlog of reforms. Much more emphasis should be placed on this crucial part of the business environment; and the EU should be prepared to assist their partners in this complex and time-consuming task.
- *Full respect of the basic rules of the market economy*
  Prices must not be fixed or influenced by government bureaucracies and this also applies to the prices of land, property, rents, interest rates, water and electricity tariffs. Where severe discrepancies between present regulated prices and free market prices have been evident, the transition period provides time for adjustment and for existing price regimes to be phased out.
- *Freedom for the employers*
  In an open market, companies must have the facility to adjust their labour force to changing conditions of demand. If competitiveness is to become the goal, companies must not be hampered by a redundant work force or be reluctant to recruit new labour. Most Mediterranean (and even some European) countries, need an urgent rewriting of their labour legislation to make it more flexible and better suited to the conditions of free market economies. Egypt is a case in point where rigid labour legislation clearly constitutes a disincentive for entrepreneurs to start new business.
- *Freedom for entrepreneurs*
  In a market economy there is no room for government agencies to approve or disapprove of business ventures. There should be no area of business, be it banking, insurance, electricity or any other sector, reserved for national companies only. Such legislation belongs to the past and is damaging to attempts to attract foreign direct investment. Legislation concerning safety, building codes, environmental and sanitary rules, however, must be respected by both domestic and foreign entrepreneurs.
- *Transparent administrations*
  Whatever administrative decisions have to be taken, they must be transparent and free from arbitrariness. This also implies abrogating or merging thousands of outdated laws and regulations. Such a 'screening' of old legislation seems particularly urgent in the case of Egypt and it

must be possible to call on administrative tribunals to review the legality of administrative decisions.

• *Efficient tax and customs systems*
Reform in this area is another key component of an overall administrative reform programme without which additional burdens are placed on the business sector thereby impairing competitiveness. The loss of customs revenue will leave no choice but for governments to overhaul their mostly outdated fiscal systems, most probably by improving the yield of value added tax. Free trade will also have very beneficial effects on the degree of corruption in the field of customs given that 'free' imports not subject to administrative controls will considerably reduce the opportunities for corruption in this area.

This indicative list is by no means exhaustive and most of the reforms will have to be undertaken anyhow, whatever the future trade regime of Mediterranean countries. The World Bank and the International Monetary Fund are increasingly linking their financial support to such legislative reform being undertaken, so the decision to enter into free trade with the EU could be said to constitute an acceleration in part due to benign external pressure.

Free Trade Among Mediterranean Partners

The measures described above concern actions to be taken by each of the countries under sovereign jurisdiction but another vital element for the success of the Euro-Mediterranean free trade area is the creation of free trade among Mediterranean partners themselves.

Each of the Mediterranean partners has too small a market to be of great value and interest for the international business community particularly in an increasingly global economy. If the Mediterranean countries want to attract a bigger share of the overall foreign direct investment to developing countries (a total of more than US$100 billion per annum) they have to offer home markets comparable in size to those of Brazil, Indonesia, China or Mexico. This requires that goods produced in Egypt, for example, can move without trade obstacles, not only to the European Union but also to the Maghrib and other neighbouring countries. The whole region must be perceived as one big market place where it is possible to invest and to trade without restrictions.

Such a scheme has been under discussion in various forms for the last 50 years – as long as the Arab League has been in existence. So far there has been only one successful experience of inter-Arab free trade which is the Gulf Co-operation Council (GCC) established in 1980. Though imperfect, the GCC did promote a common Gulf market with six participating countries doing about one quarter of their total trade (in particular manufactures) among themselves.

The negotiation of the EMPI between the EU and Mediterranean countries has given a new impetus not only to the idea of inter-Mediterranean free trade but also to inter-Arab free trade. The scheme that seems most feasible at present would consist of the core group of countries that have either concluded negotiations with the EU or are in an advanced stage of negotiations, namely, Jordan, Morocco, Tunisia and Egypt. These countries would establish a 'Mediterranean Arab Free Trade Association' (MAFTA), with free trade to be completed within five years (about ten years before completing free trade with the EU). Such an Association would, of course, be open to all other Arab countries around the Mediterranean. It would, in due time, negotiate free trade arrangements with other neighbouring countries such as Turkey, the GCC and Israel as soon as political conditions permit.

The establishment of MAFTA would be a major step towards the ultimate goal of realising a vast Euro-Mediterranean free trade area stretching from the borders of Mauritania to those of Russia and the Ukraine (perhaps even including these two countries in the future). It would make cumulation of origin really effective. It would be hailed as a bold and far-sighted political decision of Arab leaders and would turn North Africa (with a future population of some 150 million people and vast energy resources) into a much more interesting place to invest providing there is parallel implementation of the reform processes described above.

Expected Results From Euro-Mediterranean Free Trade

Assuming that the dismantling of trade barriers and the much needed internal reform processes will move ahead more or less according to schedule, the following developments might reasonably be anticipated.

Trade among the Mediterranean countries will get a big boost as barriers between them disappear and the necessary support infrastructure is improved (for example, port handling, regularity of shipping links, road and other transport links, air freight connections etc.). One should therefore assume that the future MAFTA countries will be able to intensify trade so that up to a quarter of their total external trade will be among themselves before 2010.

Trade with Turkey will rise equally rapidly. Indeed, under the terms of the EU-Turkey customs union, Turkey will have to extend free access to its market by early next century. This gesture will have to be reciprocated by the MAFTA countries and will induce major new trade flows across the Mediterranean.

One should equally expect a further increase in trade flows between Europe and the Mediterranean, especially as European goods will progressively benefit from totally free access and thus gain a preferential margin in comparison to Asian and American competitors. More important, however, is the nature of trade flows between Europe and the Mediterranean partner countries which is likely to undergo major shifts. With the improvement of technical standards, much more outsourcing should be expected to take place from European business to the southern shores of the Mediterranean, both in manufacturing and increasingly in services which will be the most dynamic elements of future development. The share of agricultural trade in overall trade flows, however, will shrink even further as a natural consequence of the remaining trade restrictions, the saturation of European demand and the increasing domestic demand of the Mediterranean countries themselves. Furthermore, there is bound to be some 'sucker effect' in favour of European products as trade barriers in the Mediterranean countries progressively fall.

One should, therefore, not exclude the likelihood that things will become temporarily worse and both the Turkish and the Israeli experience during the past decade demonstrate how difficult it is to balance trade with the European giant. As long as the deficits are compensated by surpluses in other areas like tourism, workers' remittances or foreign direct investment flows, even a big trade surplus in favour of the EU should not be a cause for concern. Also, if the balance of payments situation for any of the Mediterranean partner countries should derail, as happened in Algeria, the EU would have no choice but to assist, jointly with the IMF, in redressing the situation. This is part of the unwritten commitment it has undertaken when engaging in Euro-Mediterranean free trade.

Manufacturing industries in Mediterranean countries should be expected to undergo a profound restructuring during the next 10-15 years. The average company will grow in size, will specialise and become much more highly performing than today. However, a large chunk of the small and medium business will be eliminated. This is the price to be paid for manufacturing industries to become competitive in international markets but this process, though painful, will not necessarily be accompanied by significantly higher unemployment in manufacturing industries. Depending on the pace of reform and development, the more highly performing companies should be able to absorb the additional labour.

A much greater inflow of foreign direct investment should reasonably be expected and this will certainly accelerate the process of industrial modernisation and restructuring. The amount of investment, however, will depend essentially on the credibility that governments are able to establish with the business community based on the quality of their economic and administrative reforms. With the right investment climate, a rapid and convincing pace of internal reforms, including large-scale privatisation, and continued support from the EU and the international community for more rapid economic development, it should be possible to sustain annual growth rates of GDP of some 6 per cent, which is the minimum for any significant catching up with European levels of development.

It will, of course, be much more difficult for the region to become really attractive for large-scale private investment if the state of relations between Israel and its Arab neighbours continues to deteriorate. However, the continuation of tensions in the region must not be taken as an excuse for governments not to do their homework and put their houses in order. Both Cyprus and Turkey, but also Morocco and Tunisia, demonstrate that rapid economic development can take place in rather unruly neighbourhoods.

Conclusions

Three major conclusions can be drawn from this overall survey of the prospects, conditions and anticipated outcome of Euro-Mediterranean free trade. First, the establishment of free trade in the region is not a guarantee in itself of faster economic growth and prosperity. Free trade is no more than a device to push reluctant entrepreneurs and governments into doing things they ought to do anyhow: that is, modernise their companies in order to make them more competitive and establish a regulatory framework that encourages business initiatives instead of hampering them, as is presently too often the case. Second, free trade between the EU and each of the Mediterranean countries is not enough to generate the full potential benefit. It is necessary to complement North-South free trade by South-South free trade and the sooner this occurs, the better. Third, it appears perfectly feasible to fulfil the major prerequisites for successful and progressive implementation of Euro-Mediterranean free trade by 2015 at the latest, provided that both the Mediterranean governments and the EU continue to lend their full political and financial support to what is undoubtedly the boldest political design in European-Mediterranean relations during this century.

Development Economics, the Washington Consensus and the Euro-Mediterranean Partnership Initiative

DIANA HUNT

Introduction

The Euro-Mediterranean Partnership Initiative (EMPI) was given formal endorsement in November 1995 at a conference in Barcelona of the 15 EU and 11 southern Mediterranean states plus the Palestinian National Authority. The initiative is intended to lead to the creation of a free trade area (FTA) in industrial goods between the EU and the individual states of the southern and eastern Mediterranean by the year 2010. In the intervening period, it is intended to speed up economic and political reform in the southern Mediterranean, with some supporting aid from the EU. Spelt out in the Barcelona Declaration and in individual country treaties, the process comprises three elements: economic, political and social. While change on these three fronts is clearly interconnected, synchronisation of the changes implemented under the three headings is not guaranteed. Meanwhile, the economic component of the process has an in-built momentum in the form of an agreed timetable for moving to free trade and it is possible that this will drive the process as a whole, unless non-economic constraints supervene.

Tunisia and Morocco signed separate treaties with the EU in 1995, while Algeria has indicated a desire to do the same. Since each country already had largely free access to the EU market for manufactured exports, and since agriculture is largely excluded from the EMPI, the main consequence of the treaties is an obligation on the North African states to remove tariff and other restrictions on imported manufactures from the EU. This is to be completed within twelve years.[1] One inducement to participate is that countries of the southern and eastern Mediterranean signing up to the EMPI will have access to some increase in EU funding, to be disbursed in line with receipt of eligible applications, rather than rationed by country.

Diana Hunt is an economist based at the School of African and Asian Studies at the University of Sussex.

From the perspective of the North African states, there are a number of economic and political risks associated with these developments. Possible negative outcomes include tariff-hopping foreign investment from Europe returning to home base (seeking cost savings from a more developed production environment) and some North African owned firms being unable to compete without tariff protection. Any consequent trade creation in industrial goods between the EU and North Africa will have both positive and negative welfare effects on the North African economies, but so far as direct effects are concerned, the short-term net impact on output and employment will inevitably be negative. The initial trade creating effects will impact positively on consumer welfare through lower prices but they will impact negatively on local output, income and employment, with associated multiplier consequences. Bilateral tariff reduction may also switch trade away from more efficient third party suppliers unless tariffs on imports from these sources are also reduced. Tariff reductions will also lead to loss of import tax revenue – a source with relatively low collection costs; yet new needs, notably to attract foreign investment to boost domestic output, imply a requirement to raise government expenditure, notably on physical and social infrastructure.[2] Tax reform will therefore be necessary, and Tunisia and Morocco have already moved towards the introduction of a value added tax. Even so, for a variety of reasons (economic, political, environmental), it may not be possible to fully offset any decline in existing manufacturing production and employment by attracting new investment.

Why have the North African states chosen to adopt so risky a shift in economic strategy? The answer appears to lie partly in pure pragmatism, that is, choice of the least unattractive option. The EU is both North Africa's main trading partner and a major source of economic aid; in promoting the Euro-Mediterranean Partnership Initiative the EU made it clear that future access to financial aid would be contingent upon acceptance of the terms of the agreement. Meanwhile, some of those in a position to influence policy in North Africa take the view that increased economic integration with Europe is the only viable route out of economic stagnation and unsustainable foreign debt.[3] In the face of sustained trends towards freer international trade and a prolonged period of relative stagnation in output, employment and exports in North Africa (particularly in Algeria and Morocco[4]), many in the region see increased integration with Europe as the most promising means of stimulating increased domestic efficiency: increased efficiency of the state apparatus, an increase generally in allocative efficiency, and increased X-efficiency within productive and trading enterprises. These expectations are based largely on the assumption that the economic shocks stemming from the move to free trade will force these changes.

The concern in what follows is not primarily with the empirical evidence which can support or invalidate these expectations, crucial as such data are to developing an understanding of future economic, social and political prospects. Instead, this paper focuses on the relationship between the EMPI and the 'theoretical underpinnings' provided to it by development economics. Central to the following discussion is the nature of the 'Washington Consensus' and the beliefs, assumptions and logic which underpin the consensus itself.[5]

The Emergence of the 'Washington Consensus'

The apparently uncontested claimant to have introduced the term the 'Washington Consensus' into academic discourse is John Williamson.[6] In 1989, Williamson summarised 'the conventional wisdom among the economically influential bits of Washington, meaning the US government and the international financial institutions' as including emphasis on:

(i)   fiscal discipline (holding public spending as a proportion of GDP close to that of public revenue)
(ii)   public expenditure prioritised to areas with high economic returns (notably primary education, health care, infrastructure)
(iii)   tax reform – to broaden the tax base and lower marginal rates
(iv)   financial liberalisation
(v)   exchange rate unification
(vi)   trade liberalisation
(vii)   promotion of foreign direct investment
(viii) privatisation of state owned productive enterprise
(ix)   deregulation of production unless regulation is justified on environmental or safety grounds
(x)   provision of secure property rights.

Underlying this list are two basic macro-economic models as well as the market-based allocative model of the neo-classical paradigm. Of the two macro models, one, associated with the International Monetary Fund, emphasises the importance of demand side variables and the money supply growth rate in ensuring stability both in the balance of payments and domestic prices. The second, associated with the World Bank, emphasises the need for economies to overcome real resource constraints on the supply side (in particular, foreign exchange and domestic savings constraints) in order to achieve national growth targets.[7]

In the IMF model, the fundamental cause of economic instability is excessive domestic credit creation, normally to fund public sector budget deficits. Deficit driven credit creation expands the money supply at a rate in excess of the growth rates of real output and the demand to hold money, with consequent bidding up of domestic prices and imports. Key policy instruments in IMF programmes for restoration of foreign balance and domestic price stability include contraction of the fiscal deficit, devaluation of the domestic currency and increases in domestic interest rates (the latter to increase savings and discourage unproductive borrowing). The last two of these policy instruments act directly on domestic prices: initially on the price of foreign exchange and domestic credit, but, through these, on the price of goods and services. The neo-classical paradigm demonstrates that if allocative efficiency is to be maximised through the price mechanism, then all prices must reflect the true scarcity values of resources. The IMF also advocates general market liberalisation: both in the foreign trade sector (elimination of quotas, reduction and rationalisation of tariffs) and in the domestic economy, through state withdrawal from other forms of price determination. All the foregoing measures are represented in the Washington Consensus. The IMF's influence on national policy stems from its role in providing emergency support for programmes of balance of payments stabilisation. Much of this support is conditional on the recipient implementing a programme of domestic policy reform.

The basic model underlying the World Bank's interpretation of the causes of macro-economic imbalance is different, although it too emphasises the allocative role of free markets. During the 1960s and 1970s World Bank staff developed a model designed to identify the dominant supply side constraints to attainment of growth targets in low and middle income economies. Two resource gaps–that between the investment rate needed to achieve targeted growth and the projected rate of savings, and that between projected imports and exports–were identified,[8] either of which might constrain growth. An economy unable to raise internationally the resources needed to plug the dominant resource gap must either lower its growth target or implement domestic policy measures to reduce the gap. World Bank structural adjustment lending provides medium term support for the balance of payments and the public sector budget while domestic reforms are implemented.

The role of the IMF has, since its inception, been to assist countries in dealing with temporary balance of payments crises, while the World Bank has played a different role: that of assisting low and middle income economies to achieve their medium-term growth targets. The Bank fulfils this role chiefly by funding development projects, while also supplying technical assistance to support project implementation. However, with the emergence of the international debt crisis of the 1980s, the Bank also diversified into programme lending as well, with the latter absorbing, by the late 1980s, some 25 per cent of the Bank's new lending.[9] This programme lending is not geared to particular projects: it provides balance of payments support for programmes of structural adjustment within recipient economies. The Bank's diversification was based on the perception that emergence from debt crisis and avoidance, or at least minimisation, of future balance of payments crises in low and middle income economies entailed significant domestic policy changes, not just implementation of carefully designed investment projects. The changes would have to be geared to the creation of more flexible and internationally competitive production structures and institutional and production environments capable of attracting increased inflows of foreign capital.

In the early 1980s, the division of programme lending roles between the IMF and the World Bank was recognised to be such that the Fund would provide short-run foreign exchange support to an economy experiencing chronic instability in its balance of payments while it introduced policy reforms to stabilise the balance of payments (support conditional on reform implementation). The measures taken would be designed primarily to contract aggregate demand (and hence, imports), while paving the way for export expansion. Meanwhile, the Bank's role was to provide medium-term balance of payments support for programmes of structural adjustment. These programmes were perceived as acting primarily on the supply side of the economy. Key components of Bank supported programmes included measures to increase domestic savings and exports, and measures to raise the productivity of scarce capital. In the early 1980s, the Bank's senior economists took the view that market liberalisation was central to the attainment of these objectives. Thus, relevant policy measures included: liberalisation of foreign trade, exchange rate unification (combined with increased exchange rate flexibility), liberalisation of financial markets, and elimination of state intervention in other aspects of domestic price determination – abolition of minimum wages, urban food subsidies, public sector setting of farmgate prices and subsidies on farm inputs and equipment, *inter alia*.

Underlying the Bank's advocacy of structural adjustment is the perception that the import-substitution policies pursued from the 1950s to the 1970s usually encouraged both inappropriate and excessive industrialisation in relation to the size and resource endowments of the economies concerned. This led to the creation of unduly capital intensive industrial sectors operating in protected home markets with unit costs well above those of potential competitors in world markets. Producing only for the domestic market, firms often failed to reap the full economies of scale that capital intensive production offered. Domestic consumer welfare was lowered as a result of high unit costs, while the poor and under-employed suffered from the fact that relatively high capital: labour ratios, encouraged by policy induced price distortions, discouraged modern sector employment expansion.[10]

The Bank's economists anticipated that, given the nature of state involvement in price-setting in many low and middle income economies, price liberalisation would not only enhance overall efficiency, but also promote equity. Improvements in allocative efficiency were expected to come partly from reductions in both (i) the price of labour relative to capital (due to elimination of the minimum wage, higher interest rates and higher domestic prices for capital goods imports due to devaluation) and (ii) the import intensity of domestic production. Equity gains were expected to come from enhanced price incentives to expand farm output (including on small to medium size labour intensive farms), to expand labour intensive manufactured exports and to increase labour intensity in agriculture. Devaluation was also expected to generate shifts in the composition of consumption demand, towards domestically produced goods and towards labour intensive sectors, notably services. Thus, while real wages were expected to fall in the first instance, aggregate wage employment was expected to expand, laying the foundations for more equitable, and sustainable, growth.

World Bank economists have also persistently urged the privatisation of parastatals as part of structural adjustment packages–primarily to enhance efficiency, but also with an eye to short-run contributions to reducing public sector deficits. To achieve the latter goal, the Bank also advocates reductions in recurrent public expenditure as well as tax reform and efficiency improvements in tax administration. However, in line with its emphasis on supply side adjustment, from the late 1980s the Bank has also given increasing emphasis to the need, through a combination of public and private funding, to expand investments in physical and social infrastructure.

While the Bank and the Fund began the 1980s with quite clear perceptions of their distinct responsibilities and concerns, over the ensuing decade collaboration between the two institutions, and common focus on the same basic problems, led to increasing convergence in their programme lending conditionality vis-à-vis low and middle income economies.[11] This trend contributed to Williamson's identification of the 'Washington Consensus'.

The Ideological Underpinnings of the Washington Consensus

Many analysts of the stabilisation and structural adjustment lending of the IMF and the World Bank have emphasised the liberal ideology underlying the reforms advocated by the two institutions. This liberal ideology has in turn been linked to that which dominated policy formation in the US and

UK during the 1980s under the Reagan and Thatcher administrations. The US administration in particular was in a position to influence the Fund and the Bank by virtue of its voting share. In practice, though, it was the Bank, not the Fund, which shifted ideological stance in the early 1980s. The Fund itself has displayed a greater continuity of underlying policy focus and conditionality since its inception,[12] whereas the Bank has undergone at least two major shifts in approach, first in 1974, towards prioritising poverty reduction, and then, in the early 1980s, away from emphasis on meeting basic needs (the very concept was dropped from the vocabulary of key departments in the Bank) and towards emphasising measures to increase allocative efficiency.[13]

For many economists, the justification for the neo-liberal, market oriented ideology which dominated the 1980s is to be found in the highly influential writings of Friedrick Hayek whose influence increased from the late 1970s. Hayek's work is largely seen as providing the ideological underpinnings for the dramatic shifts in the dominant theoretical perspective of economic analysis that occurred first in some industrially advanced economies–notably the US and the UK–and then were extended via debates on policy reform to the heavily indebted low and middle income economies whose policies were influenced by the Fund and the Bank. The rolling back of the state and the switch to monetarism by the Thatcher and Reagan governments in the UK and US was more than a pragmatic response to the efficiency and equity problems posed by unfamiliar rates of price inflation in the mid and late 1970s. The Thatcherite and Reaganite revolutions were based on fundamental shifts in economic philosophy and theory regarding the role of the state, and of the market, in resource allocation.[14] They were mirrored in a similar shift in dominant perspective among senior economists at the World Bank.

The Philosophical Foundations of the Paradigm Switch

In reviewing Hayek's influence on the above, it is important to recognise that the neo-classical school of economics has two branches: the mainstream, formalist branch and the less formal tradition of the Austrian School, to which Hayek belongs. Both branches are equally oriented towards a market economy, but the less formal tradition espoused by Hayek enabled him to explore issues and ideas ignored by the formal neo-classical tradition, and, in so doing, to pave the way for the later development of what have since become significant fields of enquiry.

Concerned at the political implications of Nazism, Hayek left Austria in 1931 to take up a chair in Economics at the London School of Economics. During the 1930s he became increasingly concerned by the dominant tendencies in economic and political thought in much of western Europe and North America. In these, Hayek observed an acceptance of the superiority of the state in economic planning which in his view could only lead to totalitarianism in the political sphere. The concern of much of Hayek's writing from 1943 onwards is to re-establish the basic principles of free market liberalism in the economic sphere and of what he termed 'true individualism' in the sphere of social governance.[15]

Hayek's economic philosophy is closely associated with the neo-classical (economic) paradigm whose mainstream proponents emphasise the detached objectivity of their theoretical logic. It is therefore noteworthy that, in the preface to *The Road to Serfdom*, Hayek emphasised the political nature of his argument, observing that this derived in its entirety from certain basic values which emphasise the importance – to society as well as to the individual–of the protection of individual freedoms. Hayek sees economic and political freedoms as closely interconnected – one cannot have one without the other.

Much of Hayek's core philosophy, including the arguments which underpin his advocacy of the free market mechanism, are to be found in a few key references, most notably a lecture on individualism delivered in 1945.[16] In this lecture, Hayek contrasts 'true individualism', in the tradition of Adam Smith and de Tocqueville, with 'false' rational individualism in the tradition of Rousseau's writings on the social contract. Hayek's core theme is that a fundamental fallacy lies at the heart of all economic and political philosophy founded on individual rationality. Individuals are not fully rational: their actions are always based on imperfect information and sometimes governed by unpredictable passions. It is the erroneous assumption that individuals can behave in a consistently rational manner that underpins arguments for assignation of economic and political power to a centralised state apparatus. The high expectations of the 'rational state' include that it will co-ordinate society's pursuit of welfare and social justice. When difficulties arise in achieving social goals, such expectations generate a strong tendency to abrogate further powers to the state. However, as the growing powers of the state become increasingly intrusive in people's lives, this inevitably leads to progressive erosion of individual freedoms and to suppression of those individual talents which need such freedoms in order to flourish. Meanwhile, the fact that the state also has incomplete information, and is composed of individuals who – like others – have an incomplete capacity to process the information which they do have, opens up scope for errors on a grand scale.[17]

In Hayek's perception, true individualism is a theory of society, and of individual interaction within it, and not a theory of the individual considered in isolation. It is also a theory based on recognition of both the weaknesses and the potentialities of each individual. Social philosophers should aim to identify those organising principles for society 'by which man could be induced, by his own choice and from the motives which determine his ordinary conduct, to contribute as much as possible to the need of all others'.[18] Such a set of principles should maximise individual freedoms, but within parameters designed to minimise adverse consequences of human error and to minimise conflict between individuals. A society which maximises individual freedoms also maximises the scope for its members to evolve institutions appropriate to its future development: 'many of the institutions on which human achievements rest have arisen and are functioning without a designing and directing mind; ...spontaneous collaboration of free men often creates things which are greater than their individual minds can ever comprehend.'[19] Thus, in the economic sphere the market system has evolved over millennia in response to society's needs, but largely unconsciously, and without any grand design: yet this system is such that individuals benefit from their conduct within it in direct proportion to the benefits which their actions confer on others, without even having to be aware who those others are.

In order to minimise the consequences of human error and maximise individual freedoms in the economic sphere, Hayek concludes that the state should confine itself to facilitating the operation of the free market. The state should establish and enforce rules which enable the market mechanism to operate efficiently and equitably. This includes creating a legal system that provides clearly defined property rights so that each individual is aware of the extent of his or her power over resources.[20] Other supplementary roles of the state in support of the market system include dissemination of information, removal of avoidable uncertainty and ensuring that the system operates equitably: individuals should not be treated as if they were equal, which they are not, but they should, Hayek asserts, face equality of opportunity.[21]

Hayek assumed that the interests of the individual embrace those of the family and of other relatively small local level groupings to which s/he belongs. In his writing he strongly supports the voluntary formation of local groupings for the pursuit of common interests, contrasting such voluntary initiatives, responsive to local need, with centrally planned interventions by a state lacking equivalent local knowledge. Pinpointing an area of concern which has since become a focus of the work of Douglass North, Hayek also emphasises the importance of 'the traditions and conventions which evolve in a free society and which, without being enforceable, establish flexible but normally observed rules that make the behaviour of other people predictable in a high degree.'[22] All such behavioural rules, whether formal or informal, should clarify for all individuals their spheres of responsibility but, if the individual is to remain free to develop his/her full potential, these should not take the form of assignation to the individual of particular ends, nor the allocation to the individual of specific resources.[23]

In the political domain, 'democratic ideals spring from the basic principles of individualism.' Yet individualism does not maintain the omnicompetence of the majority: 'the whole justification for democracy rests on the fact that in course of time what is today the view of a small minority may become the majority view.'[24]

Hayek's writing is remarkable on many counts, not least for its eloquence – and for his readiness to challenge received ideas in whatever quarter they may be held. This readiness is well-illustrated in his critiques of state monopoly of the money supply.[25] His core theme is again that the system adopted should be that which is most effective in meeting the needs of the users: in this case for an efficient medium of exchange and a stable unit of account. State monopoly not only weakens the incentive to pursue these goals but creates strong incentives *not* to give primacy to these goals: instead, the state may expand the money supply faster than the real rate of growth of aggregate output in order to facilitate the funding of its own expenditures. Such monetary expansion is inflationary and adversely affects the foreign trade balance. In the long run it is bound to 'disorganise and ultimately destroy the market order'.[26] Contrary to widespread fears that uncontrolled competitive issue of money by private suppliers would lead to galloping inflation, Hayek argues that it would be in the interest of any private supplier to maintain the stability of the value of the money issued – if this were not done, no one would wish to hold it. In pinpointing the links between domestic monetary expansion, domestic price inflation and the foreign trade balance Hayek also specifies the core of the monetarist interpretation of the causes of domestic price inflation and of balance of payments crisis.

Extension of the Neo-Liberal Paradigm to Low and Middle Income Economies: the Bretton Woods Institutions and the Washington Consensus

Hayek regarded the principles of true individualism as being based on universal values, and as therefore having universal validity. However, he was not directly concerned with problems of economic and political change in low and middle income economies. Rather, he was concerned with the influence of Keynesianism in endorsing state interventionism in more advanced economies.

According to leading early development economists of the 1940s and 1950s the Keynesian demand management model was not directly applicable to low and middle income economies: aggregate demand management to achieve full employment presupposed not only unemployed labour but also unemployed capital, yet in these economies only the former existed.[27] Meanwhile, dynamic Keynesianism, reflected in the influential Harrod-Domar growth model, was preoccupied with the potentially deflationary effects of planned savings rates in excess of planned investment, whereas the overriding problem of low and middle income economies was manifestly different: there, target investment rates substantially *exceeded* actual savings rates.[28]

Yet, while the economic structures of low and middle income economies, and the dominant constraints which they faced, differed in key respects from those in industrially advanced market economies, the interventionist spirit of Keynesianism provided apparent endorsement for the interventionist approaches to policy formation adopted in these economies from the 1950s to the 1970s – approaches which in some cases were also influenced by the perceived advantages of socialist central planning as an organising framework.[29] The policy *problématique* itself was manifestly more complex in low income economies than in the industrially advanced market economies. In the latter, the goals of combining full employment output growth with stable prices and a stable trade balance dominated, and proved increasingly difficult to attain. In poorer economies, the goals were both more complex and more ambitious: to raise national savings and investment rates, to absorb the labour force into modern sector production, to expand exports and to combine all this with structural transformation in production, employment, foreign trade and economic institutions. The scope and complexity of these objectives was widely perceived to justify, for a range of reasons,[30] state interventionism.

The issues which preoccupied most early development economists included recognition that:

(i) a central problem was the need to raise the shares of savings and investment in national income;[31]

(ii) investment strategies based on existing comparative advantage in primary production offered little prospect of sustained long-run growth, owing to national and international income and price elasticities of demand for manufactures and primary goods respectively;[32]

(iii) supply inelasticity in key sectors meant that cost push inflation was an inevitable accompaniment of growth.[33]

The problems raised in (i) and (ii) above led to recommendations by most early development economists for a much larger degree of state involvement in domestic economic management than is consistent with the free market individualism of Hayek; while (iii) led to acceptance of the need for an accommodatory monetary policy. The range of state interventionism that was practised in low and middle income economies in the 1960s and 1970s in certain respects went well beyond that practised in industrially advanced economies, notably in the fields of price manipulation (via tariffs, quotas, interest rate controls, subsidies, direct government intervention in distribution, etc.) and direct state involvement in production.

Often, as Hayek had predicted, one intervention led to another. Policies implemented to keep down food prices and modern sector wage costs led given a need to expand domestic food supplies and, in the short term, to rely on primary exports for foreign exchange to countervailing policy interventions. Thus subsidies were provided to particular agricultural inputs, notably fertiliser, and in some cases farm machinery. Meanwhile, with a high role for government expenditure in the development process, there was need for increased public sector revenue to fund this. A key problem was that tax revenues did not match expenditure targets. Two domestic policy responses were heavy government borrowing from the commercial banking sector and growing reliance on expansion of the money supply at a higher rate than the growth of real output. A further source of both public and private investment funding was foreign capital: foreign aid on concessionary terms, commercial credit and private foreign investment.

Performance outcomes were mixed, for reasons that were both economic and political, domestic and external. Given these results, the problem has been to identify both the causes of varied performance and their relative importance. For some economists, including in the IMF and the World Bank, the answer in the 1980s was clear: problems leading to poor economic performance in low and middle income economies had been predominantly internally generated by inappropriate policies which relied too heavily on state intervention.[34] However, an alternative interpretation is that the difficulties experienced by poorly performing economies were not all of their own making but were, to varying degrees, also determined by external events over which they had no control (notably the oil price hikes of the 1970s; the interest rate hikes and trade recession of the early 1980s; further falls in primary product prices in the second half of the 1980s). Both the growth records of low and middle income economies, and their ability to sustain growth, varied. While neo-classicists chose to explain these facts primarily in terms of degrees of state intervention in the economy,[35] others gave greater emphasis to the nature, rather than, the degree, of state intervention and to the timing of domestic policy developments in relation to international economic trends. As we have seen, it was the influence of the former perspective that led to advocacy by the Bretton Woods institutions (the Fund and the Bank) of the policy responses identified in Williamson's list.

The Washington Consensus and the Euro-Mediterranean Partnership Initiative

It has been suggested that the EMPI has close conceptual links to the Washington Consensus in that the same ideological and theoretical perspectives underpin both.[36] Common elements between the Washington Consensus and the EMPI include the emphasis on trade liberalisation plus advocacy of a number of other policy reforms which are also listed in the Barcelona Declaration. Thus, reforms listed in the economic chapter of the Declaration include:

(i) elimination of tariff and non-tariff barriers to trade in manufactured goods and services between FTA partners;
(ii) policy design based on principles of market economy;
(iii) priority to development of the private sector;
(iv) establishment of an appropriate institutional and regulatory framework for a market economy capable of attracting foreign direct investment;
(v) programmes to mitigate the impact of structural adjustment on the neediest populations;[37]

the chapter also contains:

(vi) acknowledgement that economic development must be supported by internal savings mobilisation as well as direct foreign investment;
(vii) recognition of the importance of sound macro-economic management;
(viii) stress on the importance of developing physical infrastructure.

All these concerns are common to the Washington Consensus and the Barcelona Agreement. However, scope for policy reforms under the EMPI consistent with the principles underlying the Consensus is circumscribed by two aspects of EU-southern Mediterranean *realpolitik*: the EU agricultural policy and the bilateral nature of the free trade agreements. In practice, IMF/World Bank sponsored stabilisation and structural adjustment programmes also promote unilateral trade liberalisation (by economies over which these institutions have policy leverage). However, in the specific context of the EMPI these constraints pose significant problems for North Africa given the importance of their trade relationship with the EU.[38]

In the 1980s, the World Bank argued that trade liberalisation would force those domestic industries that could compete to do so while flushing out the 'no-hopers'. Meanwhile, general price liberalisation would also encourage: a) use of more labour intensive processes, b) production of labour intensive manufactures for export, and c), in many economies, movement of more resources into agriculture, including for increased production for export.

Revival of the agricultural sector, especially in the poorest economies, assumed a particular importance in World Bank structural adjustment programmes because of the relatively high labour absorptive capacity of this sector, particularly when production is structured around small to medium-sized farms, which is strongly supported by the Bank.[39] However, under the Barcelona Declaration restraints are accepted on sectoral adjustments to the composition of output, employment and international trade, specifically through the exclusion of free trade in agricultural products. The North African states are engaging in free trade agreements with their main trading partner which have an in-built distortion directly contrary to the underlying principles and ideology of the Washington Consensus. The EMPI confronts these states with an imperative to expand foreign exchange earnings and contain import growth, but restricts the scope for them to do so. It restricts them both directly, through the EU's restraints on agricultural imports, and indirectly, through consequent restraints on the expansion of internal markets which might come from any increased income and employment in agriculture. The larger the internal market the stronger the domestic production base from which an economy can develop the export of manufactured exports: opportunities for specialisation, for skill development, for small firm clustering to reap external economies are all enhanced. It may be the case that North Africa's economies can expand processed agricultural exports to the EU without facing equivalent restraints, but this expansion (itself partly restrained) would be easier in the context of expanding trade relations for agricultural products themselves.

While the North African states could unilaterally generate some increase in agricultural employment through land redistribution towards the small farm sector, any such redistribution is more likely to be politically acceptable in the context of a buoyant economy offering attractive opportunities for reinvestment of compensation payments. Yet the dominant consensus of recent research is that since 1985 unilateral trade liberalisation by low and middle income economies has tended to be *negatively* related with economic growth, at least in the short to medium term.[40]

The second inconsistency between the EMPI and the liberal underpinnings of the Washington Consensus is that geographically selective trade liberalisation in the form of free trade areas may, as noted in Section 1, introduce welfare lowering distortions. This will occur wherever trade is diverted from more efficient third party sources to suppliers within the FTA. Apart from comparative static adverse welfare effects, such distortions may have adverse dynamic implications for the importing economy, for three reasons: (i) where the diverted trade is in producer goods, the technology embodied in substitute goods supplied from within the FTA may be less efficient and less appropriate to the importing country's needs; (ii) any tariff revenue earned on the previous, more efficient, imports is now foregone; (iii) the importing country may become locked into relatively inefficient production technology, making it harder to compete on international markets.

These distinctions between the characteristics of the EMPI and the underlying principles of the Washington Consensus are relevant to any critique of the former. Thus, that critique may logically be approached partly, but not solely, from the perspective of a critique of the latter's neo-liberal characteristics: the initiative itself does not reflect an internally consistent application of neo-liberalism.

Development Economics and the EMPI: Critiques of the Washington Consensus[41]

At the macro level, most critiques of the Washington Consensus stem from a structuralist perspective, basic premises of which are that economic structures influence economic performance and that the real world is characterised by structural diversity between economies. While proponents of the Washington Consensus have sought to discredit the policy advice that stemmed from the early work of structuralist development economists, emphasising in particular their support for costly import substitution strategies and for state intervention in determination of economic incentives, their own menu of free market based policy reforms has stimulated a new body of critical analysis in the structuralist tradition. These critiques have been characterised both by a recognition that structural features of low income economies may constrain producer ability to respond to changed market opportunities and influence the socio-economic consequences of proposed policy reforms, and by continuing scepticism concerning the general optimality of market generated resource allocation patterns in low and middle income economies. Neo-structuralist critiques of the Washington Consensus have questioned both basic assumptions of the neo-classical mainstream and more specific assumptions, both explicit and implicit, underlying proposed policy reforms. Some have modelled the implications of alternative assumptions for growth and other macro targets.[42]
Specific criticisms levied against the Washington Consensus include:

(i) *lack of realism, manifest in*:
a) the presumption that market liberalisation and state withdrawal would generate perfectly competitive market structures and efficient resource allocation, although price liberalisation cannot ensure this when:

- economies of scale or unequal asset distribution provide opportunities for emergence of monopolies;
- externalities are significant but vary in importance between branches of production;
- elements of X-inefficiency – including inefficient management norms – are pervasive;

b) failure to recognise other empirical realities that do not fit the basic model, notably that the state, both through direct ownership and selective support to private firms, has played a key role in establishing new industries in economies ranging from South Korea to Turkey;

c) underestimation of the political, social and resource costs of restructuring.

(ii) *internal analytical contradictions/ambivalence:*
for example concerning whether public sector investment crowds out or crowds in private investment;

(iii) *failure to anticipate a range of structural constraints on the supply response to market liberalisation:*
ranging from physical resource constraints to institutional ones;[43]

(iv) *failure to identify realistic time paths for structural adjustment:*

(v) *methodological errors in analysis of policy impacts:*
including confusion of correlation with causality, undue emphasis on weak regression results and self-serving criteria for classifying country policy regimes.[44]

Many of these criticisms reflect a concern to relate policy design more closely to the structural realities of specific economies. Through both non-formal analysis and macro modelling exercises, structuralists have shown that under alternative empirical assumptions policy reforms central to the neo-liberal package (devaluation, financial liberalisation) may have the exact reverse of the anticipated effects, leading to stagflation.[45]

However, there is also some common ground between the critics and the criticised. There is, above all, agreement on the goal of sustainable growth and the need for economic reform in economies with unsustainable balance of payments deficits. Given these commonalities it might seem reasonable to propose that neo-classical and structuralist analytical approaches are potentially complementary: the basic neo-classical model provides an analytical core pointing to the need for market liberalisation, but by virtue of its simplicity cannot generate complete packages of country specific policy reforms – the latter invariably require analysis of specific country structures.[46]

However, there remains a fundamental difference in ideology between those who set prime store on the allocative role of the market, and on the role of unrestricted market competition as the basis for both efficient resource allocation and economic growth, and those who combine a pragmatic scepticism in regard to these propositions with the recognition that well managed, carefully targeted state interventions may enhance both growth and equity. From this latter perspective, consideration of the scope for reform of specific state structures and policies when these are not performing effectively is as important as any general rolling back of the state. Both sets of measures should be considered responses to specific situations, not based on dogma.

Recognition of the significance of existing economic structures in determining policy response is clearly relevant to any analysis of the likely impact of the EMPI. Equally important is the need, in the past also under-emphasised within the Washington Consensus, to consider the time path of policy reforms and of the associated policy impacts.[47] In the case of the EMPI, too, there are potentially significant elements in the time path of change implementation and, equally important, in the manifestation of the impacts of these changes, which have received surprisingly little attention. Crucial among these impacts, both politically and economically, is the likely time path of the employment impacts of the EMPI policy reforms. There is a strong probability that establishment of a free trade area between individual North African states and the EU will impact negatively on modern sector manufacturing employment in North Africa, at least in the short- to medium-term.[48] Whether this can be offset within the EMPI, as currently designed, depends essentially on any positive employment effects arising from increased inflows of foreign direct investment, both the likely scale and the timing of which are highly uncertain. Little attention, if any, has been given to identifying the scope and preconditions for the generation within North Africa of additional employment, including in agriculture and agricultural processing, and in other forms of labour intensive non-farm production.

Other Recent and Relevant Advances in Development Economics

Development economics has always embraced a variety of perspectives, drawing its inspiration both from reaction to the economics mainstream and from the latter itself. In the 1980s, although the Washington Consensus appeared to dominate policy advice, the Consensus, which in the eyes of some was incomplete even within Washington, was certainly not universally subscribed to in the wider profession.[49] Concern with the relationship between the EMPI and the Washington Consensus should not divert attention from other recent advances in development economics with the potential to offer insights into policy design, and to inform the prediction of policy impacts, including in the context of the EMPI. Notable among these advances is a cluster of theoretical developments focusing on the performance of economic institutions. The intellectual roots of key aspects of these developments can also be traced back to Hayek. However, in their emphasis on the direct interpretation of empirical reality, rather than deductive reasoning based on formal abstraction, they also have an important element in common with the structuralist approach.

Over recent decades, in both mainstream and development economics, a growing body of analysis has focused on the insights derived from dropping the formal neo-classical model's assumption of full and free access to information. Recognition that information needed by producers and consumers is costly, and that these costs are likely to be particularly significant in poorer economies, has been used to explain both absence of markets for some key resources (rural credit, for example) and the rationale for some apparently inefficient economic institutions (for example, some land tenure arrangements). An important conclusion stemming from these analyses is that where information costs are high, a free market is not necessarily the most effective allocation mechanism; assessment of the case for institutional change in the sphere of resource allocation, and of the appropriate forms of such change, then becomes more complex. By emphasising economic rationality in explaining market absence and imperfections, and the presence of alternative allocative institutions, Stiglitz and his co-researchers have highlighted the risks attaching to exogenously introduced institutional change.[50] Meanwhile, however, the current consensus in a second, broader, and less formal, body of analysis is that while societies may tend to evolve institutions appropriate to their needs, such evolution may be blocked by inertia or vested interests,[51] a conclusion which implies a potential role for external promotion of institutional change: a role for external pressure to reform state institutions and/or a role for the state in introducing lower level institutional change. Seen in this light, the key policy contribution of Stiglitz and his co-authors has been to highlight the need for caution before undertaking such interventions, including giving greater weight to prior identification of possible economic rationales for existing, endogenously generated, institutional structures – even where these appear to flout the presumed optimality of such a basic institution as the free market.

Complementary to both these branches of research in institutional economics is that of Ostrom[52] and others in the field of joint resource management. Less widely recognised, probably owing to its more interdisciplinary character, Ostrom's research, and that of others working in the same field, have nonetheless generated results that have important potential applications in the context of winding down state managed local institutions, and their transfer to the private sector. The Washington Consensus has tended to see the market as not just the best, but the only alternative basis for resource allocation and management other than state *dirigisme*. However, the conclusion of recent empirical and theoretical analyses is that for certain purposes community-based joint resource management may be as effective as, or more so than, either of the others. Progress made in identifying the conditions in which this is likely to apply offers insights into, for example, the likely effectiveness of the new institutional structures being created in the Tunisian rural sector.[53]

Another line of analysis to emerge over the last two decades, one that holds a potential relevance for policy analysis and design in North Africa, is that which focuses on domestic demand linkages and their significance for economic growth, especially in the early phases of economic development. This work, with roots in Mellor's 1976 study of the Indian economy, breaks with early structuralism in its emphasis on the potentially key role of the agricultural sector in the early stages of development.[54] As Mellor and others since have demonstrated, agricultural expansion can generate significant backward and forward demand linkages, contributing thereby to expansion of the domestic market, and so helping to provide a more secure basis for sustainable development than that offered by reliance primarily on export-led growth (especially in economies still with low skill levels). Since the 1960s developments in agricultural technology which focus on crop yield intensification (the bio-chemical revolution) have enhanced the potential role of agriculture in economic development because the new technology is susceptible to use in combination with production methods of widely varying labour intensity. Particularly on small to medium farms, these developments offer scope for raising labour absorption in agriculture while combining that labour with equipment often itself suited to domestic manufacture. Later work on domestic growth linkages has also emphasised the importance in this context of smaller-scale non-farm production, particularly in low income rural regions.[55]

Summary and Conclusion

The Washington Consensus is underpinned by a largely neo-classical and monetarist interpretation of economic phenomena, with close links to the liberal ideology articulated by Hayek. The EMPI, while clearly reflecting the Washington Consensus, represents an internally inconsistent application of the principles which underpin the Consensus. The relevant inconsistencies are due both to the failure to establish a free trade area which incorporates all productive sectors and to the potential welfare costs associated with establishment of free trade areas *per se*.

However, many of those working within the Washington Consensus were trained in the formal neo-classical tradition rather than the more empiricist, and reflective, analytical tradition endorsed by Hayek. This perspective, and its associated methodology, have also influenced their approach to the design of policy reforms for low and middle income economies. As modelling techniques develop, however, there is growing scope at the macro level for development of models which can explore the implications of varying key assumptions such as those concerning domestic supply response to policy reforms, or possible relocation responses of foreign investors, and in so doing shed further light on the likely impacts of policy initiatives such as the EMPI. For such modelling exercises to be effective, however, appropriate empirical questions must be posed first.

Also urgently needed in the case of the EMPI is more detailed analysis of the likely time path of policy change and of policy impacts, for each of the participating states. The outcomes may be critical not only to the impacts on economic welfare, but also to the political acceptance of the reform process. Meanwhile, the debate over the Washington Consensus should not overshadow other recent advances in development economics also relevant to the design of policy reforms, including in North Africa.

NOTES

1. Elsewhere in the region, Turkey and Egypt are also pursuing closer economic association with the EU under the terms of the EMPI.
2. As well as a requirement for institutional reforms, including moves towards more transparent governance.
3. See for example, Tunisia's Foreign Minister, quoted in Marks, J. (1996), 'High Hopes and Low Motives: The New Euro-Mediterranean Partnership Initiative', in *Mediterranean Politics*, 1/1, p.14.
4. World Bank (1997), *World Development Report*, Appendix Table 1.
5. It is recognised that this begs the question of whether the term consensus is fully justified.
6. Williamson, J (1993), 'Democracy and the Washington Consensus', in *World Development*, 21/8, p. 1329.
7. The basic elements of the models are outlined in Tarp, F. (1993), *Stabilisation and Structural Adjustment in Sub-Saharan Africa*, and Agenor, P.R. and Montiel, P., (1996), *Development Macroeconomics*, Princeton NJ, Princeton University Press.
8. A third gap – in domestic absorptive capacity – was also identified but did not feature in the Bank's macro model as this was subsequently developed.
9. Tarp (note 7) p.81.
10. These distortions included: formal sector minimum wages above market clearing level, low, state determined, real interest rates, undervalued foreign exchange and low or zero duties on imported producer goods – the last three in particular intended to encourage modern sector industrialisation.
11. As various authors have shown, the two basic macro models can also be synthesised. See Tarp and Agenor and Montiel (note 7).

12. This despite the dramatic changes in world currency regimes that occurred in the 1970s.
13. A widely cited illustration of the perspective adopted by the Bank in the 1980s is the Bank's 1991 *World Development Report*. Recently, the Bank has once again begun to give greater emphasis to poverty reduction.
14. The 1980s was also the period in which public choice theory received increasing emphasis in explanations of the conduct of politicians and bureaucrats. This body of theory has been described as the 'economic study of non-market decision-making, or simply the application of economics to political science' in which the basic behavioural postulate is that 'man, be he voter, politician or bureaucrat, is an egotistic rational, utility maximiser' in Mueller, D. (1996), 'Public Choice Theory' in Greenaway, D., Bleaney, M., and Stewart, I., eds., *A Guide to Modern Economics*, London, Routledge, p.65.
15. These concerns are reflected in Hayek, F. (1943), *The Road to Serfdom*, London, Routledge, and (1949) *Individualism and Economic Order*, London, Routledge, and a series of related publications over the following decades.
16. In this lecture alone are to be found, not simply a defence of the free market, but the seeds of more recent developments in economic theory, which, particularly at the micro level, have led to major advances in our understanding of the operation of economic systems (for instance, recognition of the significance of information costs). See Hayek, *Individualism and Economic Order*, Chapter 1 (note 15).
17. Compare Adam Smith: 'Great nations are never impoverished by private, though they sometimes are by public prodigality and misconduct' in Smith, The Weath of Nations Vol. I, Book II, Chap. III, 1776.
18. Hayek, *Indiviualism and Economic Order* (note 15) p.13.
19. Ibid. p. 6-7.
20. Hayek recognises that this is not always straight forward. For instance, there are 'difficult problems in connection with land, where the recognition of the principle of private property helps us very little until we know precisely what rights and obligations ownership includes. ... And when we turn to such problems of more recent origin as the control of air or of electric power, or of inventions and of literary or artistic creations, nothing short of going back to the *rationale* of property will help us decide what should be in the particular instance the sphere of control or responsibility of the individual.' Meanwhile, It should be noted that Hayek gave relatively little weight to a problem that is of increasing importance: the issue of how to deal with market failure to take account of externalities in production and consumption. This may entail a greater role for the state in the sphere of resource allocation than is seemingly implied by 'facilitation of the operation of the free market.' Ibid.
21. However, incomes and wealth will not be distributed equally – for 'if the individual is to be free to choose, it is inevitable that he should bear the risk attaching to that choice and that in consequence he be rewarded, not according to the goodness or badness of his intentions, but solely on the basis of the value of the results to others.' Ibid.
22. Ibid.p.23.
23. Ibid p.17.
24. Ibid p.29.
25. Ibid and Hayek, F. (1991) *Economic Freedom*, Oxford, Blackwell.
26. Ibid p.127.
27. Lewis, W.A (1954) *Economic Development with Unlimited Supplies of Labour*, Manchester School.Vol.22.
28. As it happened, the Harrod-Domar model was capable of application to these circumstances as well, but these were not the conditions which had prompted its development, nor the initial form of the model's articulation.
29. Support for both state co-ordination and state funding of industrial investment lies, for example, at the heart of arguments put forward in the 1940s and 1950s in favour of the 'big push' and balanced industrial growth, both intended to overcome domestic market constraints. Rosenstein-Rodan, P. (1943), 'Problems of Industrialisation in Eastern and South-Eastern Europe', in *Economic Journal*, 53, and Nurkse, R. (1953), *Problems of Capital Formation in Undeveloped Countries*, Oxford, Blackwell.
30. The reasons are discussed in various sources. See, for example, Agarwala, A., and Singh, S.

eds., (1958), *The Economics of Underdevelopment*, Oxford, Oxford University Press; Prebisch, R. (1964), 'Towards a New Trade Strategy for Development', Report by the Secretary-General of the United Nations Conference on Trade and Development, United Nations, New York; and Singer, H. (1950), 'The Distribution of Gains between Investing and Borrowing Countries', in *American Economic Review*, 40/2 [Papers and Proceedings].

31. Prevailing low shares of these variables were variously linked to distinctive class structures, the international operation of the Duesenberry effect, lack of profitable incentives to invest and the pervasiveness of uncompensated externalities. On all of these see the readings in Agarwala and Singh (note 30).

32. In separate papers Prebisch and Singer (note 32). Both argued that in international markets price and income elasticities of demand for primary products were low, whereas within low income economies income elasticity of demand for manufactures was high while price elasticity of demand for essential manufactures was low. This combination of price and income elasticities meant that it would be difficult for low income economies to sustain rising production and consumption without running into balance of trade constraints, unless they diversified their own production into manufactured goods.

33. Seers, D. (1962), 'A Theory of Inflation and Growth in Undeveloped Countries', *Oxford Economic Papers*

34. See World Bank, 199, Chapter 1 (note 13).

35. Combined, later, with levels of development of human capital.

36. See for example, Joffe, G. (1996), 'The Economic Factor in Mediterranean Security' in *The International Spectator*, Vol. 4; and Joffe, G., 'Partnership with the EU: What's in it for the Maghreb States, Text of Speech, March 1997 Royal Institute of International Affairs (RIIA).

37. By the late 1980s, these were also included, at least in principle, in World Bank structural adjustment programmes.

38. For an analysis of the composition and direction of the foreign trade of the Maghreb economies see Bensidoun, I. and Chevalier, A. (1996). *Europe-Mediterranee: le Pari de l'Ouverture*, Paris, Economica, Collection CEPII.

39. An important feature of agriculture in this context is the enormously wide range of production methods, with widely varying ratios of capital to labour, which can be used to produce a given product.

40. Greenaway, Bleaney and Stewart (note 14).

41. One of the factors which explains the durability of the mainstream neo-classical paradigm is the absence of an equally coherent counter-theory, equally susceptible to mathematical manipulation. This is apparent in critiques of the Washington Consensus.

42. See, for example, Arestis, P., and Demetriades, D. (1993), 'Financial Liberalisation and Economic Development', in Arestis, P., ed., *Money and Banking: Issues for the Twenty-first Century*, London, Macmillan.

43. North defines institutions as 'the rules of the game . . . . the humanly devised constraints that shape human action.' These range from formally legislated rules to informal codes of conduct. North, D., 1990, *Institutions, Institutional Change and Economic Performance*, Cambridge University Press.

44. Many of these criticisms are noted in Taylor, L., 1992, 'Polonius Lectures Again – The World Development Report, The Washington Consensus, and How Neoliberal Sermons Won't Solve the Problems of the Developing World', *Bangladesh Development Studies*, Vol. XX, no.2/3, p.23. See also Chibber, A. (1989), 'Aggregate Supply Response: A Survey', in Commander, S., ed., *Structural Adjustment and Agriculture: Theory and Practice in Latin America*, London, Heinemann.

45. Arestis and Demitriades (note 44).

46. See Agenor and Montiel (note 7).

47. One feature of the formalist deductive methodology of the neo-classical mainstream is its emphasis on comparative static analysis in which changes in the economic system are instantaneous and the time path of change as an object of analysis ignored. This probably helps to explain why the significance of the time path of change was underemphasised in early structural adjustment programmes.

48. Hoekman, B. (1997), 'Free Trade Agreements in the Mediterranean: A Regional Path

towards Liberalisation', and Tovias, A. (1997), 'Regionalisation and the Mediterranean'. Both papers presented to Workshop II on Europe and North Africa: Seeking an Economic Road to Security, RIIA and both included in this journal.

49. Williamson (note 6) and Taylor (note 46).
50. Stiglitz, J., (1986), 'The New Development Economics', *World Development*, 14/2 and Stiglitz, J (1988), 'Economic Organisation, Information and Development', in Chenery, H., and Srinivasan, T., eds., *Handbook in Development Economics*, Vol. 1, London, Elsevier.
51. See North (note 45).
52. Ostrom, E. (1990), *Governing the Commons,* Cambridge, Cambridge University Press.
53. Ridha Boukraa, 'Associative Culture: A Tunisian State Strategy in a Liberalised Agricultural Economy', paper presented in Workshop III of Europe and North Africa: Seeking an Economic Road to Security, Tozeur/RIIA. Unpublished.
54. Mellor, J. (1976), *The New Economics of Growth: a Strategy for India and the Developing World,* Ithaca NY, Cornell University Press.
55. Ranis, G., 1990, 'A View of Rural Development – 1980s Vintage [or Why Some of the Emperor's Clothes – and His Rice – Should Be Made at Home]', in Khan, A., and Sobhan, R., eds., *Essays in Honour of Nurul Islam*, Macmillan Press.

Global Euro-Mediterranean Partnership

NADIA SALAH

Introduction

For the first time since there has been a European political entity, Morocco, along with other countries in the South Mediterranean region, has signed an agreement which treats them as normal states or as 'mature partners' according to the term usually employed. The agreement has led to the opening of the Moroccan market to industrial products originating in Europe, although previous agreements have always been based on the principle of making exceptions in terms of most favoured nation status. There is no reciprocity in terms of free access for Moroccan products as there is for industrial goods of European origin and the reality will be that sensitive products in the agricultural sphere on both sides will not enjoy free access.

The Politics of Restriction

The ground leading to competition in industrial goods has been well-prepared within Morocco but the same is not true for the political justification of the concept of free trade. Since 1983 when the financial collapse originally occurred,[1] different Moroccan governments have followed a policy of commercial liberalisation. Prohibitions have been removed, quotas were first reduced and then removed, and finally, customs tariff protection was removed in stages. The current customs barrier is now a maximum of 35 per cent, but certain tariff and non-tariff barriers also exist, such as the calculation system of VAT, the import tax system or the compensatory dues for the four major agricultural products and related substances.

Politically however, while Moroccans have been repeatedly told that the new agreement is unlike its predecessors, the accompanying political message has been completely obscured. The various Moroccan governments have promised or at least let it be understood, that they have forced Europe (the old colonisers, the West or, more rarely, the imperialists)

Nadia Salah is Editor-in-chief: *L'Economiste*, Casablanca.

to finally recognise Morocco's true worth. It has been very instructive to observe that the discourse within the opposition political parties has not dealt with the real significance of the new agreement but, instead, has repeated this same misleading message. For them, it has been a question of determining to what degree the government has or has not forced Europe to recognise 'our true worth'.

It is an attitude which can be irritating or beguiling, depending on the circumstances, but in every case it distances its listeners ever further from reality. In this there is indeed a danger, which exists at several levels, and this ridiculous message underpins a mistake which already characterises the political links between Rabat and Brussels, between Rabat and European capitals, and which threatens to continue to affect them for a long time to come. In essence, the message makes it possible for the major differences between this agreement and its predecessors to be ignored. In particular, it obscures the fact that the Moroccan market for industrial goods must now embark on an historic and novel experience, namely the application of the rules of normal competition.

Free trade and competition are going to be a great shock for Moroccan companies, for there is little tradition in the national economic culture or political discourse which relates to competition. Indeed, the reverse is true.

'What can one sell to a people where the richest of them only has a woollen djeballa which is hardly whiter than that worn by the poorest?' asked Consul Chenier when writing to the Marseilles Chamber of Commerce at the start of the nineteenth century. Throughout the whole of the last century and at the beginning of this century, the great Moroccan merchant families were in Manchester or lived along the Senegal River. In Morocco, all they had were transit depots and sales outlets.

Given the monetary crises which continued powerfully, if covertly, to affect Moroccan policy, Sultan Hassan I and his successor, the 'regent' Ba Ahmed, at the end of the last century had hardly begun to discover international competition. They usually responded to it in political terms: residence rights against an *intuitu personae* tax or a tax on goods, or as in Casablanca, where the right to export wheat required the construction of a house.

The Act of Algeciras, which established the 'open door' regime in Morocco, in reality opened the door to the institutionalisation of political regulation, shared between the sultanate and European powers. It did not take long, however, before the door was only open to Spain and France. Since French colonialism was more dynamic than its Spanish counterpart, it imposed its own commercial principles on Morocco. In imposing them, it chose to introduce restrictions, rather than economic freedoms. With independence, socialist or 'statist' ideological preferences reinforced these reductive visions of trade and economic initiative.

The Future for the Free Market

The collapse of public finances in 1983 caused a change of approach in economic policy which was controlled essentially by government (by the so-called 'technical ministries') with encouragement or approval from the Royal Palace. Yet even today there are still very few studies, whether by journalists or academic researchers, which highlight the fact that the enforced liberalisation of the 1980s and 1990s actually generated a reduction in the level of absolute poverty in Morocco, despite demographic growth. In short, a major (albeit enforced) step towards liberalisation was thus achieved, although nobody has taken the initiative to indicate where it might lead.

As a result, Morocco is entering the era of what has come to be called 'globalisation' with dreams of a golden age involving administrative restrictions on trade and prices. It should not be overlooked that globalisation in the Moroccan context is a more limited vision for it is restricted to opening towards Europe. Although the vision of the opportunities offered by the rest of the world inform much of the public discourse, the reality is that this will be of marginal importance. Two thirds of all commercial transactions, including oil and phosphates, take place with Europe.[2]

Morocco, or, more exactly, Moroccan companies, are entering into the era of 'Euro-globalisation' with the reflexes and collective memory of a philosophy based on opposition to free trade. A circular from the Ministry of the Interior in April 1996 explained that the economic departments of the Prefectures should insist that economic institutions provide invoices because monitoring invoices remained the only way to check prices and speculation because of the effects of liberalisation. With the onset of the 'purification campaign',[3] this circular not surprisingly caused some protest in the economic world. The protests were subdued, however, for fear of the power of a ministry whose tentacles extend throughout Moroccan society. Furthermore, protesters know that the 1972 law which introduced price controls has never been abrogated.

The echoes of this regulation on price control indicate the lack of readiness of Morocco's economic elites for the world they face. A quarter of a century after it was introduced, the law can no longer be effectively applied. The vast increase in goods and services now in circulation would probably demand a body of monitors greater in number than Morocco's literate adult population. Yet the inappropriateness of the law makes it even more dangerous because its application will be discretionary and arbitrary. One economic category, for example, might be made subject to it but not others, nor, perhaps, its consumers or suppliers. A particular sector may be subjected to it at one time and not at another, or a particular company may be sanctioned whilst its competitors continue to operate untouched.

Indeed, since liberalisation began in 1983, companies have found a way of limiting this discretionary character of the law. They have formed themselves into 'professional associations' by economic sector or industry. The associations then choose (and continue to choose) a president from within the establishment and then seek to lobby the administration and the political authority. This political and ideological infrastructure – a civilian and administrative organisation with various and often contradictory levels – thus militates against commercial initiative and against free trade, even within the enclosed domestic arena. In addition, it serves a mass of petty interests so that the sum of the corresponding situational rents act as a powerful handicap to modernisation.

Social response

This tyranny of the *status quo* is counterbalanced by only four factors:

*   Morocco's elites are fearful of Islamic fundamentalism despite the fact that it has not yet been able to establish an integrated discourse with Moroccan society;
*   an unknown proportion of Morocco's female population demand an equality of status which neither Islamic fundamentalism nor under-development can provide;
*   Moroccan urban society, both in small and large urban centres, has produced a vast range of non-governmental organisations–civil society, in short–involving activists who have found support which they cannot forego in the international arena, either in terms of financial support or in terms of ideas; and
*   most important of all, both the poor and middle-class urban social strata want to 'live like Europeans', an idealised vision, no doubt, but widely spread both by Morocco's migrant community abroad and by satellite television.

These four groups see the agreement with the European Union as a motor for development and as the only way to be able to live like Europeans, to erect a barrier to Islamic fundamentalism or even to continue to operate within civil society. At the same time, this social activism (whose numerical significance is not known) has contradictory expectations about the meaning of the modernisation that the agreement with the European Union should bring. Indeed, the extent of these expectations certainly exceeds whatever improvements the agreement could possibly generate.

There are added contradictions here: on the one hand, the negative consequences of the agreement have not been explored by the political world which has, instead, used a 'we are finally being treated like adults' argument, and on the other, only a small section of the business world is worried about these negative consequences anyway. Very few studies have been undertaken, thus giving rise to the concept of the 'three-thirds', i.e. that one-third of Morocco's industrial enterprises will disappear, another third will survive and the remaining third will prosper–although it has proved impossible to find a single Moroccan study that gives these proportions. The argument that Dh40 bn will be needed over five years to fund the transition has slightly better foundations. Studies have been commissioned but their methods of calculation have been somewhat hasty.

Nonetheless, it should be noted that the transition is not going to be a passive process. The most frequent statements made on the issue deal with the efforts that Moroccan companies and government must make to raise standards.[4] This is considered an internal Moroccan affair and a matter more for companies than governmental or regulatory authorities. However, it is not clear that this approach of encouraging change will survive if the transition process involves significant disturbance in the industrial sector. This is particularly important as the four factors of social change indicated above may be made to modify their analysis of the situation. For example, how can 'to live like Europeans' have any meaning for employees who lose their jobs because of the effect of the transition process on their factories or because their companies disappear?

Ever since the agreement was negotiated there has been intense discussion, even argument, between the public authorities in Morocco and representatives of private enterprise to determine who will be responsible for guiding the transition operations. The public authorities began by considering that the Tunisian example should not be repeated in Morocco, describing it as 'a desire to control the economic structure', as 'obscuring vision', as 'the primacy of private initiative', or simply criticising it in terms of the impossibility of determining in advance which enterprise would or would not be capable of handling the process. Every possible argument against administrative control of the transition process was proposed. The possibility of financial aid, however, caused a change of opinion within the public authorities, particularly in the finance ministry and then in the ministry of commerce and industry. There is now competition to establish who should hold the keys to the coffers, even if the sums involved are small compared with the perceived need of Dh40 bn.

The Hidden Issues Within the Agreement

As has already been made clear, the phrase 'to live like Europeans' underlies the practical significance of the agreement. It has also been implicit in what has been said that issues such as competence, productivity and the organisation of production must now receive attention. In other words, issues related to difficulties in the organisation of production lead to concerns over administrative and political organisation – political governance, in short. An obligation is then inevitably created by this political issue to eliminate a series of outmoded approaches and networks and thus to exclude those who operate or profit from them. However, improvements at the level of ability and organisation in the production of goods and services are not a simple matter even when described in official reports from Brussels or Rabat. Actual movement on the ground is even more difficult.

In cases involving very small companies such as L'Economiste, for example (Dh20 m paid-up capital, 50 employees, 80 per cent of whom are university educated with 10 per cent acquiring their degrees abroad), the single modernisation operation of transferring archives to CD-ROM and putting each issue on the Internet took ten months to complete, involved one of the four most highly qualified staff members of the company, and required an entirely self-generated investment of Dh1.3 m, equivalent to 30 per cent of turn-over. Budget provisions had to be doubled and the time-demands on qualified staff, originally expected to be of negligible significance, turned out to be extremely heavy. The common denominator in the cost escalation was the absence of prior or appropriate experience in Morocco and the consequent errors that occurred. For example, software was available but one day a cable would be missing, the next day programmes were incompatible, the customs authorities blocked nomenclature inputs or diskettes had deteriorated. Preliminary studies, in short, had completely underestimated the effect of an insufficiently experienced working environment.

It requires little imagination to see that this operation, which could have been a disaster, is likely to recur in every company on a much larger scale. At the beginning, of course, this modernisation process was not a question of money, but in the end finances became a key issue to make up for errors, lost time and lapses in the completion of more traditional tasks. In personal terms, I do not know of any European financial aid packages that take these practical realities into account although they do generate experience and information which can be diffused through the press.

The task of political modernisation, which will involve the elimination of previous patterns of operation, will be more complex. The renovations suggested by the recent constitutional reform[5] will certainly involve profound change, beginning with the restructuring of the political elite. There will, however, be strong resistance, not least because habit creates considerable levels of political passivity also very evident in the debate on free trade. Indications of this passivity are seen in the refusal of the non-governmental organisations and the professional associations to enter the political field, a domain they consider reserved for the party leadership and the Royal Palace only. During the past seven years, only one political party, the former Communist Party (PPS), was able to hold its party congress. Similarly, the political proposals of the Koutla, the opposition alliance (now the government – ed.), which referred to the 1996 constitutional reforms were submitted to the king for official approval but necessitated a leak so that the press (including the party press) could get access to the documents concerned!

The hidden world in which Moroccan politics evolve clearly explains the disaffection to which it has fallen victim but also from which it may benefit. To exclude the current network of vested interest which is protected by this hidden world is the last aspect of the transition to modernisation and the one which will also be the most difficult.

The effect, however, of the closed nature of elite circles in Morocco has been moderated by the explosion of private enterprise, the reduction of economic regulation promised by the administration, the indirect control of the emerging financial market and the emergence of an effective press. This may not be sufficient, however, and there remain cases like the World Food Programme affair[6] which were certainly first revealed by the press but have been systematically delayed by constant adjournments from the judiciary. The current dependence of the political press on state aid and the dominant role of government in setting advertising tariff rates leads to fears that the renovation of civil society will be hindered whatever action is taken. Yet this development will be key to the modernisation and transition process, whether in the industrial, commercial or political spheres.

NOTES

1. In September 1983, the Moroccan government had to have recourse to the IMF for support in resolving its foreign debt burden. As a result, it began a complex economic restructuring process which is still not completed.
2. 66.4 per cent of imports and 66 per cent of exports in 1995, proportions which have tended to increase since 1993.
3. This campaign, launched in mid-1996, was designed to combat smuggling and corruption. There have also been suspicions that it has been used to settle personal scores as well.
4. The phrase usually used for the transition and modernisation process is *mettre à niveau* or to raise standards to European levels.

5. In September 1996, a new bicameral parliamentary constitution was approved by referendum, thus marking a further democratisation of the Moroccan political process. Since this article was written, Morocco has held legislative elections for the new bicameral parliament. As a result, the former koutlah opposition alliance now heads a coalition government. The essence of economic policy, however, has not changed.
6. This case involved Moroccan state officials being charged with embezzling public and donor funds, in particular from the World Food Programme's initiative to provide school meals for Moroccan children.

The European Challenge to North African Economies: The Downside to the Euro-Med Policy

JON MARKS

Introduction

There are, of course, good reasons to argue that adherence to the EMPI accords will help to speed trade liberalisation and generate growth for economies whose strategies are based on sound macro-economic policies, following many of the prescriptions most strongly advocated by the International Monetary Fund (IMF) and World Bank. Macro-economic stability will encourage investment, provided other elements of the business environment remain attractive.

There are also good reasons to believe that at least two countries in the Maghrib region – Tunisia and Morocco – can be among the most successful in implementing the EMPI and thereby gain the investment bonus needed for them to attain lift-off, becoming 'new tigers' in the Mediterranean (orbiting Europe, much as the earlier Asian tigers benefited from being satellites of the Japanese manufacturing and financial services industries).

However, it is equally clear that there are substantial risks inherent in the EMPI. The 'downside' ranges from reductions in government revenues implied by the negative budgetary implications of lowering tariff barriers (undermining efforts to control such critical indicators as the Treasury deficit); pressures on local industries caused by the accelerated opening of fragile economies to foreign competition; and the potential political consequences if the policy fails. In case of failure (a sharp upturn in job losses, for example, not offset by the creation of new, more economically viable employment), the West – and especially the EU – will be seen to have failed the Arab world.

There are strong suspicions that, in its early years at least, the main benefits of the Euro-Mediterranean Partnership Initiative could prove to be

Jon Marks is the editor of FT Africa Energy and Maghreb Quarterly Report. He is also North Africa Correspondent of Bridge News and Middle East Economic Digest.

'asymmetrical' in favour of European partners, meaning rich profits accruing to exporters of goods and services in Europe, while Arab states suffer from trade diversion. If this proves to be so, the consequences for stability in the Middle East/North Africa (MENA) region could be precisely the opposite of what the founding fathers of the EMPI have sought to achieve. There is a risk that a Euro-Mediterranean policy which is not rigorously thought out and/or is poorly implemented might add to North Africa's problems, rather than reinforcing stability and building a better future for North Africans. The potential that negative results from the programme could trigger further turbulence on Europe's southern flank should be taken into account by policy-makers.

The Political Challenge of Under-Developed Economies

Arguably, it was the need to reinforce political stability on Europe's southern flank which was chief among the preoccupations that led to the evolution of the EMPI. European analysts had long feared that instability in this area would result in mass illegal immigration, with the spectre of 'Mediterranean boat people' becoming increasingly common; agitation among migrant populations (given credence by the Rushdie affair and Algerian Islamists organising in the *banlieux* of French cities); and the increased threat of terrorism, which the Palestinian, Lebanese and Kurdish experiences had illustrated well before the emergence of the conflict in Algeria after January 1992. All of these elements served to confirm fears that North Africa had the potential to become destabilised, despite years of large-scale foreign financial assistance and political support for established regimes. The implementation of structural adjustment policies had not yet produced the sustainable growth needed to help limit social discontent.

A response was needed, especially as instability in the Maghrib has clear internal policy implications for EU member states, most notably France, Spain, Italy, Belgium and Portugal, but also others (such as Germany and the UK) where North African and other Arab opposition groups are active. Indeed, the Maghrib countries form an integral element in a southern Mediterranean region that is considered by Europe, along with the former Soviet Union (FSU), as one of the two main strategic areas bordering an enlarging EU. In a volatile context, it could be argued – unkindly – that the evolution of these concerns into plans to create a free trade area involving the EU and mainly Arab southern Mediterranean countries was a benign and imaginative expression of a dictum favoured by *The Godfather*, Don Vito Corleone: 'keep your friends close and your enemies closer'.

The EMPI formula provides an all-embracing policy which is intended to create a 'zone of stability' based around the trading bloc which will underpin the emergence of a new political configuration in a region which includes the enlarged EU, the MENA countries, Turkey and potentially part of the Balkans. The EMPI was also given impetus by the Middle East peace initiative–a process which has been notable for the EU taking a leading role in structuring the economics, while accepting a back seat in negotiating the politics.

The Economic Challenge for Under-Developed Economies

There is also more than an economic basis to the EMPI's birth as a child of the age of globalisation, which saw its zenith in 1994 when the GATT became the World Trade Organisation at a summit meeting in Marrakesh. The creation of a free trade zone encompassing both flanks of the Mediterranean – and linked into an area stretching north to the Arctic Circle, and east to the confines of the FSU – fits into the 1990s dynamic of building large trans-national trading and investment blocs, such as the American Free Trade Agreement and Asia-Pacific Economic Co-operation. The EMPI is rooted in a belief that out of the free trade blocs closer political and socio-cultural relations will flow.

The EMPI does offer real economic opportunities, giving under-developed southern Mediterranean economies a chance to integrate relatively quickly and effectively into the global economy – a global economy in which the EU ambitiously envisages a free trade area covering 30 countries and up to 800 million people by early in the next century. In fact, it is envisaged that by 2010, at least the most advanced countries of the Mediterranean basin will be open for reciprocal free trade in most manufactured goods and services through a Euro-Med partnership, based on a series of bilateral economic association agreements, the first of which was signed on 17 July 1995 by Tunisia. Morocco followed in November 1995; others are expected to follow, including Algeria, Egypt and Jordan. Turkey and Israel have also concluded complex trade accords which will draw them into this zone.

The reinforcement of political stability was a key element in devising Euro-Med but in line with the EU paradigm (and despite the neo-federalist political and social agenda of post-Maastricht Europe) the policy has a predominantly economic agenda. The European Economic Community, established by the Treaty of Rome, was after all a sophisticated customs union, intended to supersede the European Coal & Steel Community. Its greatest success so far has been the creation of the Single European Market (SEM), whose values permeate the expanded Euro-Med zone.

The policy's first real consequences will be economic and could be profound for southern Mediterranean states which must lower the tariff barriers that still (despite a decade of IMF and World Bank-sponsored adjustment) provide protection for local manufacturing and other companies. It is these who are soon to face powerful new competition from Europe under the EMPI formula. While those Arab states who so chose, will benefit from joining an enlarged zone of European economic influence – gaining advantageous trading conditions in some sectors at least similar to those offered by membership of the SEM – they will also suffer the consequences of facing much tougher competition in still protected markets. It is therefore clear that the 12-year transition periods written into each agreement must be carefully judged.

Historical Progression

The development of European Community policy towards the Maghrib is well-documented, starting during a period when Algeria was still considered part of metropolitan France, through to development of the Renovated Mediterranean Policy of the late-1980s. The EMPI fits comfortably into the schema of European-Maghrib relations, although the development of the policy (over a relatively brief period) also owes something to accidents of history, starting in 1992 when a minority group of Euro-MPs managed to block Morocco's fourth financial protocol in the European Parliament on grounds of alleged human rights abuses and the kingdom's Western Sahara policy. An embarrassed European Commission sought a solution to assuage Moroccan anger and came up with a new formula based on a free trade agreement and wider political, social and cultural co-operation, which could occupy attention while the protocol was brought back to parliament. This would bypass parliament and offer Morocco (whose interest in Europe had been underlined by its failed application in 1987 to join the Community) something new. Arguably, this policy was to prove the eventual blueprint for Barcelona.

Change within Europe has also influenced policy. The Maastricht Treaty of European Union advocates a common foreign and security policy, founded on a basic need '..to safeguard common values, fundamental interests and independence of the Union; to strengthen the security of the Union and its Member States; to preserve peace and strengthen international security; to promote international co-operation and to develop and consolidate democracy, the rule of law and respect for human rights.' According to the treaty the EU's creation involves '..establishing systematic co-operation between Member States.' To achieve this, the EU 'will gradually implement 'joint action' in the areas in which the Member States have important interests in common.'

In this context, when the EC's Foreign Affairs Council met on 18 July 1994, and invited the Commission to submit guidelines for the short and medium-term strengthening of the EU's Mediterranean policy, the Commission responded with a policy which went well beyond the traditional remit of EC co-operation with the Maghrib/Mashriq region. As well as the ideology of Maastricht, the policy drawn up with visionary zeal by the Commission embodied the ideas drawn into the Moroccan compromise and also borrowed considerably from the economic stabilisation and structural adjustment policies promoted by the IMF and the World Bank for Maghreb economies for the best part of a decade.

The prospect of creating a free trade zone was met with modified rapture across the region. The first country to sign one of the new EMPI agreements was Tunisia, the greatest 'Euro-enthusiast' in the southern Mediterranean, part of whose enthusiasm was based on already well-developed policy priorities. These included highlighting, wherever possible, Tunisia's status as a zone of social enlightenment in a tough neighbourhood (sandwiched between Algeria and Libya) and basing its economic development on attracting foreign direct investment of the very sort the EMPI was promising. Tunisian policy is rigorously implemented from the centre, where President Zine El Abidine Ben Ali controls a formidable political machine to oversee economic liberalisation heavily laced with 'Tunisian gradualism'. Ben Ali's aim is to rule over a newly industrialised country relatively early in the next century, allowing Tunisia's already relatively high living standards to come up to a European level.

Given their levels of poverty (Morocco and Egypt) and lack of potential stability (Algeria and Libya) it is probably fair to say that no other country in the region can realistically hope to achieve this aim even though several have the potential to make considerable progress towards raising living standards. Furthermore, few other Arab States have understood the EMPI's potential benefits as clearly as Tunisia. What is essential is that they see the potential consequences as clearly as possible: to implement economic policies prescribed by the EMPI in anything other than a rigorous manner could prove disastrous, leading the region (including Tunisia) to turn back on itself. But there are also clear rewards for those who work within the Euro-Med context: the Barcelona process does have an upside.

The Upside

Positive factors of the EMPI include the promise of increased resource flows to southern Mediterranean states and greater impetus to install fully functioning market economies. These factors must be maximised if the EMPI is to work.

Open Markets

This is a means to achieve critical economic goals including maintaining acceptable growth rates, promoting private enterprise and introducing a wider range of products to underdeveloped markets

More Money

The EMPI will be consolidated by the allocation of increased volumes of money. The Cannes summit in late June 1995 approved an allocation of ECU 4,685 million for 1996–2000 for the 11 southern Mediterranean partner states, more than was offered to the EC before but still fitting within the budgetary constraints set out at the December 1992 Edinburgh summit. Loans and other financing provided by the European Investment Bank (EIB) will potentially double the sum. In addition, the World Bank and other agencies will provide support within the EMPI to back industrial development and ease the balance of payments pressures which all signatories will face during their transition periods.

However, the financial incentives should not be overstated. The Cannes summit actually cut back the proposed allocation for all 11 MNCs in 1996–2000 to ECU 4,685 million. While this was more than in previous protocols, it was less than was requested by the European Commission and was expected by the southern partners – some of whom have argued that if the Euro-Med partnerships mean their economies converging with Europe they should receive convergence-type funding, as Spain, Portugal, Greece and Ireland have received. This is a forlorn hope: the European Commission initially called for ECU 5.5 billion, which was pruned back to ECU 5.16 billion prior to Cannes and to the eventual ECU 4,685 million at the summit, leaving 'satisfactory headroom within the Edinburgh Financial Perspectives'.

In contrast, the EIB provided loans worth ECU 47,128 million for regional development within the EU in 1989–93 alone. In 1994, the EIB lent a total of ECU 17,682 million within the EU and ECU 2,246 million outside. German financing to bring its eastern *Länder* up to the western level in 1994–99 is about DM 180 billion a year. This represents nearly half of all western German tax revenues but is seen as essential to bring six relatively small *Länder* up to an acceptable level.

Investment Promotion

The southern Mediterranean already complains of losing out to eastern Europe in the battle for resources. One means of overcoming this would be to mobilise increased private sector investment – the key to the EMPI process. Tunisia has seen this as a distinct advantage of the Euro-Med formula. Since at least the early 1990s, its economic policy has been tailored to attracting significant amounts of FDI (foreign direct investment) to act as the motor of its sustained growth. But despite achieving annual average GDP growth of around five per cent and investing heavily to get over its message that Tunisia can be a major investment centre in the Mediterranean, levels of FDI remain disappointing.

Energy and the Environment

While not an essential element of the Euro-Med model, the EMPI will serve to consolidate growing co-operation in a number of key sectors, such as energy, where Europe's links to the Maghrib are being strengthened by projects such as the expansion of the Trans-Mediterranean gas pipeline running from Algeria through Tunisia to Italy and Slovenia, and construction of the Maghrib-Europe pipeline which is now bringing more Algerian gas to Spain and Portugal, and will provide natural gas for Morocco. Increased co-operation also gives impetus for efforts to tackle some of the Mediterranean basin's most enduring problems, notably the environment, where EU/EIB facilities have been mobilised for projects which reduce industrial and other pollution, introduce more efficient land use and confront desertification.

Political and Security Co-operation

This is central to the Euro-Med formula, promising a new forum for conflict resolution. The prospect of regular meetings of signatory governments is a positive step. Barcelona, after all, brought Israel and Syria to the same table. The Europeans have distanced the EMPI from the parallel Middle East peace process, where Washington is the dominant player, which seems a skilful political sleight of hand that could yield future dividends. However, it also has risks: Middle East issues have the potential to weigh heavily on the EMPI framework, submerging other elements in the poison of Arab-Israeli battles.

One aim of the EMPI is to instil democracy in Mediterranean non-member countries (MNMCs) in the region (see 'The Downside'). This seems more nebulous than the partnership's security co-operation dimension, which takes the Euro-Med idea into a new sphere, while also consolidating existing ties between European and Arab security services. 'Co-operation' includes identifying extremist groups and co-operating more closely on issues of joint concern (in theory) such as drug trafficking. The creation of a corps of Mediterranean Euro-police, involving France, Spain and Italy, could be extended. Barcelona's references to military co-operation could see Europe eventually engineering a major change in the strategic configuration of the Mediterranean basin, where critics argue the *Pax Americana* still rules.

Social and Cultural Co-operation

This is to be increased and there are facilities which help to improve educational standards, increase understanding on both sides of the Mediterranean, improve the management of municipalities and the resources they manage and promote the role of women.

Flexibility

All sides recognise there are potential problems. One clause apparently added late on in the negotiating process of the ground-breaking Tunisian agreement states that in 'sensitive areas' customs duties can be phased out more slowly. Further, if signs of real damage occur to emerging industries, tariffs of up to 25 per cent could be introduced for a maximum period of five years during the transition period (on up to the equivalent of 15 per cent of total exports).

The Downside

The EMPI hinges on the promotion of free trade in industrial goods and services. The Tunisian and subsequent agreements involve a 12-year transition period, during which import duties and other tariffs are to be scrapped. But the increased competition this implies could drive local companies into bankruptcy, unless the *mise à niveau* – the raising of local industry and other infrastructure up to the level needed to compete with Europe – is handled very sensitively.

The view of Moroccan economists that a too rapid opening could prove disastrous is similar across the MENA region. In the Moroccan case, for the kingdom's many inefficient enterprises, it has been levels of tariff protection averaging some 30-35 per cent (as opposed to four per cent in Europe) which has kept them afloat. It is argued that the overnight removal of this protection would wipe out some 50-60 per cent of the Moroccan industrial sector immediately. Among other aspects of the downside:

Budgets are Under Pressure

There are major fiscal costs associated with the accords as customs receipts and other revenues due from imports are scrapped. According to initial Tunisian calculations, customs receipts – which are mainly paid from companies registered in the EU – worth TD 700 m ($746 m) a year will suffer a loss of some TD 75 m in the first year of the accord. These losses will rise progressively before stabilising therefore other forms of revenue are required.

And Money's too Tight....

Are the EU's resources and institutions–including the European Commission infrastructure–capable of meeting the challenge? Clearly large amounts of resources are needed to underpin the *mise à niveau*. Tunis has calculated an initial cost of transition of some $2.2 bn over the next four to five years, around 60 per cent of which will be required by developing small and medium-sized companies seeking to raise their level of operation through technology transfer and training. The remaining 40 per cent is slated for infrastructure and improving the business environment. Such sums must be multiplied by dozens when the other 12 signatories of Barcelona are brought into the equation, the majority of which still aspire to reach even Tunisia's current level of development.

North Africans see the integration into the EU of economies like Portugal and Greece as a model for their own development. But any hopes that funding flows will be mobilised at levels which compare with those which assisted take-off in the new southern EU member states are sadly misplaced. Indeed, the very large ambitions placed in the EMPI are in no way matched by the availability of finance to underwrite restructuring. Southern populations emerging from being state-sector dominated economies must thus put their faith in market forces, stimulated by closer links with Europe, to assure their future in the new Mediterranean.

Adding to the financial pressures, many member states have seen the EC (which follows closely IMF and World Bank policy on structural adjustment) as a means of providing support for southern economies, rather than focusing their assistance on bilateral support. Indeed, in some cases, Member States have explained that reductions in their bilateral aid and credits have been compensated for by increases in EU funding, which (they argue) they have been 'instrumental' in pushing through the Council.

Politics is Politics...

The EMPI encompasses a southern Mediterranean region stretching from the Atlantic coast of Morocco to Turkey. This includes Jordan, a country which is a bastion of the Middle East peace process but has no Mediterranean shoreline, while excluding Libya, the Arab country with the longest Mediterranean coast of all. Libya remains an intractable political problem – at least for the UK, France and some other key power-brokers in EU foreign policy. The other Arab Maghrib Union (UMA) member, Mauritania (a Lomé Convention signatory), was originally excluded from

Barcelona, but was finally included to appease other Maghrib states and Europeans, including Spain, which had lobbied for all five UMA members to take part.

Bilateral interests will probably continue to make much of the running. And, while political, social and cultural co-operation promise new levels of understanding across *mare nostrum*, the practicalities of making this happen remain somewhat obscure.

One Minister's Security Threat is Another's Democrat...

The Barcelona declaration's commitment to democracy is likely to confront severe problems. What forms of sanction the EU will apply to acts such as the suppression of dissidents has yet to be revealed. Differences of opinion over what constitutes a criminal act and what constitutes freedom of expression are more than semantic niceties as any Arab interior minister could attest. Will security co-operation include help for established Arab governments who want more assistance in countering their most implacable opponents: Islamists who have developed bases in Europe? EU governments are already under pressure to act against exiled dissidents, including those granted political asylum.

...or Boat Person

The Barcelona Declaration's social and cultural aims are worthy, but given the lack of resources available, quite how far the EMPI framework can go in building social and cultural relations is very questionable. It practically ignores key elements of North-South relations, especially immigration. The trend towards closing European borders to the majority of visa applicants from Arab countries has not been affected by Barcelona. Arab businessmen complain that their efforts to explore the single European market is severely hampered by the problems of obtaining visas. Arab critics have been angered by the application of the Schengen agreement, covering the free movement of people, which many have found adds extra constraints on immigration which were not included in the single European act.

Then There's the Farmers

Arguably opening the European market to foodstuffs and other agricultural products from Euro-Med signatories would significantly raise their exports and draw in investments as firms saw the potential for export-oriented agribusiness. This would also ease balance of payments problems and persuade rural populations that they are best served by staying on the land, rather than migrating to towns. Sadly, EMPI pays no more than lip-service to liberalising the trade in farm goods which is blocked mainly by southern EU producers.

Tunisia has been given some concessions on olive oil and cut flowers and Morocco's partnership agreement offers limited concessions on a range of crops. It is argued that these economies are not in a position to significantly increase their exports even though they would like to (the celebrated example of Moroccan tomatoes, for instance). But these arguments also fit conveniently well with the national interests of EU Member States, and have shaped EC accords since the 1970s. Farm lobbies–rather than perceptions of what is good for the South and, consequently, for EU foreign policy–remain a dominant force. For example, the Moroccan agreement was delayed by a protracted dispute with the EU over fishing, an issue in which Spanish interests dominate. Talks which started in February 1994 were only concluded in the weeks before the Barcelona Conference, a historic meeting which would have suffered badly from lack of an agreement with Morocco. The Moroccan agreement was also delayed near the end by German, Belgian and Dutch concerns about the effects on their producers of increased Moroccan exports of cut flowers, tomatoes and other products: although Morocco would only export an extra 15,000 tonnes of tomatoes, this was seen as enough by Belgian and other producers to influence prices.

The debate over agricultural trade may only finally be resolved if and when the EU decides to scrap its hugely costly Common Agricultural Policy. WTO rulings may also apply. When it comes to farm products, the EMPI formula seems redundant and European arguments that this debate is irrelevant do seem to smack somewhat of hypocrisy.

Conclusion: Who Wins?

There is a real fear that if the EMPI agreements do not produce levels of growth and investment which are familiar in Asian tigers but are virtually unknown in North Africa, their initial effects will be to create a North-South relationship which is even more 'asymmetrical' (to borrow the phrase used in studies by the former Ukrainian minister turned IMF analyst Oleh Havrylyshyn). There will be pockets of success in attracting FDI for those southern regions and corporates which use the EMPI to their benefit (such as greater Casablanca or joint venture partners in Tunisia). But initially, the most obvious benefits are to European exporters, who win out from reduced tariffs on manufactured goods and as tariffs come down, the main costs are likely to be borne by southern Mediterranean economies. This can be offset by much increased investment flows – which Tunisia, most advanced on the road to Euro-Mediterranean Partnership, claims to be seeing. But clearly, if the transition to free trade is not managed well, the FDI essential to make the EMPI work for the Arab states will not materialise.

Indeed, if increased flows of funding are mainly manifested in technical assistance and infrastructure spending, the EMPI could add to the threat of 'trade diversion', with spending going into Europe for projects which sell goods into the southern zone, rather than capital being spent in North Africa and the Middle East. In this case, southern economies may find themselves caught between living with mass bankruptcies and spiralling unemployment, or stalling reforms. This, in turn, would most likely trigger negative responses from the international financial community and a policy meant to help cure the legacy of three decades of poor economic management could help kill the generation of liberal reformers who implemented it.

Globalisation Versus Regionalism?

GRAHAME THOMPSON

Globalisation

When Paul Hirst and myself began working on the issue of globalisation[1] one of the earliest points that struck us was the lack of a clear definition of the concept. Such as it was defined, it tended to be used merely as an alternative word for the further internationalisation of economic activity, in terms of greater integration and interdependence. The most widely quoted definition in this style of reasoning emerged from an OECD study of globalisation:

> Globalisation is being driven by technological change, continued long-term growth in foreign investment and international sourcing, and the recent extensive formation of new kinds of international links between firms and countries. This combination is increasingly integrating national economies and changing the nature of global competition.[2]

Thus it seemed necessary to provide a clearer definition of globalisation that did not simply imply the extension and deepening of already well advanced international economic interactions. We thus drew a sharp distinction between what we termed a 'globalised world economy' and an 'internationalised world economy'. If there is something distinctive about the present era which distinguishes it from previous periods, then something must be said about what the nature of this new situation is, particularly if it is a potential structural shift in the nature of international capitalism rather than just as a continuation of previous trends under a different name.

Briefly put, an internationalised world economy would be one in which the principal entities remain national economies, or agents that continue to be tethered to a definite national territory. Although there is increasing integration and enmeshment between these entities, there is a continued relative separation of the domestic from the international arena, so that

Grahame Thompson is Senior Lecturer in Economics at the Open University and co-author of *Globalisation in Question*.

international processes, events and impacts are refracted through essentially national frameworks and national policies and processes. This means that an international world economy would be articulated upwards, so to speak, from the national actors to the international level or sphere. Relatively distinct national economies and nationally embedded actors would be articulated together to form such an international economy. The principle private agents in this kind of an economy would be multinational corporations. These would maintain a clear national base with a nationally formed management style and personnel. They would still be effectively regulated and policed by home country authorities, and continue to operate mainly in respect to their home-base country.

In contrast to this is a globalised world economy. This is an economy that exists above the national economies, and agents, autonomously from those national economies and that bears down upon those economies and actors, stamping them with their particular character and form. It enfolds them within its own dynamic. Thus it is articulated downwards, so to speak. It would determine what can and cannot be done at the national level, by both public and private agencies. This would be an economy that escapes governance – one typified by unorganised and uncontrollable market forces. The principal private actors here would be trans-national corporations which represent organisations that are disembodied from any national-base. They would source, produce and market genuinely internationally. They would seek competitive advantage and the most secure and lucrative returns by roaming the globe for cheap but efficient production locations. They would have an internationalised management style and personnel. Thus the image here is one of footloose capital searching the globe for competitive advantage.

These two contrasting images of different types of world economy are presented starkly so as to try to differentiate any new globalised economy from other previously formed sets of internationalised economic relationships. They represent ideal types, and are constructed to aid analytical enquiry rather than being direct representations of any actual or potential economy. It seemed incumbent upon us to provide a relatively rigorous definition of what a globalised economy would look like if we were to say what was different about the present from previous periods of internationalisation. The internationalisation of economic activity has been going on almost since civilisations began, and certainly since the 1700s. So the question that needs to be addressed is what is new and distinctive about the present period?

I have spent sometime on these definitional issues since they are often neglected or misunderstood. These definitions are self-consciously conceptual and deliberately polarised. They have also proved controversial, since commentators have often mistaken these ideal typical analytical distinctions as measures of actual economies and of globalisation itself. In so doing, however, perhaps unwittingly, other contrasting definitions of globalisation have emerged, which it will be worth briefly considering.

The first of these confuses the analytical distinction made above with a distinction between actual forms of the economic mechanism, accusing it of providing a single 'end-state' for the international system – *the* globalised economy.[3] This is seen as a single equilibrium, so to speak – the end result of a series of stages, mechanically unfolding one after another. By contrast, it is suggested, globalisation is an ongoing *process* (or sometimes a set of ongoing *practices*), where there may be a number of outcomes (multiple-equilibria) depending upon the 'path' by which that process evolves and the present 'phase' of globalisation is just one of its many possible forms. This position thus sees globalisation as a process that has been going on for many centuries, and does not feel the necessity of providing the kind of distinction discussed above. In effect, the outcome of its approach is to revert back to a conception that stresses the increasing intensity and extensivity of the internationalisation of economic relationships.

The problem with this kind of approach, however, is its relative lack of analytical rigour. To begin with the criticism that the conceptual distinction sketched out above is incompatible with the idea of a process is a misplaced one. It would be perfectly possible to render this distinction into the framework of a process in which one form of the international economy gives way to another. But to do any proper analytical work it is always necessary to interrupt such processes and ask where exactly we are in respect to them. To do this requires that processes are further specified in respect to their 'periodisation' and are given a certain structure. This is in effect what the Hirst and Thompson definitional activity allowed us to do. In addition, we would argue that all processes have some end in mind if they are not to be meaningless. The Northern Ireland peace process, for instance, has some idea of what peace amounts to, which at a primitive level is shared by all parties involved despite the fact that they might have different ideas of the ways of achieving it. If processes involve some human deliberation and agency, then they must have an end or objective in sight. The admission of potential multiple equilibria does not excuse the specification of what those equilibria would exist/consist in, so we are back at the same point from which the accusation of an end-state began.

The second criticism of our definition arises from a different quarter. The approach suggested above emphasises cross-border interactions and in this sense it is fairly conventional. An alternative approach, indeed one that provides an alternative definition of what is the unique feature of this period of 'globalisation', is to suggest that borders are no longer the key feature of the present international system. The 'global is the local' is one way of putting this, thus the way globalisation works is to imbricate international, and not necessarily cross-border, features at the local level. They become part of the fabric of the local. Features of the commercial world like accounting conventions, legal frameworks, credit rating measures, ISO 9000 quality standards and the like, embody the process of globalisation unnoticed as it were, and do not obviously involve a definite flow of something across a border that can be measured. What is distinctive about the present period of globalisation, it is argued, is the emergence of processes whereby the international world is increasingly governed by these kinds of (mostly Anglo-American) commercial practices.

Clearly, this is a feature of the international system, one that does give significant power to those agencies responsible for setting the standards. The agencies responsible for these standards both claim and exercise a kind of public power, yet they are not in any way obviously publicly accountable for those powers. They are potentially different types of semi-public/semi-private organisations.

However, forms of international standard setting have been a feature of the international system at least from the 1870s onwards, when it was the British that were in the position to establish credit ratings for instance. Before the First World War it was Norway and Britain that set the standards for the sea-worthiness of commercial shipping, them having captured this largely because of the size of their merchant fleets. For all intents and purposes it is the US Federal Aviation Agency that sets the air-worthiness standards for international air craft, but this was achieved long before the advent of globalisation. And one could go on to multiply these kinds of examples, so there is nothing essentially new about this approach which enables international standard setting to operate as the defining feature of a newly globalising world economy.

Other definitions of globalisation could be added that operate along similar lines as these – the idea that it is a strategy, for instance, and thus in the minds of decision takers, particularly in private businesses. But I would defend the original definitional clarification against all these alternatives because I find it gives the clearest basis on which to begin an empirical investigation into the nature of the contemporary international system. However, there may be a further legitimate and rival claim that speaks for the nature of the international system, that of regionalisation.

Regionalisation

Regionalisation signifies a process that draws states and groups together on the basis of their proximity, perhaps because of economic advantages such as transport and information cost economies, or perhaps because security or environmental issues can have a region-wide impact. In addition there is a possibly more pronounced *institutional* integration process that often accompanies such regionalisation which attempts to manage and regulate these local integrative processes, which can be termed regionalism. Clearly, there could be a parallel institution building moment to the globalisation process – globalism – but this is both more difficult at the global level and also less developed (though by no means non-existent).

There are perhaps two main forms of regional institutional integration current in the present period; so-called closed regionalism and open regionalism. Closed regionalism refers to the process most pronounced in Europe, and to a lesser extent in North America, which attempts to establish a common policy for all regional members, common internal and external criteria of operation, and strong common institutions that manage the system. On the other hand the open regionalism of the APEC countries looks towards the integration process being led by market forces without any strong institution building measures driven by political objectives. Ostensibly it remains open to outside interests and remains non-discriminatory with respect to those interests, relying on more relaxed and informal mechanisms of common interest building. It leaves the individual members to decide their own internal and external support measures, allowing the pace and extent of change to be established by a series of separate consensus-seeking inter-governmental negotiations amongst the parties and not according to some carefully planned timetable. These inter-governmental negotiations establish non-binding initiatives and conditions conducive to trade liberalisation, but not necessarily to internal liberalisation or common standards.[4]

While there is at least some consensus amongst commentators that a region is a subsystem of the whole, one marked by geographical adjacency and contiguity of its component parts, this does not advance far the definition of what can or cannot be considered a region. Clearly spaces like the European continent meet this criteria well, and regions have also been proposed (and constructed) for various purposes around seas like the Mediterranean and the Black Sea. But constructing them around oceans like the Pacific, as APEC tries to do, may be stretching the idea of region too far. However, this depends upon a range of other criteria that need to be brought to bear when defining a region, which are not just geographical.[5]

The first of these would be shared characteristics of various kinds – a river basin, religious affiliation, political characteristics, common diseases, etc. The second would be the extent and degree of interactions between areas, which itself can be divided into: a) types of interaction, for example, economic, cultural, security; b) attitudes accompanying these interactions, for example, benign co-operation *versus* mutual suspicion or fear; c) intensity of interaction, and finally; d) what boundaries consist of (are they solid or porous?) and how well they would fare in respect to an intruding power that is not part of the region. Thirdly, we might consider the perceptual level; do potential members consider themselves to be related in some manner, and what is the rhetoric of any potential regionalism?

These criteria, along with the more obvious one of geography, can be used to identify the extent and scope of different regional configurations. There can be little doubt that definite patterns of regional integration based upon these criteria are in play at the international level. In addition they allow us to open up two somewhat separate aspects to regional integrations, namely the economic and the security aspects, which may contain their own different modalities and dynamics.

Global, Regional, or Both?

When looking at the question of whether the empirical evidence supported the main claims of the strong globalisation thesis, the Hirst and Thompson study concluded that the balance of the evidence could not sustain those claims. In particular, the degree of integration and interdependence being experienced in the early 1990s was in many respects no more than had been experienced a hundred years earlier during the high Gold Standard period.[6] The key economic differences between the high Gold Standard period and the present are that there has undoubtedly been a growth in the internationalisation of production and, on the other, in the development of large scale short-term international capital flows – including derivative instruments based on them. But neither of these two developments is sufficient to meet the claims that a new and radically different era is upon us that meets any reasonable definition of a globalised economy, particularly in the light (but not the letter) of our conceptual clarification discussed above. We continue to live more in an internationalised world economy than in a globalised one. Our analysis found that the degree of internationalisation of production had been severely exaggerated – most international firms still meet the criteria of being multinational rather than transnational. The emergence of short-term capital flows–which has occupied so much of the attention of the strong globalisers – is clearly important, but only holds the significance it does for those who subscribe to a monetarist version of how the economy works or of how best to manage it. Without these as overriding concerns, it is international trade and real capital flows that should occupy attention since it is they that genuinely augment the system rather than simply redistribute success and failure around it (which is largely what short-term capital flows actually achieve).

This may sound an heroic position given the events in East-Asia during the Winter and Spring of 1997-1998, but careful analysis shows that it was the economic fundamentals of the economies concerned that both precipitated the crisis in the Asia-Pacific area and will determine how it is resolved.[7]

One of the key features of the international system can be illustrated by Figure 1. This shows which member of the Triad (the USA, the European Union and Japan) dominated the inward foreign direct investment (FDI) in particular countries over the period of the late 1980s and early 1990s. Intra-Triad relations alone were responsible for 75 per cent of FDI flows during the 1980s, some 70 per cent of trade in 1992, and a similar percentage of GDP (whereas they accounted for only 14 per cent of the world's population). After the mid-1980s the growth of FDI eclipsed that of trade growth so FDI now figures as the central driving force in the international economy (both of these are, however, expanding at a faster rate than is world GDP). Although the growth of FDI flows declined somewhat in the early 1990s, and the direction of these flows moved more in favour of the non-Triad countries, the older pattern began to re-establish itself again after 1992. This intra-Triad dominance was reinforced by the important subsidiary flows of investment between the Triad itself and a geographically discrete group of smaller clustered states shown in the square boxes of Figure 1. Relatively isolated clusters of main actor and client states were emerging, therefore, which were geographically discrete and stabilising. Thus whilst intra-Triad investment relationships were particularly dense, a pattern of further discrete but robust inter-linkages between each of the Triad members and more marginalised country clusters was also evident. These country groupings tend to be regionally specific and adjacent to one or other of the Triad members. Further, this testifies to the relative lack of integration in FDI flows and stocks since the boxed clusters indicate a geographical and regional discreteness in the relationships between countries. The direction of FDI relationships is first amongst the Triad countries themselves and then secondly between one or other of the Triad powers and its cluster of client states, rather than between the clustered boxed states themselves.

There are a number of issues here and the first concerns the intensity of the relationships involved and the consequences of these. Broadly speaking, the intensity of the relationship between the core Triad members and their adjacent clustered regional allies is greater in the case of trade than it was in the case of FDI.[8] This is just another way of saying that multilateral trade integration is lower than is integration in the case of FDI, even though, as we have seen it remains extremely geographically discrete in the case of investment flows and stocks. But despite this there is a more multilateral set of integrative linkages between all the countries shown in Figure 1 where

FIGURE 1: FOREIGN DIRECT INVESTMENT CLUSTERS OF TRIAD MEMBERS,
1990. (ECONOMIES IN WHICH A TRIAD MEMBER DOMINATES INWARD FOREIGN
DIRECT INVESTMENT STOCKS/FLOWS)

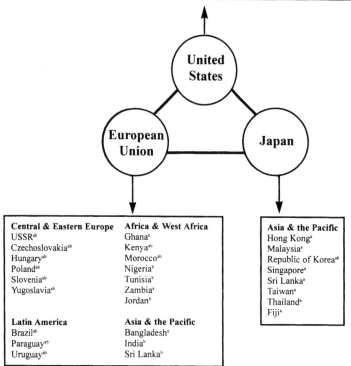

Latin America		Asia & the Pacific	Africa & West Africa
Argentina[b]	El Salvador[b]	Bangladesh[a]	Ghana[b]
Bolivia[ab]	Honduras[b]	India[a]	Nigeria[a]
Chile[ab]	Mexico[ab]	Pakistan[a]	Saudi Arabia[ab]
Colombia[ab]	Panama[ab]	Philippines[ab]	
Dominican Republic[b]	Peru[b]	Taiwan[ab]	
Ecuador[ab]	Venezuela[ab]	Papua New Guinea[ab]	

United
States

European
Union

Japan

Central & Eastern Europe	Africa & West Africa
USSR[ab]	Ghana[a]
Czechoslovakia[ab]	Kenya[ab]
Hungary[ab]	Morocco[ab]
Poland[ab]	Nigeria[b]
Slovenia[ab]	Tunisia[b]
Yugoslavia[ab]	Zambia[a]
	Jordan[b]

Latin America	Asia & the Pacific
Brazil[ab]	Bangladesh[a]
Paraguay[ab]	India[b]
Uruguay[ab]	Sri Lanka[b]

Asia & the Pacific
Hong Kong[a]
Malaysia[a]
Republic of Korea[ab]
Singapore[a]
Sri Lanka[a]
Taiwan[a]
Thailand[a]
Fiji[a]

Note: a in terms of average inward FDI *flow*, 1988-90
         b in terms of inward *stock*, 1990
Source: Hirst and Thompson 1996 (note 1) Figure 3.6, p. 65.

investment is concerned, so that the geographical discreteness (and any
associated clientism) is potentially less important in terms of investment
than it is in the case of trade. Investment relationships are more open to
cross-integration between the core countries and the different sets of
clustered states than they are in the case of trade relationships, which are
more intensively linked and hence more closed to these cross-fertilisations
as between regionalised blocs and clusters. In other words, there are more

cross relationships between the countries shown in the boxes where investment is concerned than where trade is concerned.

In fact, since this analysis was completed there has been a growth of precisely this aspect to the relationships depicted. Mainland China, for example, is not included in the countries shown in Figure 1 but became the largest single developing country recipient of inward FDI during the 1990s. Most of this was organised by overseas Chinese business interests, so an alternative supply network to those depicted in the figure has emerged. In addition there has been a rapid growth in some inter-cluster trade and investment relationship, particularly amongst the Mercosur countries in the southern cone of South America (see Figure 2, below). These trends are tending to obscure the picture that emerged from Figure 1, but as yet they are not strong and even if they continue it will take a very long time before the established pattern depicted by the figure is undermined. If we were to add just ten of the most favoured other countries in terms of FDI flows that were outside the Triad in the early 1990s, then these would all have accounted for 90 per cent of FDI flows during the 1980s. Thus the Triad will continue to dominate for the foreseeable future.

This has two possible further implications. First it means that protectionist sentiment on the part of the different trading blocs and major states is likely to be lower in the field of investment than it may have been in the case of trade. Secondly, it would seem to make investment as potentially liable to genuine multilateral regulation as trade has been, which itself was highly amenable to this form of management in the past. Both of these features could thus act to undermine any intense and inward looking development of regionalised trading blocs. Given that investment is tending to displace trade as the main driving force for international integration, the likelihood of competitive and antagonistically poised trade and investment blocs emerging is reduced. Thus the potential for the security of the system needs to be considered in this context. There are more incentives for continued minimal co-operation between the Triad blocs than for outright dissent amongst them. The international division of labour is now so advanced that it would be difficult for it to unwind and degenerate into open hostility.

But this optimistic note should not divert us from the seemingly clear trend towards the formation of explicit trading blocs in the international system. Figure 1 captured the *de facto* nature of regional integration, that driven by the ordinary commercial decision of private economic agents – but this does not necessarily directly coincide with the *de jure* nature of that integration, which is driven by explicit intergovernmental policy towards the creation of regional trading blocs like the EU, NAFTA and APEC. Here we encounter the difference between the regional*isation* of economic activity on the one hand and the development of regional*ism* on the other as a mechanism of governance for the regionalising economies.

Figure 2 shows that some 61 per cent of international trade was accounted for by formal regional free trade arrangements in 1994. This clearly remains the dominant contemporary expression of the international economy. The table divides trading arrangements into three separate areas: Europe, the Americas and the Pacific Rim. Europe and the Pacific Rim accounted for about 25 per cent each, while the Americas contribute the remaining 11 per cent. Clearly the EU is a major bloc, with the much more diverse APEC of similar importance (here APEC excludes the USA/NAFTA trade). The NAFTA comprises perhaps a surprisingly small bloc, which is mirrored by the Americas total as a whole.

FIGURE 2
REGIONAL FREE TRADE ARRANGEMENTS – SHARE OF WORLD TRADE, 1994 (%)

EU		22.8
Euro-Med		2.3
	Europe Sub-total	**25.1**
NAFTA		7.9
Mercosur		0.3
FTAA		2.6*
	Americas Sub-total	**10.8**
AFTA		1.3
Australia–New Zealand		0.1
APEC		23.7*
	Pacific Rim Sub-total	**25.1**
TOTAL		**61.0**

Notes: FTAA = Free Trade Area of the Americas
            AFTA = ASEAN Free Trade Area
            * Excludes cross-sub regional totals.
Source: Adapted from: Bergsten (1996) p.196[9]

According to Frankel, Stein and Wei,[10] all these regional arrangements show more bias towards trading between the countries within them – at the expense of trading outside of the regional bloc – than might be expected, even after adjusting for natural determinants of trade such as size, GDP per capita, proximity and common borders. Thus there would seem to be some trade diverting aspects to regional bloc formation. Overall, however, what this analysis suggests is that although there is a very clear trend towards the regionalisation of the world economy, this is buttressed by a continued relatively robust commitment to multilateralism at the same time.[11] These two processes are not incompatible. In addition, these two trends do not square very well with a strong move towards the full globalisation of economic activity, for reasons already outlined.

A further implication of this analysis is to stress the *strategic* interrelationship between the three main player countries/groups within the international system – the Triad – which potentially displays a dynamic that is different to that driven by the growth of purely economic inter-dependences. For instance, the analysis by Sandholtz *et al*[12] stresses the way that a Triad of economic powers based upon the USA, Germany and Japan is redefining the nature of international security, but a security in which the issue of comparative international competitiveness is considered to be critical.

Two features animate this analysis: the collapse of the Cold War and the decline of US hegemony. The first is seen as heralding the potential end of geo-politics as a new geo-economics based upon international competitiveness replaces it. The emphasis shifts from a predominantly militarily driven system of inter-state/bloc rivalry, based upon deep ideological and systemic socio-economic organisational differences, to a system based around peaceful economic competition between states/blocs with military matters subsidiary to this (at least in the first instance). The second implicates the USA's ability to manage the newly evolving system and to secure its own strategic objectives. The decline of hegemony is put down to a decline in economic power and the loss of international competitiveness, so the remedy is obvious – to restimulate the American economy. How this should be done, however, is a question which has preoccupied many American analysts since the 1970s.

The geo-economics approach has the advantage of setting the problem of managing all aspects of domestic economies squarely within an international system, and one where state/bloc rivalry between the advanced industrial states continues to figure prominently. The thrust of the approach is to look for the possible consequences of a different or similar competitiveness record amongst the Triad (in terms of its security implications). Although the nodal points of the approach adopted by Sandholtz *et al.* are represented by single countries (the USA, Germany and Japan) a feature of the analysis is to link these to the formation of definite economic blocs (indicated by East-Asia, NAFTA and the EU). An obvious potential problem here is whether such an East-Asian bloc, formed around Japan, is actually emerging – though the analysis conducted around Figure 1 above and the recent East-Asian crisis, which has strengthened the hand of the yen in the area, lends some support to this. The EU looks the most coherent bloc, with NAFTA a long way behind in terms of institution building. Insofar as there is an East-Asian bloc based upon Japan, it is driven by commercial activity rather than by any institution building. Explicit and complex institution building is eschewed by the 'Asian way', and is certainly rejected within the wider APEC process, which is the classic case of an open regionalism.[13]

Managing the Regionalised but Multilateral International System

Given the patterns and trends identified above what are the implications for the overall governance of such a system? The analysis has suggested that although there are strong trends towards the regionalisation of economic activity, this can still be set within the framework of a continued commitment to multilateralism. As an intermediate stage in the process of governance the idea of regionalism was introduced, associated with the emergence of explicit and formal inter-governmental and even super-governmental agencies of economic regulation like the EU, NAFTA, Mercosur and APEC. Outlined in this section is a way of reconciling the existence of co-operative regional trading arrangements with the benefits of a modified multilateralism. These two features can be mutually reinforced by conceiving the international system as a kind of 'regime'.[14]

To do this what needs to be considered further is a way of moving from models of the international system that rely upon national economic actors with strict neo-realist utility functions of the form $U_a = V_a$, where U is the utility of country A and V is the pay-off to country A. In this case the state-players are concerned only with their own absolute advantage. With these kinds of strictly independent utility functions player-states do not care what other player-states might achieve or not achieve in terms of gains from any co-operative relationships. Strictly speaking, therefore, it rules out the analysis of situations characterised by common but mixed interests.[15]

Instead we could suggest that utility functions may in fact be interactive, where common and mixed interests prevail, so that the relative position of power gain becomes important.[16] Here any attempt to forge co-operation between the state-players in a system might be more dependent upon the perceived changes in relative capabilities that the co-operation would bring about. If this were the case the utility function would not just involve the term V_a, but also an additional term W_b designating the partner state B's payoff. One way of thinking about W_b would be to view it as negatively contributing to the state-players' utility, so that if the capability 'gap' between any two players were to increase, the individual state-player A would feel threatened. In this case the utility function becomes:

$$U_a = V_a - V^k(W_b - V_a); \ 0 < k$$

with k representing the state-player's coefficient of sensitivity to potential capability advantages or disadvantages perceived to arise as a result of co-operation. Note that with this formulation it is only gaps in gains favouring partners that reduces the utility a state enjoys from co-operation. Thus this could lead the relatively disadvantaged state-player to avoid co-operation altogether, even though the joint action promised it some individual absolute gain. This would happen if the gain gap $(k(W_b - V_a))$ was sufficiently in its disfavour to outweigh the absolute individual gain (V_a).

Clearly, in this example, state-players' utility is at least partially interdependent so that one state-player's utility affects another's which could be seen as a characteristic of the process of European integration. The case of 'defensive positionalism' analysed through the gain gap mechanism just described captures a good deal about the suspicious manner in which governments approach co-operative institution building in an increasingly interdependent world.

However, there is a further consideration that needs to be brought into the analysis. These models rely upon suspicion and a lack of goodwill on the part of state-players. They begin from a position of radical non-co-operation, non-trust and non-integration and ask how co-operation, trust and integration can be built up. But the problem is that any system already has some co-operation, trust and integration built into its operation. Therefore, we need to begin from a different position, one that recognises the already prior existence of these attributes in some or other form.

Let us suppose, then, that the aim is to maximise the utility of the system overall (which I call a 'regime'). It is assumed that the utility of the regime/system in time period 1 (U_{s_1}) is in some way additive of the utility of the individual state-players A, B, C, etc.:

$$U_{s_1} = U_{a_1} + U_{b_1} + U_{c_1} + \ldots\ldots + U_{n_1}$$

and that the utility of each individual player-state is itself a combination of its own absolute advantage gain in this period and some inherited goodwill derived from the co-operative regime in the previous period. Thus:

$$U_{a_1} = V_{a_1} + j(U_{s_{t-1}}); \ 0 < j$$
and
$$U_{b_1} = V_{b_1} + h(U_{s_{t-1}}); \ 0 < h$$

where j and h are the goodwill sensitivity indicators for state-players A and B respectively, inherited from the regime in the previous time period $(U_{s_{t-1}})$. Thus we can rewrite the regime/system utility function in the present period as:

$$U_{s_1} = [V_{a_1} + j(U_{s_{t-1}})] + [V_{b_1} + h(U_{s_{t-1}})] + \ldots + [V_{n_1} + \propto (U_{s_{t-1}})]$$

This way of characterising the international situation has the advantage of making it dynamic by building in some hysteresis, or inherited activity from the past. Clearly the goodwill factor is the crucial one. It represents a number of things: the co-operation, trust and integrative benefits already built into any system that claims to be social. The 'goodwill coefficients' express the individual state-players attitude towards these features. Thus the analytical problem from this point of view is not to ask how co-operation, trust or integration can be built from nothing, but how can the system and the players be made more trustworthy or trusting, or differently trustworthy and trusting; or how can different forms of co-operation or integration be fostered; or how can the (existing) integrative regime be modified to suit state-players interests and expectations, etc.

The point about this reformulation of the nature of international competition is to stress the way interdependence and integration have established a framework of co-operation within which national players under normal conditions *must* co-exist. Those approaches that insist on the continued use of realist theoretical credentials are in danger of missing this point. The challenge is to explore the operation of 'regimes' (as loosely described above) that bind together the main economic actors into various forms of reciprocal relationships – a thorough going multilateralism. These relationships are more likely to result in continued co-operation than to disintegrate into hostile zero-summed solutions, though this is not to say they are necessarily stable or that it is impossible for them to degenerate into something worse. As it stands, however, the prospects still remain positive for the security outcomes of the drift away from geo-politics and towards the geo-economics of a competitively orientated world economy.

What About Europe?

Here, we enter the difficult terrain of the future of the EU and whether it can establish itself as a coherent bloc or remain so. It now looks very likely that EMU will begin on time and involve enough of the members to make it at least an initial success. But it must be said that the EU has done best when it has looked outside of itself to its external environment and negotiations. There has been less dispute between its members in these instances than when the Union focused in upon internal developments. In some ways there are too few disputes in the international system, between the Triad for instance. The USA tends to gets its way too easily and too often. With more conflict the Union could exercise its powers more clearly, and this would tend to provide the political conditions for a more coherent internal decision making process to develop. The key to the internal deepening of the Union clearly remains the relationships that unfold in respect to its external profile. The widening of the Union, for instance, requires a deepening of its internal structure for that widening to be a success. There are two sets of issues that arise here, both of which concern what happens around the Union's borders in the near future.

The first concerns what happens towards the east. The successful integration of any new members to the east will require a radical restructuring of their own economies and polities if this process of widening the Union is not to undermine the development and achievements of the Union so far. But if the Union is to provide some serious 'ladder' process by which potential members can climb to be ready for union, then this will itself require a comparable process of deepening of the Union amongst the existing members at the same time. This is why the present monetary union process has come at just the wrong time, despite its likely successful launch. The process of monetary union is itself deflationary, which has coincided with a general recession in some of the Union countries while existing economies, particularly the French and German, need internal restructuring to re-establish or maintain their own international competitiveness. This is a less than ideal situation, and one that could easily lead to a longer-term destabilisation of the European economy.

On the other hand we have the issues that arise to the south, something of particular interest to the readers of this journal. The economic relationships between the EU and the countries around its southern perimeter are more complex than those between the EU and its eastern candidate members because of a basic asymmetry in the revealed comparative advantages displayed by the two areas.[17] The countries to the east display a complementary sectoral comparative advantage structure to the existing EU countries, whereas those to the south show no such complementarities, and indeed few comparative advantages in any sector of production. Thus whilst there seems to be the basis for a mutually advantageous sectoral trade between the EU and the countries to the east, there seems little such basis for mutual sectoral trade advantage for those countries to the south and the EU.

But what happens around the Mediterranean, and particularly amongst the Muslim countries, will be crucial to the political development within Europe. This is because of the large Muslim populations within the Union, which have the capacity to destabilise, or more likely to be used to destabilise, its internal political developments. Obviously, of particular significance here are developments in the most important of the Mediterranean Muslim countries, notably Turkey, Egypt and Algeria. If these become radicalised, the present uneasy political equilibrium within many of the key Union states could be severely shaken, which will itself dramatically affect the moves towards a deepening of the Union. As usual, these potential political developments cannot be read off very easily from the economic ones discussed in this article, and I am not sure what direct contribution the kind of analysis it has offered can make to what will be highly contingent and very unpredictable events.

NOTES

1. Hirst, P. and Thompson, G. (1996), *Globalisation in Question:The International Economy and the Possibilities of Governance*, Cambridge, Polity Press; and Hirst, P. and Thompson, G. (1996), 'Globalisation: Ten Frequently Asked Questions and Some Surprising Answers' in *Soundings*, No.4, Autumn, pp 47–66.
2. OECD 1992, p.195. This definition of globalisation was recently repeated almost verbatim in the European Union (1997), 'Annual Report for 1997'in *European Economy No. 63*, Brussels, European Commission, p.45.
3. Perraton, J., Goldblatt, D., Held, D. and McGrew, A. (1997), 'The Globalisation of Economic Activity' *New Political Economy*, Vol.2, No.2, pp. 257–77; and Perraton, J. ' A Critique of Hirst and Thompson' in Holden, B.B. (ed) '*Global Democracy: A Debate*' (forthcoming).
4. Yamazawa, I. (1998), 'Economic Integration in the Asia Pacific Region' in Thompson, G.F. (ed) *Economic Dynamism in the Asia-Pacific: The Growth of Integration and Competitiveness*, London: Routledge.
5. Mansfield, E.D and Milner, H.V (1997), 'The Political Economy or Regionalism: An Overview' in Mansfield, E.D. and Milner, H.V. (eds) *The Political Economy of Regionalism*. New York, Columbia University Press; and Buzan, B. (1998), 'The Asia Pacific: What Sort of Region in What Sort of World?' in McGrew, A. and Brook, C. (eds) *Asia-Pacific in the New World Order*, London, Routledge.
6. See Hirst and Thompson 1996 (note 1); and Thompson, G.F. (1998) 'Where do MNCs Conduct Their Business Activity and What are The Consequences for National Systems?' in Quack, S., Morgan, G. and Whitley, R. (eds) *National Capitalisms, Global Competition and Economic Performance*, Berlin, De Gruyter .
7. See, for example, Thompson, G.F. (1998) (ed) *Economic Dynamism in the Asia-Pacific: The Growth of Integration and Competitiveness*, London, Routledge.
8. United Nations, *World Investment Report 1993. Transnational Corporations and Integrated International Production*, New York, United Nations, Chapter VII; and United Nations (1996) *World Investment Report 1995. Transnational Corporations and Competitiveness*, New York, United Nations, Chapter I.
9. Bergsten, C.F. (1996), 'Globalising Free Trade', in *Foreign Affairs*, 75/3, May/June.
10. Frankel, J., Stein, E. and Wei, S-J. (1993), 'Continental Trading Blocs: Natural or Supernatural?', *NBER Working Paper No.4588*, Cambridge MA, National Bureau of Economic Research; and Frankel, J., Stein, E. and Wei, S-J. (1994), *APEC and Regional Trading Agreements in the Pacific*. Washington, D.C., Institute for International Economics.
11. See Thompson, G.F. (1998) *From 'Embedded Liberalism' to 'Trilaterally Minimal Multilateralism'? Governance of the International Economy*, Centro de Investigaciones Interdisciplinarias en Ciences y Humanidades, Mexico, Universidad Nacional Autonoma de Mexico.
12. Sandholtz, W., Borrus, M., Zysman, J. (1992), *The Highest Stakes: The Economic Foundations of the Next Security System*, New York, Oxford University Press.
13. Yamazawa (note 4).
14. See also Thompson (note 11).
15. Thompson, G. F. (1993) *The Economic Emergence of a New Europe? The Political Economy of Cooperation and Competition in the 1990s*, Cheltenham: Edward Elgar. Chapter 1.
16. Grieco, J. M. (1990) *Cooperation Amongst Nations*. Ithaca, New York, Cornell University Press.
17. Padoan, P.C. (1997), 'Regional Arrangements as Clubs: The European Case' in Mansfield & Milner (note 5) Table 5.1, p. 112.

Regionalism and the Mediterranean

ALFRED TOVIAS

Are We Heading Towards a World of Trading Blocks?[1]

The successful completion and further implementation of the Uruguay Round in 1993 (including the creation of the World Trade Organisation) have not promoted any movement away from trading blocks although the process is slower than before 1993 and likely to remain so. Pressure on Argentina and Brazil to enter NAFTA (North American Free Trade Area), for example, has been slowed since agriculture was adequately covered by the Uruguay Round. In addition, APEC (Asia-Pacific Economic Co-operation) will take much more time to emerge as a real trading block than if the Round had failed. A scenario of confrontation, however, could rapidly develop[2] if any of the two existing trading blocks (that is the EC/EEA and the US/NAFTA):

- lose interest in the multilateral process of negotiation;
- become entities which systematically exclude would be candidates for new initiatives;
- maintain or increase the average level of protection against non-members;
- resort to bilateral reciprocity for the granting of trade concessions;
- impose unilaterally retaliatory measures and resort to threats;
- discriminate against foreign producers within the block.

So, while the WTO (World Trade Organisation) and GATT (General Agreement on Tariffs and Trade) machineries act as a reminder for all of the advantages of multilateralism, there are clear signs of the world trading system shifting towards what can be called 'regionalism', if not 'regional trading blocks'.

Professor Alfred Tovias is Deputy Director of the Helmut Kohl Institute for European Studies at the Hebrew University in Jerusalem.

What are the Implications for Countries in the Periphery of the Blocks?

If we assume for a moment that we are heading to a world of regional trading blocks, remaining outside any block would create an underdog of a small economy, with the danger of one or several trading blocks ganging up against it. In a world of blocks with no MFN (most favoured nation) treatment there is no question that small trading countries must enter one block (no matter which) rather than none. Of course there is a price to pay for this. Apart from the cost of trade diversion for member countries, an additional disadvantage of being in a block for countries such as Mediterranean Non-Member Countries (MNMCs) is that exporters do not try to adjust to world standards but rather to the block standards. This is what happened to Australia in the 1950s and 1960s with very bad results. The same happened to Eastern European members of the ex-COMECON. Thus, if allowed, small countries should try to enter, or to be closely associated with, more than one block. For MNMCs the basic issues are:

- whether new or existing blocks will be relatively open;
- whether they will be open to new membership or at least associate membership, even to countries which do not belong to the region; and
- whether membership in one 'club' precludes simultaneous membership of other clubs.

If emerging blocks remain fairly open, there is not much point entering into a specific block. If one of them is inward-looking while others are not, it is an open question if MNMCs would gain more by trying to enter the inward looking block than by not entering. First, unless the inward-looking block has a lot of leverage on the rest of the world, including on the other blocks, entering may not only lead to losses from trade diversion, but also put in jeopardy MNMCs' access to the other blocks.

Theoreticians stress that all other things remaining equal, trading blocks should be more protected (and protective) than their individual members and that this allows them to reap the benefits of the enlarged leverage obtained through union – the block may conduct a strategic trade policy where the individual member of the club may not. Of course the outcome of the block's moves depends on who is facing it. If it is another block of similar size, the final outcome of the strategic game is unpredictable, because of the risks of retaliation. But if the 'other' is not a block but a small economy (like that of any MNMC), the outcome of a trade war seems clear cut. The worst case scenario is of course different trading blocks ganging up against a small country (in the military domain this corresponds to the situation of Poland in 1939). This is what countries like Korea, Taiwan and so on, seem to have feared since the mid 1990s with the emergence of both the European Economic Area (EEA) and the North American Free Trade Area (NAFTA).

However, MNMCs were not in the position of Taiwan or Korea. Between 50 per cent to 75 per cent of MNMCs exports entered duty-and quota-free under preferential treatment given by the EC (and in the case of Israel also by the US and EFTA) with almost no restrictions. Moreover, MNMCs have benefited from limited preferential access into some other OECD countries such as Japan, Canada and Australia under the GSP (Generalised System of Preferences) programme since the mid-1970s. So MNMCs were not 'stranded' countries even before Barcelona, when the Euro-Mediterranean Partnership Initiative was launched.

What is the Interest of MNMCs in Joining the EU 'Hub'?

The fact that Arab countries have embraced the Euro-Mediterranean Partnership underscores the strategic reorientation of some of these countries' foreign policies towards Europe after the end of the Cold War (for example, Egypt). But beyond political choice, what lies behind the aspiration of MNMCs to be part of the European Trading Block, and is the EU the 'natural trading block' of the MNMCs?

It is evident that the EU15 is now a confederation in the making and MNMCs are not a part of this process. This is a challenge, which nowadays materialises with the further deepening of the EU to become a monetary union by 1999. The challenge is compounded by the fact that the EU has decided to enlarge again east and south, after having done so in 1995 with the inclusion of Austria, Sweden and Finland. Negotiations for the inclusion in the EU of Hungary, Poland, the Czech Republic, Slovenia, Estonia and Cyprus by 2002 or 2003 started in the spring of 1998. Note that Slovenia and Cyprus are in fact MNMCs.

Other MNMCs (including Malta, whose electorate recently decided not to enter the EU) cannot remain passive in view of these developments given their trade dependence on the EU (ranging from 40 per cent to 80 per cent, with the exception of Jordan). The larger the area of geographical discrimination in international trade, the more non-members in the periphery suffer from exclusion. The movement towards regionalism and the creation of huge trading entities will continue, in large part because of lack of traditional opposition to the idea by the US.[3]

Natural trading blocks are linked to economic geography. In distribution activities what counts is the delivery time and economic distance and this is valid for MNMCs too. Highly perishable products (some personal services or goods such as live animals, fruit, vegetables and so on) and bulky products (such as cement) are highly sensitive to economic distance. Electricity does not travel well over long distances.

The short geographical distance between MNMCs and EU member countries (for example, MNMCs and Western Europe are at most one hour away in terms of time zones) facilitates real time commercial intercourse (for instance, opening and closing times are practically the same; there is no 'jet lag' when travelling to Europe; quick feedback from markets is possible; highly perishable and bulky products are tradeable). Another factor connected to geography is the fact that MNMCs and parts of Western Europe share the same oceanic and meteorological factors, conferring easy knowledge of the natural conditions prevailing in the trading partner. Moreover local consumption and cultural patterns and standards largely overlap with European ones, and the climate is similar to that of Southern Europe.

Of course MNMCs have neighbours other than Europe (themselves, some parts of Sub Saharan Africa or Central Asia), but there are limited possibilities for MNMCs to direct their exports to any of them, not only due to states of war or hostility with some of them, but also because of their limited absorption capacities. Unfortunately this will not change in the short to medium term, whether there is perfect peace among countries in the EU's periphery or not.

There are several factors which will increase the relative importance of the EU for MNMCs as a trading partner, at least in relation to the US or Japan. First and foremost are its past and future enlargements. With time, the EU will come closer to the Eastern Mediterranean after having come closer to the Maghrib with the incorporation of Spain and Portugal to the EU. This will happen when Cyprus or Hungary join the EU. Secondly, because of the end of the Cold War, the US will rely less on Israel, Turkey, Morocco or Egypt as strategic partners. It also has plans to extend the NAFTA agreement to all the Western Hemisphere the NAFTA agreement (the so called Enterprise for the Americas) or create a huge FTA around the Pacific (the APEC project). Thirdly, the fact that most MNMCs citizens have had access to European TV programmes for several years has already had, and will continue to have a tremendous influence on MNMCs' local culture and behaviour. Because of the language barrier, the influence of France on the Maghrib is preserved by this channel to the detriment of the overwhelming presence of the US elsewhere in world media.

Will Joining the EU 'Hub' be to the Detriment of Relations with Other 'Hubs'?

Reverse preferences to be conceded by Maghrib and Mashriq countries to the EU in the context of the Euro-Mediterranean Partnership are significant insofar as average MFN tariffs in these countries are non-negligible (for example Jordanian MFN tariff rates average 25 per cent). A preliminary assessment of the impact of these preferences on MNMCs consists in comparing the likelihood of trade creation and trade diversion effects. The latter are particularly awkward for those countries still relying largely on tariffs as a source of fiscal revenue. Trade diversion effects are the ones which might negatively affect MNMCs relations with other 'hubs'. In this respect, the US is unlikely to remain silent for long, particularly regarding the future of their exports to Egypt, the second highest US aid recipient after Israel. Not by coincidence, Israel realised in the early 1980s that morally and politically it was untenable to discriminate against the US in the Israeli market and overcame this problem by concluding a free trade agreement with the US as early as 1985. Maghrib and Mashriq countries could do the same or reduce MFN tariffs in parallel to the implementation of their free trade area with the EU. The other side of the coin, however, is that this would imply additional adjustment efforts deriving from an even larger trade liberalisation programme.

To get a sense of the potential importance of the trade diversion issue, below is a sectorial analysis of the issue, using United Nations Commodity Trade Statistics of Tunisia and Egypt (1993), disaggregated by product group at the SITC (Standard International Trade Classification) two digit level and by country of origin. In the case of Tunisia there are five SITC categories regarding which the share of US-originating Tunisian imports is quite high; therefore, the potential for trade diversion against the US seems non-negligible.

Categories		**Corresponding US share (%)**
SITC 67 :	iron and steel	13.7
SITC 75 :	office machines and automatic data processing machines equipment	22.1
SITC 76:	telecommunications equipment	19.2
SITC 79:	other transport equipment	43.9
SITC 81:	prefabricated structures, sanitary plumbing, heating and lighting fittings	65.3

It is noteworthy that in some categories other MNMCs would be highly discriminated, should Tunisia decide not to enter into FTAs with them.

SITC 67:	iron and steel	17.2
SITC 56:	manufactured fertilisers	15.5

Other developing countries are important as suppliers of:

SITC 52:	inorganic chemicals	50.8
SITC 67:	iron and steel	15.1
SITC 63:	wood and cork manufactures	61.8
SITC 75:	office machines	27.9
SITC 76:	telecommunications equipment	22.4
SITC 82:	furniture	28.1
SITC 83:	travel goods	33.9
SITC 87:	professional and scientific instruments	14.6
SITC 88:	photographic and optical goods	22.5
SITC 89:	miscellaneous manufactured products	24.7

The potential for trade diversion against the US in the case of Egypt is much larger, both because the size of the market and because of a higher import dependence on non EU imports. It appears that in the following SITC categories, the share of US originating Egyptian imports is at least 15 per cent.

SITC 64:	paper and manufactures	15
SITC 74:	general industrial machinery	20.8
SITC 75:	office machines and automatic data processing machines	28.2
SITC 87:	professional and scientific instruments	23.1

Noteworthy here is that in SITC categories 52: inorganic chemicals and SITC 61: leather manufactures, other MNMCs account for more than 20 per cent of total Egyptian imports; thus the margin of trade diversion in favour of the EU is high unless Egypt enters into FTAs with them. In the case of Egypt, Japan would also suffer from trade diversion. For example its share in Egyptian imports of road vehicles (SITC 78) is about 15 per cent and of photographic and optical goods (SITC 88), 20.8 per cent. But in the case of Egypt, what is much more striking is that other non developed and non Mediterranean countries have a share higher than 20 per cent for a huge number of SITC categories such as SITC 52, SITC 53, SITC 56, SITC 57, SITC 59, all SITC 6 categories, SITC 73, SITC 76, SITC 78, SITC 81, SITC 82, SITC 83, SITC 84, SITC 85, SITC 88 and SITC 89. In some cases, namely rubber manufactures, wood and cork manufactures, textile yarn, fabrics, road vehicles, travel goods and clothing the share is higher than 50 per cent of total imports.

Also systematically neglected from the analysis of trade relations within free trade areas between the EU and MNMCs are the so called shifting effects. These must be accounted for in addition to the better known trade diversion effects, particularly if the countries forming the FTA are neighbours and if the rates of tariff protection applied by them differ widely, which is exactly the case here. For instance in the early 1990s the average tariff protection in Jordan reached the 25 per cent mark or in Egypt about 31 per cent whereas the CCT (Common Customs Tariff) turns out to be around five per cent, a huge difference. The Israeli tariff is on average 8.5 per cent. In that case (assuming that other MNMCs tariffs *vis-à-vis* the rest of the world have not changed by 2010), it is easy to foresee European and Israeli exporters shifting part of the products previously sold in their local market to sell them at a higher price in neighbouring non-industrialised Arab markets (since the latter are protected by high MFN tariffs not applied to EU and Israeli exports). To replace whatever is sold in the Arab markets, EU and Israeli consumers can buy from the world market at the same price as before (in the case of the EC, the world price plus the CCT). Observe in passing that prices in the FTA would not be at all unified, as in the case of a Customs Union. Shifting is not worthwhile if your partner is far away, but if he is your neighbour, which is the case for Spain regarding Morocco, Italy regarding Tunisia or Israel regarding Jordan and Egypt, it is worthwhile. It goes without saying that Arab MNMCs have nothing to gain from shifting effects described here, rather the contrary. As in the case of trade diversion, they will end up buying imports at higher prices than before, lose tariff revenue, see a deterioration in their terms of trade and consequently suffer from a deterioration in their balance of payments. What is more to the point here is that there will be net trade diversion against the rest of the world, which might not remain passive.

The crucial difference between the FTA solution being proposed to Arab MNMCs as part of the EU-Mediterranean Partnership, and the Customs Union solution applied to relations between the EU and Turkey, is that the latter had to align its tariff on a very low CCT, thus avoiding many of the negative trade diversion and shifting effects described above which might afflict the Arab MNMCs.

Being part of the European trading block will also necessitate progressively adopting rules, norms and standards decided in Brussels and imposed on MNMCs without the latter participating either in the decision making or even in the decision shaping (Norway, Iceland and Liechtenstein have had some input into the latter as non-EU members of the EEA). Not only is there a cost in renouncing sovereignty without the MNMCs being heard in Brussels, but furthermore in relation to our subject, adopting Brussels rules, norms and standards to facilitate trade between MNMCs and the domineering trading partner, the EU, might be uneconomical if applied to only 50 per cent or 80 per cent of your foreign trade. It might be worthwhile from an economic viewpoint to adopt the EU standard or norm as the 'national' one. But then, links of this kind with your 'hub' might jeopardise your relations with other 'hubs' and particularly with the US.[4]

What is the Interest of the EU in Having FTAs with MNMCs?

It seems that beyond the official rhetoric of European policymakers, whereby the economic side of the Partnership will be good for MNMCs because they will have to open their economies and 'shake' themselves, the interests of the EU itself in proposing the Partnership are very clear it will:

- equilibrate EU relations with Central and Eastern European countries,
- compensate for the increasing US influence in the Eastern Mediterranean, and
- increase EU exports to MNMCs while not increasing imports from them.

MNMCs which decide not to lower their MFN tariffs until 2010 might become a 'dumping ground' for expensive European products, which the EU is unable to sell elsewhere, since it would have a huge preference margin on average of 25 per cent to 30 per cent (as explained above). On the other hand, the EU seems unwilling to 'shake' itself where it hurts. Instead of more South-North trade it prefers to increase aid (an agenda which is the exact reverse of 'trade, not aid').

In a recent empirical evaluation of the effects of the new FTAs between the EU and North African MNMCs, it has been shown that the principal and most direct beneficiary of these agreements will be the EU exporter of industrial products to Tunisia and Morocco, particularly of machinery and textile products. Almost half of the expanded exports will be on account of exports currently originating in other OECD countries.[5]

Will the Partnership be to the Detriment of Relations of the EU with Other Potential 'Spokes'?

Here the answer is a relatively short no! To begin with, the Partnership is based on FTAs which allow each partner total freedom in deciding to have FTAs with other partners. Secondly, European economies are traditionally geared to exports, particularly those in Northern Europe. Exporters will, as in the past, press EU policy makers persistently to sign agreements with groups of countries not yet open to them, such as Mercosur or ASEAN. In fact this author expects the EU to propose industrial FTAs to clusters of emerging economies wherever they are. The reason is quite simple. Following a mercantilistic logic, the EU knows it is not offering wide changes in market access to prospective partners since the post-Uruguay Round average CCT will turn around three to four per cent (Where tariffs count, as in agriculture, there is nothing to talk about, says the EU.) In return, the EU expects to get preferential access to economies with still significant tariffs and quantitative restrictions.

Will MNMCs be Second Rate Members of the European Trading Block?

Formally speaking the Euro-Mediterranean agreements come very close to the Europe agreements which the EU concluded with Central and Eastern European countries in the early 1990s. The status of MNMCs will remain inferior to that awarded to EFTA countries in the EEA and on a par with the present status of Eastern European countries, but not for long. A first batch of Eastern European countries, Estonia and Cyprus, shall enter the EU by 2002 or 2003, placing relations between the EU and the future members at a correspondingly higher level. A second batch might follow shortly afterwards and enter not later than 2010, when the Euro-Mediterranean FTAs will finally be in place.

By then MNMCs will still be very far from being part of the European Single Market, as EFTA members are already and CEEC soon will be (either as part of the EU or alternatively as part of the EEA, which might be accepted by some of them as an intermediary step in spite of early objections). To illustrate this point regarding MNMCs, the EU refused in negotiations with Israel on the 1995 association agreement to discuss mutual recognition of diplomas and professional qualifications, basically for political reasons – to make a distinction between European and non European countries. If the past is of any guide, one might expect that it will be the most recent members (the 'conversos' using Spanish terminology of the time of the Inquisition) which will be most opposed to erasure of distinctions between members and non members. One might expect however that with time the logic of the Market (or more simply the Single Market) will prevail; that it is to the advantage of the EU to extend its Single Market to countries in its outside periphery. By 2010, this will be particularly the case for banking, insurance and professional services.

Should the 'Spokes' Link Among Themselves?

Since the 1994 Marin Paper, the European Commission's position, defining the long term objective of the Euro-Mediterranean Partnership as the creation of a Euro-Mediterranean Free Trade Area by 2010, contemplates free trade among MNMCs, and not only between them and the EC. The Commission calls this MEFTA, the 'Mediterranean Free Trade Area', which should follow closely the pattern set by EFTA in 1959 and by CEFTA, the FTA established among Central and Eastern European countries in 1993. In the end by 2010 a huge Euro-Mediterranean Free Trade Area of 600 to 800 million people and about 40 countries would emerge. About 60 per cent of their total trade would be within the region.

The idea of inciting Israel, Turkey, Malta and Cyprus to reach FTA agreements with other MNMCs is particularly welcome since the four have been offering for many years substantial reverse preferences to the EU, with the result of diverting trade away from other MNMCs. There is no doubt that trade between Israel and Turkey has been negatively affected by the 'hub and spoke' system privileging their trade with the EU. In fact, if no FTAS are signed among MNMCs, the hub and spoke system that emerged in 1975-76, with the then EEC as the 'hub' and partner countries and regions as the 'spokes', will be actually deepened by 2010.

One reservation must be noted here, however. By early next century Israel and Turkey, two of the spokes in the hub and spoke model, are expected to have implemented several additional FTA agreements. The most relevant to the present discussion is Israel's FTA with Turkey, which itself established a Customs Union with the EC that has been in force since January 1996. As a result of this (and after a transition period of five years), Turkey will have to apply the EC Mediterranean Policy agreements in its relations with Maghrib and Mashriq countries, including free access to Turkish markets for industrial products and facilitated access to the Turkish market for agricultural products. It is to be noted that Turkey and Israel have already decided to forge ahead and apply free trade relations, by signing an industrial FTA agreement which will enter into force soon. This is a first step towards a linkage between the 'spokes' of the Euro-Mediterranean system.

Seen from an Israeli perspective, to have FTAs with Arab MNMCs has an important advantage in relation to the present situation: politically, if implemented, they would put an end to discrimination that Israel makes in favour of the EU, the US, Canada, Turkey and EFTA which can be taken as offensive by neighbouring countries at peace with Israel. The US certainly would not object, since it already has an FTA with Israel and, with the EU, is the country most eager to promote economic integration in the Middle East.

The obvious question arising from this analysis is whether the system can be completed by linking up the remaining spokes. The answer is a cautious 'yes', if the aim of MNMCs is to prevent the system from being increasingly lopsided. It is also important to unravel the 'hub and spoke' system that has emerged over the years, so as to deter firms (particularly those in MNMCs) from being tempted to locate in the 'hub' and not in the 'spokes'.

That the system is tending to become even more lopsided than before does not need much elaboration. As explained above, the EU is gradually expanding south and east. Much as the EC's interest in the Maghrib increased after Portugal and Spain joined it in the mid 1980s, the EU's interest in the Mashriq can be expected to follow a similar pattern after Cyprus and, later, Bulgaria, Rumania and maybe Turkey become member states. The EU's relative economic size is also expected to rise. This will give Europe stronger political clout as a third party in regional political arrangements among MNMCs which, since World War II, have been a US-USSR duopoly, and since the disintegration of the Soviet Union, almost a US monopoly. The successive enlargements of the EU have brought it to leading positions in international organisations such as the OECD and EBRD. The EU is quite likely to become a leading shareholder in a Middle East Regional Development Bank, in spite of its deep reluctance to be involved in the project. Ensuing from the above is the fact that we are witnessing the emergence of a steadily expanding trading block which includes most of the European continent, that is, the EU, the EFTA countries in the European Economic Area (EEA) and the CEEC ('Pan-Europe'). Being part of such a block could be of just as much value as the real thing to non-European countries wishing to join the EU as full members. Membership may in some cases be logical from an economic viewpoint, but not very acceptable to the club members from a political viewpoint. Full membership of Mediterranean countries in other continental blocks, such as NAFTA or APEC, seems even more remote, principally for geographical reasons (but the option should not be totally excluded). The best, if not the only option open to MNMCs is therefore to proceed in two simultaneous courses of action: deepen as much as possible the MNMC's ties with the EU (the 'hub'), and intensify links within MNMCs (the 'spokes'). It is important in this context that in preferential agreements concluded among the 'spokes' the same rules of origin be used as the ones prevailing in the bilateral association agreements that MNMCs have signed or will have signed by then with the EU. Following the Euro-Mediterranean conference of November 1995 in Barcelona and the Madrid European Summit of December 1995 all the rules contained in the different bilateral association agreements are going to be harmonised in the near future.

How Should the 'Spokes' Link Among Themselves?[6]

To begin with, as baffling as this might sound, many MNMCs must still 'normalise' trade relations among themselves. In fact for the coming years, 'normalisation' of trade relations between MNMCs is the name of the game, that is, MFN treatment and WTO like relations; the establishment of FTAs among MNMCs goes far beyond 'normalisation'.

Imagine a plausible near future scenario, in which all countries in the Mediterranean are GATT and WTO signatories and maintain a formal state of peace (i.e. no boycotts) with each other, but no new regional trade initiatives are possible for political reasons (such as a 'cold peace'). Such a state would automatically imply that all countries in the region apply non-discriminatory treatment to each other and maintain open borders to trade. Although according to all empirical studies consulted, the trade potential among MNMCs is not large, there can also be potential regional spillover effects regarding extra-regional exports, which may be more important than inter-regional trade. Producers in any one country in the region may be unable to offer distributors in foreign markets a sufficient variety of products or services, and may not justify opening a local office. In a state of peace and 'normalisation of trade relations', multi-country business trips would be more attractive, and cross-border accessibility could also be an incentive to direct foreign investment. In addition to that, improved transportation and communication links can encourage buyers to open regional purchasing offices or become partners in trading companies in the region. So 'normalisation' of trade relations would already be a step towards making the present system less lopsided than it is now.

At present, when psychological, economic and other obstacles still undermine the prospects of any form of economic integration (such as FTAs), at least in the Eastern Mediterranean, it may be useful to begin by joining forces to achieve an improved access to European markets. A significant step in that direction would be an agreement by the EC to modify the provisions concerning the rules of origin, included in existing bilateral agreements between the EC and individual countries. The modification would redefine area products as those 'sufficiently transformed' in the territory covering the EC and all MNMCs. In the jargon of political economics this provision is known as 'cumulation of origin', although it should rather be called 'cumulation of value added for the purpose of defining origin'. The EC has in fact accepted in principle such a request as part of its own intention to multilateralise its network of bilateral agreements within the framework of the Euro-Mediterranean Partnership.

It is clear that in addition to widening the region's access to the European market, the implementation of cumulation would promote trade in intermediate goods and services between any two partners in the region, thereby making use of potential complementarities between them. There is a vast potential of collaboration in the textile and clothing sectors and one can also think in terms of large regional intra-industry trade flows in the chemical and agro-food sectors. In the long run, the more countries that are included in the scheme (including some in Eastern Europe), the higher the potential for promoting regional and sub-regional economic cooperation and maybe eventually integration. The EU may attribute a special significance to such process as a catalyst for firms in the region to work together and think regionally rather than nationally.

Cumulation has a slight drawback in relation to more advanced forms of cooperation: it is a technical solution to overcome problems derived from the strict application of origin rules. It tries to bypass the political context. Furthermore, cumulation is also going to benefit European consumers rather than local consumers in MNMCs.[7]

So the question arises why not go all the way and conclude industrial FTAS among MNMCs?

There is first the question of political feasibility. The FTA solution would tend to alter the institutional status quo in countries where state ministries are heavily involved in the organisation of foreign trade (as in Syria). Bureaucracies would tend to oppose the conclusion of such wide ranging agreements.

Then there is the crucial question of why the omission of agriculture. One can understand, for instance, in the case of EFTA that the almost total exclusion of agriculture from the 1960 Stockholm Treaty helped member countries avoid serious political and economic obstacles to achieve an agreement. Among MNMCs, however, the situation is radically different. Countries in this region have a competitive advantage in the production of agricultural products such as cotton, fruit, dried fruit, vegetables, flowers, olive oil, tobacco, rice, poultry and sheep meat, some of which are not easily exportable to distant markets while they can be traded regionally. The agricultural sector is very important in terms of national production and employment. Unlike their European colleagues, MNMC farmers are not well-organised and therefore governments are relatively free of political pressures from agricultural lobbies. Non-tariff barriers (NTB) are very significant. The obligation of all WTO members to proceed with the tariffication of their NTB's has made agricultural protection more transparent than before. Unlike industrial products, most agricultural products are entirely locally produced, simplifying the issue of product origin definition.

The picture depicted above points to the fact that there is a large potential for intra-regional trade if future FTAs among MNMCs would include agriculture in addition to industry. The first step towards such an agreement could be that each MNMC would grant its partner in a FTA similar conditions to those accorded to extra-regional partners with which they have FTA agreements.

Of course, to make agricultural free trade a reality, countries would have first to reach an agreement on what to do with agricultural subsidies which are widely used by some of the states, such as Jordan. More generally, non-tariff barriers are said to be the plague of Arab countries' trade regimes. Therefore any wide ranging option such as FTA agreements dealing only with tariffs and even quantitative restrictions would probably be considered unrealistic or unjust by some of the potential partners.

The main policy conclusion is that MNMCs should not commit the error of the EU in excluding agriculture from any free trade area agreement. If choosing as a long term aim the one proposed in the Euro-Mediterranean Partnership for 2010, MNMCs should go all the way beyond what was actually agreed in Barcelona in November 1995 and tackle the issue of agricultural subsidies as well.

NOTES

1. On this issue, see, for example, Anderson, K. and Blackhurst, R. (1993) (eds.), *Regional Integration and the Global Trading System*, New York, Harvester Wheatsheaf; Cable, V. and Henderson, D. (eds.)(1994), *Trade Blocs? The Future of Regional Integration*, London, RIIA; Devos, S. (1995*), Regional Integration and the Multilateral Trade System: Synergy and Divergences*, Paris, OECD; Geiger, T. and Kennedy, D .(1996) (eds.), *Regional Trade Blocs, Multilateralism and the GATT*, London, Cassell; Hine, R. (1992), 'Regionalism and the Integration of the World Economy', in *Journal of Common Market Studies*, 30/2, pp.115–24; Kelly, M. and Kirmani, N. and Xafa, M. (1988), *Issues and Developments in International Trade Policy*, Washington DC, International Monetary Fund; Langhammer, R. (1992), 'The Developing Countries and Regionalism' , in *Journal of Common Market Studies*, 30/2 (June), pp.211–32; Lorenz, D. (1991), 'Regionalisation versus Regionalism-Problems of Change in the World Economy', *Intereconomics*, 26/1, pp.3–10; Melo, J. de and Panagariya A. (1992*), The New Regionalism in Trade Policy, An Interpretive Summary of a Conference*, Washington, World Bank; Oman, C. (1996), *The Policy Challenges of Globalisation and Regionalisation*, OECD Development Centre , Policy Brief No.11, Paris, OECD; Schott, J., (1991), 'Trading Blocks and the World Trading System', in *The World Economy*, 14/1 (March), pp.1–20 and Tovias, A., (1988), 'Trade Discrimination in the Thirties and Eighties' , *The World Economy*, 11/4, December, pp.501–14.
2. De Sebastian, L.(1995), 'Trading Blocs and The Stranded Countries' in Ahiram, E. and Tovias, A., *Whither Israel and the European Union?*, Frankfurt, Peter Lang, pp.147–64.
3. For a more thorough analysis of these ideas see Tovias, A.(1994), 'Israel Between Europe and America: The Status of Israel in a World of Rival Trading Blocks', in *History of European Ideas*, 18/5, pp.697–710.
4. This is true of course, unless the EU and the US agree on some common standard, or unless the EU adopts an already-existing world standard.
5. Tovias, A., 'Impacto comercial de las futuras zonas de librecomercio', a research report prepared for the Catalan Institute for the Mediterranean, not yet published.
6. This section draws from Tovias, A. (1997), *Options for Mashrek-Israeli Regionalism in the Context of The Euro-Mediterranean Partnership*, Brussels, Center for European Policy Studies, CEPS Paper No.67.
7. For more details on the question of cumulation, see Tovias, A.(1997), 'The EU and Mediterranean Countries' in Demaret, P., Bellis, J.F. and Garcia Jimenez, G. (eds.), *Regionalism and Multilateralism After The Uruguay Round: Convergence, Divergence and Interaction*, Brussels, European Interuniversity Press, pp.95–113.

Free Trade Agreements in the Mediterranean: A Regional Path Towards Liberalisation

BERNARD HOEKMAN

Why Go Regional?

There are three basic options for governments seeking to liberalise trade and investment regimes: unilateral action, multilateral liberalisation based on reciprocity, and preferential (discriminatory) liberalisation. For a small country – one that cannot influence its terms of trade – unilateral free trade is the best policy. If, in the context of multilateral negotiations, other countries reciprocate, this will increase the gains from unilateral liberalisation efforts. However, given the small country assumption – which applies to the countries in the Mediterranean region – there are few if any gains to be expected from making liberalisation conditional upon reciprocity by trading partners. Preferential liberalisation through the negotiation of a free trade agreement (FTA) will also be an inferior strategy. The reason is simple: the world market is always larger than a regional one. By not discriminating across potential trading partners, domestic firms and consumers will be allowed to buy goods and services from the most efficient suppliers, wherever they are located. By granting preferential treatment to specific countries, trade *diversion* may occur – the elimination of tariffs may induce consumers and firms to source from suppliers located in a partner country that are less efficient than those located in non-member countries. It may be the case that trade *creation* – the elimination of domestic sourcing by firms and consumers in favour of imports of goods produced by more efficient suppliers in the partner country after the

Bernard Hoekman is a senior economist in the International Economics Department of the World Bank. This paper draws in part on material contained in Hoekman, Bernard and Simeon Djankov (1997), 'Towards a Free Trade Agreement with the EU: Issues and Policy Options for Eygpt', in A. Galal and B. Hoekman (eds.), *Regional Partners in Global Markets: Limits and Possibilities of the Euro-Med Agreements*, London, CEPR and ECES.
Comments and suggestions received from participants in workshops at the Royal Institute for International Affairs and the Egyptian Center for Economic Studies are gratefully acknowledged.

elimination of trade barriers – is sufficient to offset the welfare loss caused by trade diversion. The point, however, is that through unilateral liberalisation such losses do not occur: net gains are greater.

The case against regional (preferential) trade agreements is particularly strong in the context of small countries that already have duty free access to partner country markets but maintain tariffs on imports originating in these countries. This is the case for the Mediterranean countries, which were granted duty-free access to EU markets for industrial (non-agricultural) goods under Cooperation Agreements negotiated in the 1970s. In such cases, as argued by Panagariya,[1] Mediterranean countries that enter into a FTA with the EU will lose the tariff revenue presently collected on imports of EU origin. Given that tariffs are relatively high and often account for a significant share of total revenues (Table 1), and that the EU accounts for 48 percent of total imports into Mediterranean countries, this revenue loss is substantial. The static benefits that arise to Mediterranean countries of the FTA are unlikely to offset this loss. Benefits consist of efficiency gains, which will tend to be substantially smaller than the fall in tariff revenue. Of course, dynamic benefits (induced growth effects) may well ensure that longer term returns are positive. The point, again, is that these benefits can also be attained through unilateral liberalisation, without the associated losses.

TABLE 1
TRADE TAXES IN MEDITERRANEAN COUNTRIES, 1996

	Share of Import Duties in Total Government Revenue (%)	Average Collected Tariff (revenue/imports %)
Morocco	17.6	19.5
Tunisia	25.6	18.7
Egypt	9.7	19.0
Jordan	25.2	12.3
Syria	12.9	25.6
Turkey	2.3	1.8

Source: IMF Government Finance Statistics Yearbook, 1997; International Financial Statistics, 1997.

These are powerful logical arguments which raise two questions. First, what might explain the pursuit of preferential trade agreements by Mediterranean countries? Why not pursue trade liberalisation independently, and lock these changes in through the World Trade Organisation (WTO)? Second, what are the necessary conditions for regional integration to be welfare enhancing for the countries involved? Possible economic explanations or motivations for regional integration include the following:

Credibility and Associated Dynamic Gains

A regional integration agreement (RIA) may offer a stronger mechanism for locking in (anchoring) economic reforms than the WTO. In part this may be because the RIA addresses policy areas that are not covered by the WTO at all, or where WTO disciplines are weak. For example, investment or factor market policies are not addressed by the WTO. WTO disciplines pertaining to services policies are relatively weak.[2] Thus, reforms in these areas may be anchored through a RIA in ways that are not available in the WTO. Even with respect to trade policies, the traditional domain of the GATT, WTO disciplines may be weaker than under a RIA. Credibility under the WTO arises in large part from the binding of tariffs. The most that can be done in this connection is to bind tariffs at applied rates. This is something many developing countries have not done, in part because of the mercantilistic bias of the multilateral negotiating process (governments wanted to keep 'negotiating chips'), and in part because they did not want to be bound by GATT rules. Although governments are increasingly asked to reduce the difference between bound and applied rates in multilateral trade negotiations, there is no WTO requirement to bind at applied rates. This remains a voluntary step for developing country governments, increasing the political difficulty of doing so. In a RIA binding is not voluntary, but required, and the level at which rates are bound is zero.

Credibility may also be enhanced if enforcement of binding commitments is stronger under a RIA. Under the WTO, the ultimate enforcement is retaliation by 'principal suppliers', the countries with whom a tariff concession was originally negotiated. Such retaliation, if it occurs, will take the form of increases in tariffs on exports of the country violating a binding. This may not constitute a sufficient deterrent threat. A RIA may not make allowances for the permanent reimposition of tariffs.

Harmonisation and mutual recognition

A RIA may involve harmonising regulatory regimes and administrative requirements relating to product standards, testing and certification procedures, mutual recognition agreements, common documents for customs clearance (for example, the EU's Single Administrative Document), coordination and cooperation on linking computer systems of Customs, etc. These are areas where the WTO is restricted to general principles (that is, national treatment and MFN). While such cooperative efforts can be pursued unilaterally, formal agreements may be necessary to induce the administrative bodies involved to cooperate. The greater is the share of exports going to partner countries, the greater the benefits of elimination of such non-tariff barriers.

Security of Market Access

A RIA may allow the countries involved to agree to eliminate the possibility of imposing contingent protection, such as anti-dumping actions against partner country exports. The greater the share of total trade that occurs between partner countries, the greater the value of enhancing the certainty of market access. In the multilateral context such an agreement is unlikely to be feasible any time soon,[3] but has proved possible in regional contexts.[4] Harmonisation or recognition of administrative requirements and procedures may also help to improve the security of market access. An important area in this connection relates to product standards and their enforcement.

Transfers

A RIA may involve transfers from richer members to poorer ones. Such transfers may be financial, or take the form of technical assistance. If such transfers are conditional upon membership of the RIA and are *additional* to status quo ante flows, they will help offset transitional fiscal losses and the costs of trade diversion.[4] Given the generally declining trend in official aid, and the emergence of the central and eastern European countries as new 'claimants', taking past transfers as the basis for an 'additionality' test may not be appropriate. To some extent the EMPI may lock in current transfers that otherwise could be vulnerable. If so, there would be additionality.

Political Economy

Non-economic considerations, especially foreign policy, may imply that there is a stronger political constituency for regional, as opposed to multilateral, liberalisation. Hence the chances of attaining liberalisation, albeit on a preferential basis, may be greater. Of course, from an economic perspective it remains important that policymakers (and voters) have enough information regarding the extent to which the attainment of non-economic objectives are associated with possible economic losses, and that efforts are made to minimise such losses.

Facilitation of General Liberalisation

The main way to limit possible losses is to liberalise economic activity more generally, that is, on a most-favoured-nation (MFN) basis. Available quantitative economic studies suggest that adjustment costs for Mediterranean countries associated with liberalisation on an MFN basis are not likely to be much higher than those emerging from regional liberalisation with the EU.[5] If the multi-dimensional nature of an EMPI and the financial and other assistance from the EU allow preferential free trade to emerge, the message from the economic literature is that the additional political cost of generalising the reductions in trade barriers should be limited. Moreover, the additional gains are likely to be very substantial.

The Agreement with Tunisia

The first Euro-Med Partnership Initiative agreement negotiated with Tunisia, was initialled in April and signed in July 1995. An agreement with Morocco followed in October 1995. Discussions are ongoing with Egypt, Jordan and Lebanon. In terms of what the EU is willing to offer, there is likely to be very little variance across agreements. What follows therefore discusses the Tunisian EMPI agreement.

The EMPI has six major elements: (1) political dialogue; (2) free movement of goods; (3) right of establishment and supply of services; (4) payments, capital, competition and other economic provisions (for example, safeguards); (5) economic, social and cultural cooperation; and (6) financial cooperation.

Free Movement of Goods

As noted above, Mediterranean countries already benefit from duty-free access to EU markets for manufactured goods under Cooperation Agreements with the EU. Thus liberalisation will mostly occur on the Mediterranean side. Tunisia chose to separate products into five groups, each of which is to be liberalised according to a different timetable. Tariffs and surcharges on products listed in Annex 3 (equal to one-third of total imports) will be eliminated over a five-year period in steps of 15 per cent. Goods in Annex 4 are to be liberalised over a 12-year period transition period, in steps of eight per cent per year. Products listed in Annex 5 will commence tariff reductions four years after the entry into force of the agreement, with reductions spread out linearly over the remaining 8 years of the transition period (that is, annual cuts of 11-12 per cent). A small number of manufactured products in Annex 6 (mostly bread, pasta, and carpets) are exempted from tariff reductions. Finally, tariffs on manufactured products that are not mentioned in one of these four Annexes will be abolished upon the entry into force of the agreement. They are all either intermediate inputs or machinery, and accounted for 10 per cent of 1994 imports from the EU (Table 2).

Goods to be liberalised immediately have the lowest average tariffs, and tend to be intermediates and capital goods. Those to be liberalised last have the highest average rates, and include most consumer goods that are produced in Tunisia. A possible factor underlying the back-loaded nature of the tariff reduction process is that the government may have been concerned with the revenue implications of a more uniform move to free trade with the EU. The dependence on trade taxes in Tunisia – as in the other countries of the region – is relatively high (Table 1). Some 26 per cent of government revenues are derived from trade taxes. The EU accounts for 68 per cent of

TABLE 2
TARIFF LIBERALISATION COMMITMENTS BY TUNISIA (INDUSTRIAL
PRODUCTS)

	Share of trade		Share in domestic output	Share in total tariff revenue	Import weighted average tariff	Number of 6-digit lines Total=5019		Share of machinery & Intermediates	
	Exp.	Imp.					% of total	by line (%)	by import value (%)
ANNEX 3: 5 year transition	16	24	20	12.5	26.7	1810	41	93	87
ANNEX 4: 12 year transition	7	29	22	9.2	30.4	1127	26	94	89
ANNEX 5: 8 year transition starting in year 5	75	36	43	32.9	33.8	944	22	8	4
ANNEX 6: Exempted	1	1	1	n.a.	n.a.	37	1	0	0
Industrial goods not listed in an Annex: Immediate liberalisation	1	10	14	3.6	21.6	470	10	100	100

Source: Own calculations based on COMEXT and World Bank data. All data are for 1994.

total imports, and generates 58 per cent of total tariff revenue. Most of the tariff revenue generated from trade with the EU is currently collected on the imports of consumer goods (Annex 5), which account for 33 per cent of total revenues, as compared to 12 and nine per cent, respectively, for Annexes 3 and 4 (Table 2). The goods to be liberalised immediately generate only 3.6 per cent of total revenue.

Agriculture

Little will change as far as agricultural trade is concerned. Although the objective of the EMPI is to gradually liberalise trade in this sector, all it does in concrete terms is to largely lock in the status quo (existing preferential arrangements), while offering only limited improvements in access for specific products through expansion of tariff quotas and reduction/ elimination of tariffs for specific quotas. Negotiations to improve on existing agricultural concessions are to be initiated after 1 January 2000. Continued restrictions on imports of agricultural products reduce the benefits of an EMPI for Mediterranean countries. The unwillingness (inability) of the EU Commission to significantly expand export opportunities was an important stumbling block for Morocco in reaching agreement with the EU.[6]

The relative importance of agriculture varies significantly across Mediterranean countries. It is least important to Jordan, where it accounts for eight per cent of GDP, and most important in Egypt, Morocco and Syria, where it contributes some 20 per cent to GDP (Table 3). In terms of exports, agricultural produce is by far the most important for Morocco, where it accounts for 30 per cent of total exports. It is therefore not surprising that this sector was a high profile one during negotiations.[7]

TABLE 3
AGRICULTURE IN MEDITERRANEAN COUNTRIES, 1994

Country	Share in GDP	Share in Employment	Share in Exports to EU	Share in Total Exports
Algeria	12.0	17.3	1.2	2.1
Egypt	19.8	39.9	4.4	5.7
Israel	12.4	15.3	14.2	8.4
Jordan	7.9	6.2	4.7	3.2
Lebanon	12.2	19.3	14.2	15.2
Morocco	21.2	43.4	23.4	29.3
Syria	21.1	22.9	2.1	5.2
Tunisia	15.4	26.2	12.1	11.3

Source: World Bank (1995a, b); UN COMTRADE database.

Establishment and Supply of Services

The right of establishment (that is, freedom to engage in FDI) is an objective in the EMPI. Modalities to achieve this objective are to be determined by the Association Council. No specific language is devoted to this subject; no time path or target date is mentioned for its realisation. The absence of the right of establishment may be interpreted by the financial markets as a signal that this continues to be a 'sensitive' issue. No specific commitments are made on liberalisation of cross-border supply of services (that is, trade). As with the right of establishment, liberalisation is an objective that is to be pursued by the Association Council. The EMPI simply refers to the obligations of each Party under the General Agreement on Trade in Services (GATS). These do not imply much, if any, liberalisation (Hoekman, 1996). Mediterranean countries made very limited commitments under the GATS, subjecting some six per cent of their service sectors to the national treatment and market access principles, as compared to 26 per cent for the EU.[8]

Competition Policy, State Aids and Procurement

The EMPI requires the adoption of the basic competition rules of the EU, in particular with respect to collusive behaviour, abuse of dominant position, and competition-distorting state aid (Articles 85, 86, and 92 of the Treaty of Rome), insofar as they affect trade between the EU and each partner country. Implementing rules are to be adopted by the Association Council within five years (as opposed to three under the Europe Agreements). Until then, GATT rules with respect to countervailing of subsidies will apply. For the first five years after entry into force of the EMPI, Tunisia will be regarded as a disadvantaged region under Article 92.3(a) of the Treaty of Rome. This implies that state aids can be applied to the entire territory of Tunisia during the first five years. The Association Council is required to adopt rules to enforce competition policy and subsidy disciplines after the initial five-year period. The agreements also provide for enhanced transparency of state aid, each party agreeing to provide annual reports on the total amount and distribution of the aid given. Anti-dumping remains applicable to trade flows between partners, despite the agreement by Tunisia to apply EU competition disciplines. Liberalisation of government procurement is not required. Reciprocal and gradual liberalisation of public purchasing is, however, an objective of the EMPI.

Rules of Origin

These are a key determinant of access to EU markets. Even though in principle Mediterranean countries already have duty-free access to EU markets for manufactured goods, in practice rules of origin may be such as to require the use of EU inputs in order to benefit from duty-free treatment.[9] Less restrictive rules of origin in an EMPI may then imply an effective liberalisation of trade in manufactures. The Tunisian agreement allows for cumulation for rules of origin purposes for products produced in Algeria and Morocco as well as the EU and Tunisia. This may help create backward and forward linkages between the Maghreb countries and enhance the potential for intra-industry trade. The extension of cumulation to other Mediterranean countries as well as Eastern European nations would be more beneficial, helping to offset the hub-and-spoke nature of the EU's web of trade agreements. To be effective, more liberal rules of origin must be complemented with a reduction in barriers to intra-regional trade (see below).

Economic Cooperation

One-third of the Articles of the Tunisian EMPI deal with cooperation in economic, social and cultural matters. The prime objective underlying economic cooperation is to target 'first and foremost' activities 'suffering the effects of internal constraints and difficulties or affected by the process of liberalising Tunisia's economy as a whole, and more particularly by the liberalisation of trade between Tunisia and the Community' (Article 43). Methods of economic cooperation mentioned in the EMPI include information exchange, provision of expert services (consultants), joint ventures (the Euro-Partenariat programme, for example), and assistance with technical, administrative and regulatory matters. Economic cooperation is largely oriented towards upgrading Tunisian infrastructure broadly defined (both physical and regulatory) and providing support for restructuring of the economy.

Financial Cooperation

Under the EMPI, financial protocols will not be renewed. Instead, the EU envisages earmarking a total amount of assistance – grants and loans – for all the Mediterranean countries. Individual allocations out of this total would not be predetermined, but would in part be endogenous – depending on country performance, including the implementation of the EMPI. Although not spelled out explicitly in the EMPI, the Articles in the EMPI on financial cooperation put emphasis on the link between EMPI implementation and the provision of financial resources. How future financial transfers will compare to past flows remains to be seen, although the absolute value of transfers is expected to increase. Some ECU 4.7 bn has been earmarked to support Mediterranean countries, to be complemented by an equivalent amount of European Investment Bank resources.

Dispute Settlement

The Association Council deals with disputes. In the case of a dispute that cannot be addressed through consultations with the Council, one of the Parties may appoint an arbitrator. The other Party is then required to appoint a second arbitrator within two months, and the Association Council appoints a third one. Decisions by the three arbitrators will be taken by majority vote, with the Parties required to implement them. However, it is not clear what the sanctions may be in case of non-implementation of arbitration decisions. In a number of areas that are particularly relevant from a market access viewpoint binding obligations have yet to be established, e.g., as regards product standards.[10]

Evaluation

In principle, the liberalisation of trade required under the EMPI should do much to induce firms to upgrade their production capacity and improve their efficiency. Although in the long run the EMPI is likely to be beneficial to all of the countries involved, being a discriminatory arrangement the exercise may be economically welfare-reducing in the short- to medium-run. Computable general equilibrium models of free trade agreements between the EU and Morocco, Tunisia, and Egypt all suggest trade diversion may be significant. Indeed, in some cases it is estimated that a static welfare loss will occur.[11] The major potential advantage of an EMPI is that it provides a commitment mechanism, allowing a gradual reform path to be more credible than otherwise. Credibility may be enhanced through the binding nature of the agreement, the implicit linkage that has been made between official financial transfers from the EU and implementation of the EMPI, and the offer of wide-ranging technical assistance to help Mediterranean countries improve the administration of their regulatory regimes (e.g. customs; certification of product standards). However, the absence of binding commitments in the areas of foreign direct investment and supply of services, the exclusion of government procurement, and the maintenance of antidumping and broadly worded safeguard provisions imply that the EMPI does not go significantly beyond existing multilateral (WTO) disciplines.

Tunisia's transition path to free trade with the EU is relatively long (12 years), with liberalisation of goods competing with domestic production only starting five years after the entry into force of the agreements. This may well reduce the incentives to initiate rapid restructuring, and may create problems in implementing tariff reductions in the future (for example, through pressure for safeguard protection). By lowering of tariffs on intermediates and capital goods first, domestic industries are granted some up front compensation for the adjustment costs that must be incurred later, and are given time in which to restructure. This strategy also ensures that tariff revenues will initially decline slowly, giving more time to create alternative sources of funds for the government. But the possible downside of the strategy should be recognised. The tariff reduction strategy implies that effective rates of protection may increase during the transition, thereby giving rise to welfare losses and creating possible perverse incentives to invest in the 'wrong' activities. Insofar as such investment occurs, the costs of implementing EMPI tariff reduction commitments increase and political opposition to liberalisation may emerge.

The fiscal argument for the tariff reduction strategy is not very compelling, except perhaps for countries such as Lebanon which depend heavily on tariff revenues. Clearly a necessary condition for more general liberalisation is that alternative tax bases are developed and that efforts are made to reduce expenditure. As argued by Havrylyshyn and Galal and Hoekman,[12] while the fiscal loss resulting from trade liberalisation is important, options for compensating revenues and reductions in the size of government are also significant and should render the problem manageable.

Much clearly depends on the extent to which complementary actions are pursued to improve the functioning of the economy. Four policy areas are of importance in this connection: (i) reducing the role of the State; (ii) generalising trade liberalisation beyond the EU to the rest of the world; (iii) liberalising access to service markets; and (iv) signalling that the economy is open to foreign investment. Actions to reduce the role of the state are clearly important not only for fiscal reasons but also to change expectations and create avenues for inward investment. Privatisation of state-owned enterprises will generate revenue, open up investment opportunities for foreign (and flight) capital, and limit possible claims on the budget as the state-owned enterprise sector becomes subjected to greater competitive pressures. Although the EMPI may help ensure that state firms confront harder budget constraints over time – provisions on state aid to industry will start to bite after five years under the EMPI – such disciplines are relatively weak. There are important political economy issues here. Many Mediterranean countries have a significant stock of educated workers that are employed either directly by the government administration or by state-owned firms. Many also have large pools of unskilled, underemployed labour. In addition, some countries such as Egypt have a substantial stock of unemployed university graduates.[13] Implementation of the EMPI may not be politically feasible if increased job opportunities for the unskilled and the educated unemployed do not materialise, or if job losses in the state sector become too large to be politically manageable.

Greater employment opportunities for the unskilled could emerge through the creation of firms specialising in labour-intensive production and by improving access for agricultural exports. The latter has been excluded; a necessary condition for the former is the existence of adequate infrastructure and the absence of red tape restricting export production (regulations, tax administration, customs). For many of the more highly educated, potential job opportunities lie in the service sector. Realising this potential requires fostering competition in services activities and allowing establishment by foreign providers (see below). Even then, realism suggests that in countries where the existing labour force employed in services is already significant, net losses may well occur initially. FDI can do much to stimulate both labour-intensive and more skilled activities, be they in services or manufacturing, but it will only materialise if the regulatory and institutional environment is conducive to private sector investment. In the absence of improvements in the legal and regulatory framework, opening up to trade with the EU may result in greater competition from imports without much in the way of new investment. If so, the political viability of EMPI implementation will decline and the liberalisation dynamic may falter. A strong case can be made that using EU grants to fund worker compensation schemes could do much to facilitate downsizing of the public sector.[14]

The EMPI is likely to create substantial incentives to pursue additional preferential agreements. Indeed, this is an objective of the EU – one of the goals of the Euro-Med initiative is to promote the integration of the economies of the Mediterranean countries. This may not only help to reduce static trade diversion losses, but may also be important insofar as the negotiation of bilateral agreements between the EU and each of the Mediterranean countries will otherwise result in a so-called hub-and-spoke system. A problem with such an arrangement is that it creates incentives for firms to locate (invest) in the hub, in this case the EU, as this gives them barrier-free access to all the 'spokes'. The potential for investment diversion can be reduced if all trading partners remove barriers on each others' trade – cooperation is required. In this connection it is noteworthy that the Arab League decided in 1997 to begin to establish a free trade zone among members in 1998, with full free trade to be achieved over a ten-year period. The recent Arab League FTA may to some extent have been motivated by a desire to avoid the negative implications of the emerging 'hub and spoke' network of bilateral Euro-Med agreements.

Intra-regional trade between countries of the Middle East and North Africa is limited. In part this reflects the similarity in endowments, in part the non-competitiveness of processed and manufactured goods that are produced. If the Persian Gulf states are included, intra-regional trade is not insignificant (it stood at some \$8.3 bn in 1990, or eight per cent of total exports). Relative to the participation in world trade, these levels are actually not that low.[15] Thus, the trade of Egypt, Jordan, Syria and Turkey with other countries in the Middle East and North Africa is four times more intensive than trade with the world as a whole.[16] The only major economy in the region where intra-regional trade is clearly too low is Israel. However, if attention is restricted to Mediterranean nations (that is, the Gulf countries are excluded), intra-regional trade becomes much smaller. Such trade represents less than three per cent of total trade of Mediterranean countries. Given the differences in the factor endowments and per capita income between Israel and some of its neighbours, intra-regional trade should be able to grow substantially. More generally, a convincing case can be made that the scope for greater intra-industry trade is significant, and that much of the potential for greater intra-regional trade comprises intra-industry exchange.[17]

As mentioned previously, the EMPI does little to assure investors of national treatment or to grant the general right of establishment. This is a significant difference from the Europe Agreements concluded between Central and Eastern European (CEE) countries and the EU, where such establishment is permitted immediately for most activities, and a transition path is spelled out for the remainder. By signalling the fact that they are open to FDI and willing to lock this in, the CEE countries increased the incentives for foreign firms to establish and transfer much needed know-how by reducing political risk. FDI is especially important in the services area, where establishment often remains the best way to contest a market. More generally, it is of great importance that policy attention centres on enhancing the performance of service industries. An efficient service sector can play a crucial role in determining the competitiveness of manufacturing and agricultural producers on both world and domestic markets. Telecommunications, information technology, port services, financial intermediation, and business support services are all key inputs into other sectors of the economy. By limiting commitments on services to those made in the GATS, a country risks sending a signal that liberalisation is not on the immediate agenda. It may also end up increasing the effective taxation of other sectors of the economy.

The last point can be illustrated by simulating the effect on manufacturing of elimination of tariffs but maintenance of protected service sectors. This can be most easily determined by calculating the effective rates of protection (ERP) that would apply once free trade in merchandise with the EU has been achieved. Such an exercise has been done for Egypt and is reported in Table 4. It is assumed that the cost inefficiency of the services industry is addressed to varying degrees (ranging from 25 to 100 per cent reduction in the assumed tariff equivalents). It can be seen that the manufacturing average ERP becomes positive only if service price wedges are reduced by at least 40 per cent. In short, in the absence of a significant programme of services liberalisation, free-trade in goods with the EU will translate into a much greater shift in the terms of protection under which the Egyptian manufacturing industry is operating than what is suggested by its current structure of nominal protection.[18]

Conclusions

The EMPI option provides a unique opportunity for Mediterranean countries to credibly pursue far-reaching liberalisation of trade in a gradual fashion. The EMPIs should induce greater competition in product markets and encourage investments to upgrade the efficiency of production in partner countries. The extensive provisions for technical cooperation with a view of harmonisation and mutual recognition of regulatory procedures (e.g., in the area of customs clearance, product standards) should do much to reduce transactions costs associated with trade. However, the EMPI does little more than contain hortatory language as regards the liberalisation of service markets and foreign investment. This may affect negatively the desired investment and supply response. By not committing to a concrete transition path to achieve a liberal environment for these areas, an opportunity may have been missed, especially considering the magnitude of the (flight) capital owned by nationals of some of the countries in the region.[20]

Absence of commitments in these areas may be related in part to the issue of privatisation and the role of the State. Without public sector reform

TABLE 4

IMPACT ON ERPs IN EGYPT OF REDUCING TARIFF EQUIVALENTS FOR SERVICES
(ASSUMING FULL ILLIMINATION OF TARIFFS ON IMPORTS FROM EU)

SECTOR	Service Share	0% Cut	25% Cut	50% Cut	75% Cut	100% Cut
Chemicals and products excl. petroleum	32	-64	-56	-48	-40	-32
Clothing: assembled and pieces	44	77	81	84	88	92
Cotton ginning and pressing	12	-23	-22	-20	-19	-18
Cotton spinning and weaving	22	-24	-20	-17	-14	-11
Crude petroleum and natural gas	89	-29	-22	-15	-8	-1
Food processing	23	-11	-8	-4	-1	2
Furniture	26	-10	-7	-4	-1	2
Glass and products	26	4	9	13	18	22
Iron steel other base metals	25	2	3	3	5	7
Leather products excl. footwear	28	-22	-18	-14	-10	-6
Machinery and appliances	27	-28	-24	-19	-15	-10
Mineral products n.i.e.	19	-10	-7	-4	-2	1
Other extrative industries	54	-25	-19	-14	-8	-2
Other manufacturing	62	-8	-5	-2	0	3
Paper and printing	52	-29	-20	-10	-1	9
Petroleum refining	32	-25	-15	-6	4	13
Porcelain china pottery	34	36	40	44	48	52
Rubber plastic and products	37	-10	-6	-2	2	6
Footwear	24	33	42	50	59	67
Transportation equipment	43	-10	-4	2	8	15
Wood, wood products excl. furniture	37	-10	-7	-4	-1	2
Mean	33	-9	-4	1	5	10
Standard Deviation	17	29	28	28	28	28

Source: Hoekman and Djankov (1997)[19]

– at a minimum the introduction of hard budget constraints – the impact of EMPI-based trade liberalisation may be muted. New employment opportunities may not emerge if barriers to entry continue to exist. The recent literature evaluating alternative explanations for the success of particular countries in attaining and sustaining high rates of economic growth concludes that while openness to the world economy is very important, in itself it is not enough. Equally important are efficient public institutions, domestic competition, a well-functioning service sector (finance, infrastructure, distribution, etc.), investment in human resources (education), high rates of private saving and investment, and a stable macro-economy. These factors cannot all be 'imported' through an agreement with the EU. Some, however, can be included by Mediterranean governments in the EMPI, thereby reducing the burden of unilateral pursuit of the reforms needed. Prominent examples are liberalisation of services and the right of establishment.

As noted in Section II, one way for the EMPI to be unambiguously welfare-improving is if it is used as a deliberate strategy to offset political economy constraints on MFN liberalisation, in part through the use of the financial and economic assistance that is on offer. A publicly announced timetable for such MFN liberalisation of barriers to trade and investment, in conjunction with a programme of shifting towards alternative sources of revenue, would do much to provide a strong signal to domestic producers and foreign investors that the ultimate objective is not regionalism, but integration into the world economy. Assuming the EMPIs are implemented, there is some reason to be optimistic that this path will be pursued. The dynamic incentives that are created by the EMPIs are towards further liberalisation. Mediterranean countries have an incentive to pursue regional liberalisation in order to attenuate detrimental hub-and-spoke investment incentives. The recent Arab League free trade agreement suggests that governments are well aware of this incentive. They have an incentive to reduce trade barriers more generally on an MFN basis so as to reduce diversion costs. Indeed, implementation of the EMPIs (and the Arab League agreement) may induce other major trading nations – perhaps led by the US – to seek to conclude similar free trade agreements with the countries in the region. The most obvious candidate in this connection is Egypt, and preliminary discussions on this topic were held between the two parties in 1997. Finally, WTO members can be expected to exert pressure on Mediterranean countries to reduce MFN tariffs so as to lower the margin of preference that will emerge in favour of EU products.

NOTES

1. Panagariya, Arvind (1995), 'The Case Against Preferential Trading', presented at the ERF conference on Liberalization of Trade and Foreign Investment, Bogazici University, Istanbul, September 16-18.
2. For a detailed treatment of the WTO, see Hoekman, Bernard and Michel Kostecki (1995), *The Political Economy of the World Trading System: From GATT to WTO*, Oxford: Oxford University Press.
3. Ibid.
4. For example, the EEC, the EEA, the FTA between Australia and New Zealand, and most recently the FTA between Canada and Chile.
5. Additionality may not be easy to determine. For example, the Mediterranean countries already receive significant financial assistance from the EU, both through bilateral official aid, and through the Financial Protocols that are agreed every four years under auspices of bilateral Cooperation Agreements. What matters then is the comparison between the present discounted value of the expected transfers under status quo arrangements (Cooperation Agreements) and those that are expected under the new regime (the EMPI).

6. In Galal, A. and Hoekman, B. (eds.) (1997), *Regional Partners in Global Markets: Limits and Possibilities of the Euro-Med Agreements*, London, CEPR and ECES; and Havrylyshyn, Oleh (1997), 'A Global Integration Strategy for Mediterranean Countries: Open Trade and Other Accompanying Measures', Middle Eastern Department, IMF (August).

7. After lengthy and heated negotiations, Morocco obtained improved access to EU markets for tomatoes, citrus, and cut flowers. For example, an additional 15,000 ton quota was given for tomatoes, of which 5,000 may be shipped in October, and 10,000 during November-March. Preferential treatment ceases in April, when EU produce comes to market. Agricultural market access conditions for Egyptian produce in EU markets is currently the major contentious issue in the negotiations between Egypt and the EU.

8. For a recent analysis of the potential for production and trade in agriculture in the MENA region, see De Rosa, Dean (1997), 'Agricultural Trade and Rural Development in the Middle East and North Africa: Recent Developments and Prospects', Policy Research Working paper 1732, World Bank.

9. The share of the service sector where commitments were made – even if not guaranteeing national treatment and market access also differed substantially. The EU scheduled 57 per cent of its services; the Middle East and North African Members of the WTO only 16 per cent.

10. Local content requirements are often 60 per cent, i.e. to benefit from duty-free access to the EU, 60 per cent of the value added must originate in either the EU or in the partner country. Alternatively, if a change in tariff heading criterion is used, the value-added equivalent may exceed 60 per cent. See Hoekman and Kostecki (note 2) for a summary discussion of origin rules.

11. Disputes on matters relating to state aid (in the first five years of the EMPI), antidumping, and state trading are explicitly referred to the WTO by the EMPI (Article 36).

12. Many of the available studies are summarized in Havrylyshyn (note 6) and Galal and Hoekman 1997 (note 6).

13. Havrylyshyn (note 6) and Galal and Hoekman (note 6).

14. Diwan, Ishac (1997), 'Globalization, EU Partnership and Income Distribution in Egypt', in Galal and Hoekman (note 6).

15. World Bank (1995), *Will Arab Workers Prosper or Be Left Out in the 21st Century?*, Washington D.C.: World Bank.

16. See Yeats, Alexander (1996), 'Export Prospects of Middle Eastern Countries', World Bank Policy Research Working Paper 1571 (February); Ekholm, Karolina, Johan Torstensson and Rasha Torstensson, 1995. 'Prospects for Trade in the Middle East: An Econometric Analysis', presented at the ERF conference on Liberalization of Trade and Foreign Investment, Bogazici University, Istanbul, 16–18 September, Lawrence *et al.* (1995). Existing intra-regional trade is to some (unknown) extent driven by barter deals and a web of preferential, commodity-specific 'protocol trade' agreements. These involve preferential tariff rates on specific lists of goods of Arab origin. Some of the intra-regional trade may therefore consist of the 'wrong' goods, i.e., those in which countries do not have a comparative advantage.

17. Yeats, Ibid.

18. Havrylyshyn (note 6).

19. Hoekman and Djankov (note 6).

20. World Bank (1995), *Claiming the Future: Choosing Prosperity in the Middle East and North Africa*, Washington D.C.: The World Bank.

Globalisation, Culture and Management Systems

RIADH ZGHAL

Introduction

If one excludes the atypical case of public bodies (as elements of a centralised economic system) which owe their existence to both political and social decisions, all companies, wherever situated, are concerned with effective economic objectives and financial outcomes. The theoretical currents of contingency planning which have developed through research into comparative management have shown up differences in management style, participant strategy and company operation overall.

Concepts designed to explain these divergences in analysis have moved from the economic environment either towards a psychology of the manager who 'satisfies rather than maximises',[1] or towards organisational psychology where systems of organisation become 'cultural answers to the problems encountered by humans in their efforts to reach their goal',[2] and which are a product of the culture in which they exist.[3]

The new concept is globalisation, a phenomenon furthering the integration of economies towards the interests of the international consumer rather than inside national frontiers. However, it is not yet clear whether or not this change will encounter resistance, bringing about local rigidity or at least an exclusive and defensive local reaction in societies or states which are not prepared to confront international competition, and thus risk falling into poverty and misery. Neither can one exclude the divergent and historical experiences which generate the differences in business management among the most economically sophisticated societies.

Societal Effect, Organisational Effect and Globalisation

An article by Mueller[4] rejects analysis based on societal influences on management systems arguing that this approach exaggerates the traditional

Professor Riadh Zghal is Professor of Management at the Faculté des Sciences Economiques et de Gestion, Sfax University, Tunisia.

contrasts between states and underestimates organisational and globalisational effects. Mueller notes convergence between management systems which he explains by four principal factors:

- international spread of technology
- economic development
- industrial policy, and
- management styles.

The transfer of technological advance across frontiers is accompanied by improvements in national welfare. The process of industrialisation is achieved through the adoption of common systems of organisation – bureaucratic organisation as described by Max Weber. He recognised two essential characteristics of bureaucratic organisation: its potential for material improvement and its universal applicability. Mueller argues that forces in the industrial environment compel businesses in different countries to adopt similar responses to modern technological development. Thus parallel paths for mass production destined to satisfy mass consumer markets emerge.

In the European automobile industry, for example, work categorisation has evolved in similar ways: in labour intensive sectors a dual post system has developed, whereas a triple post system has evolved in capital intensive areas. Technological development has a tendency to standardise organised work: greater functional integration, greater interdependence between different activities, faster response capacity and greater cost implications for system failure.

Overall, it appears that in certain industrial contexts, there are technological advances and global strategies which affect businesses similarly in various countries. Such strategic orientations shape the internal structural models of companies.

Recent developments designed to overcome linguistic, commercial and structural barriers also question the significance of institutionalised national barriers. The ease with which technology, knowledge and information spread at the global level weakens the argument that knowledge used by one nation to obtain high productivity is inaccessible to any rival country.[5] Furthermore, capital is not only volatile, but circulates globally across national boundaries. There is also an international market generated by managerial mobility. Multinationals have less and less specific cultural or national identity. They are institutionally located outside states and respond less and less to national industrial policy. Although such theoretical claims to the comprehensive effects of globalisation have been criticised, they still retain an inherent logic.

The dominant role of economic and demographic development on national life would favour greater homogenisation between industrialised societies and reduce the ability of political leaders to impact significantly on policy options. Mueller cites the work of authors like Amoroso, Shonfield and Baglioni[6] in this regard. Amoroso sees industrial globalisation as a threat to the social compromise established in well-off Western European societies. We know that the specificities of each of these societies are based on the social compromises that have evolved through each particular national history. Signs of convergence were, however, identified in the 1960s. Shonfield noted signs of convergence in institutional structures, particularly in economic planning in Western countries. Baglioni's study identifies common objectives between governments of all countries: all aim to raise GNP, increase productivity, lower inflation, reduce budget deficits, and restrain salary increases. In recent years, there has also been an attempt to restructure the labour work market and expand privatisation, as cornerstones of state policy. Mueller notes however that, in the case of European states, societal concerns have intermittently resurfaced in the wake of Europeanisation. This leads to the conclusion that reality is ambivalent and 'that for each example of globalisation there are counter-examples of national differentiation'.[7]

The organisational effects to which Mueller refers stem from the spread of management systems across national frontiers which then influence their new environment. In this respect he notes that multinationals are considered by strategic management theory and economic internalisation theory to be 'relatively effective mechanisms for trans-boundary knowledge transfer.'[8] 'Best practice' in management also undergoes an internationalisation process in commerce and business. Hence in the 1960s and 1970s it was predicted that the American style of management would dominate the world, but there has been a shift towards Japanese management styles. The styles tend to become a component of the global model towards which the different countries converge. The components of this model are: 'lean' production (for instance in automobile manufacturing), multi-tasking, integrated engineering and accelerated production procedures, combined development of horizontal and vertical learning capacity through self-management team work and integration of supplier-producer networks.

This process of the international diffusion of common management practices confirms the theoretical view of the organisational effect as unifying management styles across national boundaries. Other arguments to justify this conclusion can be found in the similarity of management practices observed in local enterprises in different countries. The author includes amongst his examples the case of Ford-Europe, which practices the same management style in Spain and Great Britain even though this may mean changes in traditional working conditions in British or Spanish plants. He demonstrates how organisational effects can neutralise societal effects through multi-national operations.

What will be the consequence of the neutralisation of societal influences through technological advance, industrial policy, globalisation and organisational change? The arguments put forward by Mueller certainly seem well-grounded and realistic. But the angle from which he views the issue is too remote from the real *modus operandi* working of small, medium and large companies which form national industrial structures. To demonstrate the effects of official industrial policy, the author focuses on the way in which the policies of different states converge. This, however, obviously distances us from the actual companies themselves even though state industrial policy is strongly influenced by industrial evolution. The effects of technology, organisation and globalisation are emphasised mainly through complex industrial sectors such as car manufacturing or multinational corporations which are heavily competitive on an international scale. Yet this is only one specific component of the national industrial fabric – the visible part of the iceberg turned towards the international scene. Although diffusion of Weberian-type organisation models and American or Japanese management styles has an effect in formal terms, it is less evident that organisations counter differential social influences once the reality of structure and human behaviour and interaction are taken into account. The main point of this analysis is its emphasis on global isomorphism which then creates convergences between organisational systems, together with state and business management. These convergences are only partial, however, because they cannot completely ignore national and cultural specificity, as demonstrated both in developed and developing countries.

The Effect of Institutions and Social Values

Developed Countries

Work by sociologists who question the concept of globalisation from an ideological point of view[9] emphasise the role of social participants in the entrepreneurial dynamism and the life of the companies. This role is particularly evident in comparative research carried out between different countries. To illustrate this, two European studies will be discussed here. The first, by Arndt Sörge[10] concerns Germany and Britain. The second, by Michel Bauer and Benedicte Bertin-Mourot[11] compares France, Germany and Britain.

Sörge belongs to the school of societal development created by the Laboratoire d'Economie et de Sociologie du Travail in Aix-en-Provence

(LEST).[12] The principle behind this approach is one which wishes to recontextualise human 'artefacts'. In other words, it seeks to integrate the functional and evolutionary modes of societies which receive or import these artefacts or goods and on this basis, the author looks at the application of micro-electronics to industrial products by British and German businesses.

The choice of micro-electronics essentially tests the primal role of societal influences by contrasting them with globalisation because, the author argues, 'micro-electronics is rightly regarded as an internationalised technique developed, produced, commercialised and utilised in a truly homogenised world market', with few elements 'which can halt the globalisation of hardware and software'.[13] In terms of innovation, micro-electronics products link businesses with teaching, research and development institutions. This is also the result of activities generated by all social participants – from large companies and state enterprises which finance research and training to the technicians who actually modify products or techniques in order to improve output. This transfer of innovation means that it is recontextualised in a structured space[14] or '..filled with regularity of behaviour', and transected by mobility or flows of ideas, information, materials and people.

Starting from this analytical framework the author compares ways of exploiting micro-electronics development in 26 businesses in Germany and 27 in the United Kingdom, spread over four types of industries. The following contrast was noted between the two countries: in the UK the emphasis is put on buying sophisticated components which are then integrated into the product. By contrast, in Germany less complex components are used but they can be adapted, since it is felt that available products are not adequate and must therefore be tailored by the manufacturer to requirements.

On the other hand the diffusion of technical innovation is more balanced between different industries in Germany, whereas in Britain it is concentrated in high technology industries such as electronics, electricity, aeronautics, space and defence.

The difference in such diffusion patterns is explained by general societal characteristics which predate technical change: 'Innovation spreads and takes shape according to recognised societal influences'. These influences are mainly the interaction between organisational, socialisational and educational arenas, industrial sectors and the labour market.

The author notes differences between these spheres and their interactions, including: the importance of training workers in electronics, very pronounced in Germany and practically absent in Britain; the flow of workers from the craft to the industrial sector; the flow of workers towards activities similar to or part of the German concept (the first type of flow is absent in Britain). Differences can also be noted in product strategy – in Britain the emphasis is on enterprise specialisation, in Germany the strategy varies little between different industrial branches and types of product.

Michel Bauer and Bénédicte Bertin-Mourot think that differences in management style and economic performance arise from the different management hierarchies in the three European countries of France, Germany and Britain. They identify education, inheritance, enterprise, administration and political learning as the capital pool from which managerial expertise emerges. The study places Germany and France at opposite extremes with Britain in the middle ground. In France the domain which generates most senior management is *'les grandes ecoles'* (ENA, HEC, Polytechnique), followed by social environment in terms of inherited patterns of behaviour. In Germany, to become a senior manager it is necessary to spend on average of twenty years in a company. Managerial educational backgrounds can vary for every type of university postgraduate and specialised education is represented.

This demonstrates to what extent management styles are determined, well before their formation, by social choices and the values that society links to knowledge, as well as predetermined personal experience and competence. This is amplified by the onus of social structures and relatively rigid social hierarchies. It is then easy to imagine to what extent the different sources of legitimisation of managerial power have consequences on the behaviour of social participants within the enterprise, including the managers themselves, whether they are external to the company (social background or the 'grandes ecoles' in France) or reflect internal business factors (experience and competence in Germany).

Whether they are based on the recontextualisation of innovation or on adapted managerial frameworks, these studies show that in developed countries the relationships between management styles and social institutions are significant. It is the structures, the values and the transfers which distinguish the social spheres through which companies operate. This creates a homogeneity encouraging company integration with the social sphere which, in turn, generates a dynamic between the two arenas. Then there is a dialectical interaction between social and economic dynamic, which gives development its characteristic of continuity.

This is not the case in developing countries where industries appear as transplants, and imported innovations. At the same time, certain African experiences show that the integration of social institutions and enterprises, produces an innovative and efficient management style.

Developing Countries

Mamadou Dia[15] notes the fact that de-linking management systems and motivation on the one hand and societal cultures on the other hinders the effectiveness of public services and of large, modern companies in Africa: 'The absence of congruence between organisational cultures and societal cultures erodes the responsibility and productivity of Africans working in modern enterprises'.[16] By analysing the African management systems, both in prescriptive and analytical terms, the author seeks to show that crisis in Africa is located in the disconnection coupling of formal and informal institutions. On the other hand, contrary to conventional pessimism about Africa, the region possesses substantial capacities which can be mobilised and good practices which can be built upon. The use of these capacities is, according to Dia, dependent on the reconciliation of the formal and informal institutions and the empowerment of local communities as well as the individuals involved.

Dia's investigations into sub-Saharan Africa companies have revealed several examples of economically successful companies in the formal and informal sectors. They have shown that managerial success is based on two strategies linked to societal culture: first, a neutralisation strategy for factors unfavourable to economic efficiency; and secondly, the integration of positive cultural parameters into the construction of a management system which is both coherent and congruent with social values and structures.

Chanlat and Kamdem[17] challenge the opinion that there is a fundamental paradox between Africanism and modernity. They analyse in detail three cases of successful management in the formal sector of Cameroon outlining three models:

1. The 'techno-paternalist' model: This borrows from the expatriate European culture in terms of work discipline and the realisation of economic objectives, as well as from African paternalist culture which provides solidarity and comprehension. Management practices include principles of consensus (through the spoken word) and communication, and access to the top of the management pyramid. The model has two facets: a techno-economic and a social aspect.
2. The model of 'commercial excellence', inspired by the specific requirement of its target populations, is based on product innovation. At the level of human resource management, the model is also based on the two categories of modern and traditional values. Concertation, comprehension and solidarity on the one hand, responsibility and competitiveness on the other.

3. The third model, described as 'monastic' shows similar patterns to the previous model in terms of product innovation. It involves seeking the cultural niches to develop economic activity. It is characterised by the establishment of a rigorous code of conduct based on the values of discipline, work, integrity and austerity. Room is also provided for the spoken word as paternalism and benevolence are instruments used to mobilise labour effectiveness. This two-dimensional model is powerfully congruent with Bamileke culture from which the employees of the company studied originated.

In the same pattern of intermixture of the modern and the traditional, Alain Henry's[18] investigations in Togo identify a culture which is both new and is rooted in a wider inherited culture. The author made a detailed study, in a Togolese company, of the spread of the global technique of procedure manuals. Even if this is an alien technique which has been imported, it has found a favourable terrain and can be exploited to two ends: to endow employers and employees with defence against anti-economic social pressures and to produce efficiency. The procedure manual formula has been well accepted because those involved in operations contributed to the drafting process and it is in tune with local attitudes. The procedures help to protect against 'memory failures', considered human nature, and place limits on behaviour. They ensure an immunity against vengeance – a sort of psychological and social armour – which protects against corruption in a hostile environment. The formal procedure performs the role of arbiter and this corresponds to the ancient traditional culture of the *nganga*, an indispensable mediator in African society.

Dominique Desjeux[19] emphasises the similarities, both in content and structure, in participant strategies in various social areas. Models exist which are normally considered appropriate to the economic sphere (such as *tontine*) or social relations (such as ethnicity), which in effect underpin the whole of social life, either as a rationale or as a problem-resolution model. For example, in Congo, the *tontine* is a collective savings model which has a 'circular and egalitarian' distribution base – each, in turn, receives from the *tontiniers* the same sum. The same principles govern the village, urban elite activities and the political sphere. The same is true of ethnicity and sorcery, which beyond their cultural implications, constitute a structural component within the social mechanism.

In conclusion these observations demonstrate that social actors – whether or not they belong to the organisation – develop their own strategy within the limits of the cultural framework in which they move.

Culture and Management in Tunisia

The interdependence between management system and cultural environment is reflected in the need to adapt culturally determined human behaviour in the work place. To speak of culture as a determining factor in behaviour is to speak of an internal logic which members of a particular society share and which appear as customs – an unspoken agreement that everyone respects as if it were the pledge which determines social membership.

Initial empirical research into the links between culture and organisational behaviour carried out at the beginning of the 1980s led to the identification of a cultural configuration with three variables.[20] This configuration has an explanatory value and can predict many patterns of behaviour observed in organisations. It embraces one component based on an equality and dignity value, another component which exemplifies tendencies towards vagueness, and a third which attaches importance to the relationship defined by a sense of belonging to the social group.

Equality and Dignity

The first answer given by a worker to our questions was: my father told me: 'stay *aziz*, when you work'. This qualifying adjective '*aziz*', translated as 'dignified', does not reflect the wealth of the term. In the morality of traditional Arab society, to be *aziz* is also to be proud, independent, free and respectable because of the fundamental principle of equality between men. The distinction must be made between selling one's ability to work against a salary and selling oneself; between the work of a free man and that of a slave. In proverbs and sayings, popular culture tends to assimilate salaried work and enslavement. Here are two examples:

The olive tree is wealth, work to serve men is debasing.
Only misery pushes a free man to work for a free man.

The value attached to the equality-dignity equation is paralleled by a refusal to work under another person's authority. There is a basis for this within Sunni Islam which does not recognise an intermediary between Allah and human beings. The Qur'an reminds us of the identity of human nature, the fraternity which links all believers and which demands justice. The only difference which legitimates inequality is that of knowledge and piety. The *hadith*[21] takes the principle of *tawhid* or oneness of human nature and exhorts humility and equality of interaction between men – rich or poor, strong or weak.

But if the sacred texts exalt the value of equality, they remain ambiguous about the hierarchy of human society: differences between rich and poor, nobles and common mortals, the educated and the ignorant. Justice is the regulatory value which can prevent the excessive use of privileges, the belief in the identity of human nature and the equality of all in front of God. This brings moral compensation to the impoverished.

Paternalism

Confronted with concrete reality, these paradigms of being and work encompass a fundamental contradiction which needs to be resolved. On the one hand is the social hierarchy, unequal distribution of resources and the necessity for most persons to work for someone else, and on the other is the absolute belief in universal equality, together with the necessity to safeguard individual dignity which is jeopardised by the submissive assumptions of the workplace.

One solution is resignation to the situation, an attitude sustained by a belief in destiny, the *nektoub* or the path chosen by God for the life of each individual. Another solution is to erect barriers between the period of time spent in work and the time available outside it. Each period follows a separate system of values and the inter-dependent relationship is not total. Paternalism is a third way to resolve the dilemma created by this theoretically humiliating subordination and the relationship of paternalism is based on:

- the belief that the hierarchical boss of the underling has a favourable opinion of them.
- the desire to see workers' interests, even those outside work, taken into the hands of their managers, and
- the primacy of affective relations in determining patterns, goals of rights and duties for everyone in their social relationships. From this derives a tendency to develop forms of charismatic power and fluid situations.

Ambiguity

In general, organisations assure coordination by instituting relatively precise rules so that everyone can orient themselves and anticipate the behaviour of others. What has been observed in Tunisian companies is a degree of unwillingness to formulate precise rules to deal with specific problems. Alternatively, when it is necessary to formulate rules, they are designed to be deliberately ambiguous, leaving the way open to multiple interpretations. In other examples the limits concerning each person's responsibility are ill-defined or even undefined. In management meetings, questions for debate are often interrupted before reaching a clear decision.

The current wave of deregulation, removing rules where they do exist, avoiding the need for precision and clear attribution of responsibility, is treated here as a cultural parameter which dictates behaviour. Links exist between this phenomenon and Islamic philosophy which accentuates forgiveness and divine clemency: disobedience does not automatically carry sanction. In the Qur'an, clemency is invoked ten times more often than severity.

Ambiguity is not only manifest in organisational life, but also in social settings. In a changing society, values and norms are constantly subjected to shocks. Responses to new situations, demand both inventiveness and consensus. Uncertain responses are without a doubt the result of the uncertainty of the situations, because reactions to them are unpredictable.

Social Relations and Identity

The fluidity associated with paternalism provides a favourable environment for the development of relationships and social identity. Faced with lacunae and ambiguity in social definition, social identity becomes the only guarantee of trust and of predictability in the reactions of 'the other'. At the organisational level, active networks of solidarity which link individuals in the same family, region, school or place of work illustrate the attraction of social identity as a point of reference in a fluid social environment. In essence, individual behaviour in Tunisian organisations can only be understood if reference is made to the interlinked aspects of the country's innate cultural configuration: attachment to values of dignity and equality, paternalism as a means of regulating situations in which inequality is inevitable, deregulation and social ambiguity and the attraction of relations based on social identity.

Each of these elements taken in isolation can be found in other cultures, but the originality of Tunisian culture rests in its singular configuration linking a specific set of cultural parameters together. The phenomenon of social ambiguity or fluidity can exist in all societies, but to different degrees. The same is true of the phenomena of dignity and social identity as behavioral factors. Studies carried out in Algeria also refer to these phenomen. Riffault[22] demonstrates that the Tuareg of Southern Algeria, when integrated into salaried employment, live a double life: that of work and that of traditional tribal life where the dependent relationship implied by the sale of labour power is eliminated. Henni[23] demonstrates that the Algerian company functions on a confraternal basis: each individual is member of a traditional network which confers an identity, a confidence and wealth. In the company, the investment in the relational network produces 'capital', in the sense that the greater the number and relevance of these relationships 'the greater are the possibilities of production and reproduction because of administrative means and privilege'.

Ben Chikhi[24] notes that patterns of management in Algerian companies do not have a company identity. Workers define status by family, region, location and religion and refuse to let their social status be devalued at work by either managers or by state administration. The quest for social contact outside the work environment causes inefficiency at work because the constraints of this social ethic are often opposed company objectives.

The importance of workers' cultural profile can be measured in terms of social and organisational dysfunction whenever it is disturbed, as well as by the elements which compose it. It has been noted that, in Tunisian companies organised along the lines of formal administrative hierarchy and impersonalised power, based on regulation and competence, there are multiple negative reactions to performance:

- no intrinsic value is attached to work in consequence of any presumed or real effect of such relationships on career development,
- employees perceive the ideal manager in terms of his amiability, civility and respect for them, rather than in terms of his competence, and
- power is centralised, but is contingent because of the differences in social background between those who express it and those to whom it is applied. Moreover the fluidity or ambiguity which surrounds procedures, values of equality and dignity, both of which undermine respect for managers and employers, renders power ineffective.

As a result, those invested with hierarchical power face a dilemma because of the contradictions between a bureaucratic organisational system associated with objectives of economic efficiency, and a cultural configuration which orders individual behaviour but which is generally irrational in terms of the system itself.

If the organisation were to accept the prevailing cultural norms, however, it might generate a relatively satisfactory performance. Indeed, a comparative study of productivity levels within different workshops of the same factory demonstrates that when deregulation was maximised in one workshop, productivity did not fall to the same levels as elsewhere in the plant.[25] In this firm the workforce was dissatisfied over its remuneration, with low salaries and presumed injustices in revenue distribution. It also refused to increase efficiency because of fear that this would lead to job losses. It was, therefore, disposed to minimise productivity and commitment. In this context, the manager of the workshop in question drew up a work schedule based on the following principles:

- reduce the social distance between him and his workers, and
- introduce flexible management emphasising multi-tasking and job

rotation: a machine operator could operate more than one machine and could undertake manual work; a machine operator assistant could also operate the machine and replace the machine operator himself.

This flexibility reduced the social and professional distinctions between workers, reducing boredom and fatigue since workers could replace one another in physically demanding jobs and compensate for absences in key posts. In effect, the consequent flexibility in time management was amplified by workers' ability to exploit multi-tasking, for there were now always replacements available – to such an extent that the section manager has claimed that his own absence had no repercussions on the rhythm of work.

This type of organisation creates a kind of community within the workshop, where social and professional differences are reduced, and where levels of negotiated productivity are of general concern. This approach does not totally eliminate feelings of frustration and injustice, because many believe they are more hard-working than others and receive no compensation for their extra efforts and competence. Nonetheless, a degree of equilibrium in relations in the workplace is achieved because attitudes towards the administration, which is judged to be responsible for innate injustice in remuneration, are redirected. In terms of work efficiency, this workshop has the highest level of activity, compared with two other production shops which are managed in a more coercive way.

This pattern of organisation could be compared to avant-garde management styles so that any culture-based explanation can be eliminated from the argument. This, however, would be to forget that we are dealing with a generalised organisational environment which is under-producing and which is not oriented towards an approach designed to improve organisational patterns. The workshop manager has merely adapted his management style to fit the culture profile of the workers without any idea of creating a theoretical management construct. Conflicts are not eliminated but are merely channelled upwards, towards the general management structure, so that they do not harm the general work productivity.

The values associated with work, as demonstrated by the research carried out nation-wide in Tunisia, corroborate research undertaken on Tunisian immigrant workers in France.[26] They are particularly associated with a need for respect, with paternalism, and a rejection of discipline, even at the managerial level, based on an avoidance of direct intervention. In every case, pride derived from cultural origin plays a key role: so that attempts are made to eliminate the inherent contradiction by identifying the manager as a father-figure or by replacing salaried work by entrepreneurship.

Conclusion: Globalisation or Persistence of Differential National Management Systems?

The answer to this question cannot reflect one extreme or the other. Arguments for the globalisation of management systems identify a phenomenon of managerial transfer or spill-over. However, it has not been demonstrated that the phenomenon is generalised for it only involves certain categories, sectors and aspects of the societal environment. The same is true for the diffusion of management methods as is true of technology. They may be available and accessible, but their adoption depends on factors other than those implied by the diffusion process. The use of such technologies must be seen in context as the anthropologist Malinowski reminds us when he points out 'adoption ends at the point at which change begins.'[27] This is the reason why certain models are altered by the actors themselves and become unrecognisable to those who originally invented them. The structures and the characteristic values of the social environment give shape to the borrowed model.

Finally the diffusion of dominant models does not negate the organisational capacity for inventive solutions when confronted with a specific problem. This may not only be a result of economic activity, but could also reflect the social inter-related environment. After all, the starting point of a global management system is the creation of such a system within a specific geographical area, in a specific socio-economic context. Diffusion beyond geographic boundaries corresponds to relative values of acceptable management at the international level, such as performance, participation, responsibility, internationalisation of competition and acceptance of international norms of quality and management. The companies concerned with this international space, structured on values which are themselves underpinned by international institutions, would be the most competent to borrow and diffuse international management systems. Companies most concerned with national or local environments provide a privileged space for managerial innovation derived from the environment itself. Thus the economic and managerial world becomes one of cross-currents of national or regional differentiation and globalisation. Globalisation is stimulated by a need for international integration through an ideology based *inter alia* on the denial of frontiers and on values of excellence. Differentiation feeds on the very nature of the national industrial fabric. It does not respond in every respect to the criteria of globalisation. It is also constricted by forces which reinforce structures of societal values, ordering choice and behaviour by reactions based on perceptions of social survival threatened by extreme tendencies beyond national control.

If globalisation corresponds to domination, then it will be manifest in transnational companies, managed according to comparable systems and norms surrounded by a desert of discarded and outclassed initiatives. But if the globalisation implies exchange, negotiation and mediation between the different and conflicting interests, then the process of creativity through managerial differentiation will expand exponentially to develop original interactions with different currents within the globalisation process.

NOTES

1. March, J.G., and Simon, H.A. (1964), *Les organisations, Problèmes psycho-sociologiques*, Paris, Dunod.
2. Crozier, M. (1973), The Determinants of Organization and Behavior in Modern Organizational Theory, in Naghandi, A.R., *A Model for Analysing Organistions in Cross-Cultural Settings: A Conceptual Scheme and Research Findings, in Modern Organizational Theory*, Kent State University Press.
3. d'Ibarne, P.H. (1989), *La logique de Honneur*, Paris, éd. du Seuil. Hofstede, G. (1980), Culture's Consequences, International Differences in Work-Related Values, CA, Sage Publications Inc; Neghandi, Ibid.
4. Mueller, F. (1994), Societal Effect, Organizational Effect and Globalisation, in *Organization Studies* 15/3, pp.407–28.
5. Ohmae, K. (1990), *The Borderless World – Power And Strategy In The Interlinked Economy*, London, Collins.
6. Amoroso, B. (1992), 'Industrial relations in Europe in the 1990s: new business strategies and the challenge to organized labour' in *International Journal of Human Resource Management*, 3/2 pp.321–46; Baglioni, G. (1990), 'Industrial relations in Europe in the 1980s, in *European Industrial Relations: The Challenge Of Flexibility*, Baglioni, G. and Crouch, C. (eds.) 1-41 London, Sage; Shonfield, A. (1965), *Modern Capitalism*, Oxford, Oxford University Press.
7. Mueller (note 4) p.416.
8. Ibid.
9. Enriquez, E. (1995), *Fantasme d'emprise totale, fantasme d'autonomie*, W.P. Colloque Entreprises et Sociétés, Montréal .
10. Sörge A., (1995), *Effet sociétal, internationalisation et entreprise, cadre d'analyse et résultats de comparaisons européennes*. W.P. Colloque Entreprises et Sociétés, Montréal.
11. Bauer, M. and Bertin-Mourot, B. (1995), *Les dirigeants d'entreprise en France, en Allemagne et en Grande Bretagne: une étude comparée*, W.P. Colloque Entreprises et sociétés, Montréal.
12. Maurice, M., Sellier, F., Silvestre, J.J. (1982), *Politique d'Education et Organisation Iindustrielle en France et en Allemagne*, Paris, PUF.
13. Sörge (note 10), p.1.
14. See Giddens, A. (1984), The Construction of Society, Berkeley CA, University of California Press.
15. Dia, M. (1996), *Africa's Management in the 1990s and Beyond, Reconciling Indigenous and Transplanted Institutions,* Washington DC: The World Bank.
16. Ibid, p.4.
17. Chanlat, J.F., and Kamdem, E. (1995), *La dynamique socio-culturelle de l'entreprise africaine, le cas de triois entreprises africaines*, Montréal, W.P. Colloque Entreprises et Sociétés.
18. Henry, A. (1995), *Les entreprises africaines face à un environnement hostiles*, Montréal, W.P. Colloque Entreprises et Sociétés.
19. Desjeux, D. (1995), *Le fonctionnement des organisations en Afrique: Modèles Culturels de résolution des problèmes, stratégies et réseaux sociaux*, W.P, Colloque Entreprises et Sociétés,.
20. Zghal, R. (1994), Culture et Comportement Organisationnel, *Les Cahiers du MIRS,* No 1

Février, Paris, Conservatoire National des Arts et Métiers, CNRS.

21. The words of the Prophet and the second source of Islamic doctrine.

22. Riffault, M.C. (1974), 'Salariat et culture traditionnelle, une application à partir du sud algérien', in *Spécificités culturelles et Industrialisation*, Actes du VIIIe colloque de l'Association International des Sociologues de Langue Française, Tunis 1971, RTSS No. 36–39.

23. Henni, A. (1992), 'Le Cheikh et le Patron', in *La performance, Théories, Perceptions, Pratiques*, Tunisia, Publications de la Faculté des Sciences Economiques et de Gestion de Sfax.

24. Benchikhi, S. (1987), 'Non-Identité au Travail et Société en Algérie', *Travail et Développement, Revue Tunisienne des sciences du Travail*, No 9.

25. Zghal, R. (1992) 'Hiérarchies et processus de pouvoir dans les organisations', in *Elites et pouvoir dans le monde arable pendant la période moderne et contemporaine*, Universite de Tunis, CERES.

26. Zghal, R. (1995), Relations de Travail et Condition d'Emigré, in *Les Quartiers de la ségrégation, Tiers monde ou Quart monde, Institut Maghreb-Europe*, Karthala, Paris.

27. Malinowski, B. (1958), *The Dynamics of Culture Change*, New Haven CT, Yale University Press.

Social Feasibility and Costs of the Free Trade Zone

AZZAM MAHJOUB

The Social Costs of Adjustment to the Free Trade Zone

The free trade zone forms the commercial element of the Euro-Mediterranean Partnership Initiative agreement between the European Union and Tunisia. It has at least four specific characteristics:

- it exists between one single country, on the one hand, and a group of countries on the other,
- it takes place between economies of unequal levels of development,
- it involves economies at different levels of integration, and
- it involves economies with different levels of mutual protection.

These characteristics mean that this free trade area differs from the classic definition of a free trade area where two or more countries of similar levels of development and protection agree to dismantle the protective systems controlling their own commercial transactions. The free trade area being created here is thus characterised by a manifest asymmetry. Whilst the European Union is already open to Tunisian goods, Tunisia must now undertake a unilateral dismantling of its system of protection towards imports coming from the European Union. This uniqueness and asymmetry of the proposed free trade area, which will have unequal and uncertain consequences, requires special conditions for its introduction and care in the interpretation of the way its impact is evaluated.

The analysis of the social impact of the free trade area is closely linked to its economic effects which specifically and primarily affect economic activity and public finances. Yet these impacts produce reactions which will significantly affect the consequences and prospects of the free trade area as far as economic and social development are concerned. As a result this analysis must put forward a speculative rather than a prospective

Professor Azzam Mahjoub is Professor of Economics at the Faculté des Sciences Economiques et de Gestion, University of Tunis, Tunisia.

conclusion, although it will also take the opportunity to recognise the major social difficulties and constraints which are normally eclipsed by economic and financial imperatives.

The creation of a free trade area between the European Union and Tunisia involves the effectively unilateral removal of protection against European products without any corresponding concession by the Union since virtually all manufactured products have free access to the European market. Only a few agricultural products have seen their export levels towards the Union increase as a result of the removal of barriers to commercial exchange, but the exclusion of agricultural products from the free trade area will remove this advantage. The positive commercial effects which can be expected from the creation of a free trade area in manufactured goods can only be indirect. For the Union's partnership country, they will have to arise from the increase in competitiveness associated with the decline in the price of imports from Europe, and through the adjustments leading to increased productivity as a result of removing protections from the economy. At the same time, any evaluation of the quantitative effects of the creation of a free trade area cannot be separated from the macroeconomic policy associated with the removal of customs protection and these impacts turn out to be highly diverse when set against the basic hypothesis behind the process.

The hypothesis implicitly assumes that the introduction by government of a recessive macroeconomic adjustment policy (based on reductions in public expenditure or exchange rate alterations) will affect global economic activity on a very small scale: There will be a degree of global stagnation but a differentiated pattern of sectoral growth underlining the need for industrial restructuring and the displacement of labour towards low capital-intensive sectors. The introduction of an active macroeconomic adjustment policy, designed to exert a degree of control over the potential consequences of the free trade area, could involve compensation for net fiscal deficits as a result of the removal of customs protection through an increase in indirect taxation, or adjustment through growth based on significant increases in foreign investment.

• Firstly, although increases in indirect taxation will compensate for declines in customs receipts, they will also generate perverse effects which will seriously affect economic growth. Prices will rise, so that domestic investment and consumption will decline and jobs will be lost, particularly in industries designed to service the domestic market. This decline in economic activity will, in turn, lead to a reduction in tax revenues – the global taxable revenue will decline despite the rise in tax rates – and will worsen unemployment despite its implicit assumptions that mechanisms exist for the spontaneous reallocation of labour through the control over sectoral movements in the labour force.

- On the other hand, the macroeconomic effect can be reversed if adjustment is carried out through capital inflows, even though the same dispositions continue to apply to budgetary and monetary policy. The results of a study of the impact of the free trade area on the Tunisian economy suggest that, in this case, the process could result in accelerated growth through a significant capacity to absorb additional investment in certain sectors and in improved outcomes for employment and fiscal receipts.[1]

Thus the effects on economic activity and employment are highly variable, depending on national ability to capture and mobilise significant flows of direct foreign investment and on the capacity of the industrial fabric to absorb major changes in investment levels. The major challenge is the degree of economic flexibility that can coexist in the transitional period of exchange rate liberalisation whilst macroeconomic equilibrium is preserved. During the introduction of a free trade area, however, Tunisia was not able to enjoy slow or moderate growth. The adjustment process was made even more difficult because Tunisia initially faced a high levels of protection and high unemployment. Studies which were undertaken estimated that up to 60 per cent of industrial production was threatened by tariff removal for imports from the European Union. Half of this production reflected activities which could be competitive and half protected activities where there was no real comparative advantage.

As a result, the protection of the same level of activity after the free trade area is in place, would essentially mean the transfer of 30 per cent of industrial activity – in other words, a third of it would have to be abandoned and the resources deployed elsewhere, which involves a veritable transformation of the Tunisian economy. Thus, to what extent would it be possible to carry through such a massive reallocation of productive resources in order to render the Tunisian economy itself competitive and to what extent would this 'competitive third' remain competitive?

Social Impacts of Free Trade Adjustment Difficulties

For a country like Tunisia where under-employment is the norm (unemployment levels are at 16 per cent), the social consequences of deregulation are considerable. At present the major source of competitiveness in Tunisian industry is the textile and clothing sectors which absorb more than half those in employment, however, even this competitiveness is artificial and will disappear, not because of the introduction of the free trade area but because of the disappearance of the Multi-Fibre Agreements.

The social impact of the introduction of the free trade are with the European Union also arises in terms of the effects it will have on public finance given that customs receipts form an important component of budget revenues. There is much anxiety with respect to public finance (the budget deficit was above four per cent of GDP) where revenues depend on duties and import taxes and a significant effort to redirect access to budgetary resources from domestic sources will have to be made. This will require two basic conditions: firstly a general fiscal reform and secondly the development of fiscal revenue-generating activities. This is difficult to envisage in a context of profound industrial change and reconversion which have specifically required tax incentive measures.

For Tunisia, the fiscal shortfall inherent in the introduction of the free trade area with the European Union has been calculated to be equivalent to around 65 per cent of customs revenues, or a reduction of more than 18 per cent in overall fiscal revenues. This impact creates a dilemma for government which is tempted to adopt 'spontaneously' policies of demand management through either reductions in public expenditure or increases in indirect taxation.

In view of the fact that public expenditure is an essential part of the introduction of new productive resources, policies of reduction in public expenditure are incompatible, on the one hand, with policies designed to encourage investment, and inappropriate, on the other, in the context of liberalisation promoted by industrial reconversion which requires more sustained state budgetary intervention. Thus the reaction to declines in fiscal receipts through policies of public expenditure reduction can only lead to general recession in the critical context of the introduction of a free trade area. If this process is viewed dynamically, such a recession which will lead to a reduction in fiscal receipts can only worsen the negative budgetary management consequences.

In the second case, where the decline in fiscal receipts is translated into a search for other fiscal compensatory resources through increasing other indirect tax rates, the consequences will be similar even though the means are different. In effect, the increase in the indirect tax burden will cause a decline in consumption and thus in investment, as well as in production and employment. Even if it were assumed that the free trade area would have no effect on activity through demand management – a view which is unlikely, not to say unrealistic – Tunisia would have to raise its VAT rates by around 50 per cent to compensate for the fiscal shortfall caused by tariff liberalisation. Such conditions lie quite outside political and economic realism.

Thus, whatever the governmental reaction to customs liberalisation, there will be a serious risk of decline in state social expenditure. The introduction of the structural adjustment programme has not yet had a social cost because of policies protecting social sectors through an increase in public expenditure for social purposes by 14 per cent in real terms from 47.5 per cent of budgetary expenditure in 1987 to 52.5 per cent in 1993.[2] The introduction of the free trade area is a new challenge in terms of fiscal adjustment and the preservation of the social environment.

The Social Feasibility of the Free Trade Area

It should first be recognised that the free trade area is not a techno-economic problem in the strict sense of the term. It has differentiated social redistributive consequences and its social feasibility is both a function of the reactions of different social groups – in terms of potential pressure to reorient and redirect the rhythm of adjustment through confrontation or passive or active resistance – and of the responses made to them by politicians. Given the fact that we can establish the overall social cost of the free trade area, we must briefly take account of the differentiated redistributive social costs, because the political feasibility of the free trade area is dependent on the political leadership's ability to enlist support for the reforms as part of the construction of a broad and coherent coalition in favour of the free trade area itself.

Two scenarios arise from a macro-economic analysis of the social impact of the free trade area.

1. Free trade adjustment in the economic arena, in terms of adjustment policy and reconversion is either is non-existent or has had imperceptible effects. Furthermore, external capital inflows are of little significance. The state reacts, either by reducing public expenditure or by increasing VAT, in order to compensate for the fiscal deficit. All simulation models suggest that the adjustment will be recessionist in nature, accompanied by worsening unemployment.
2. The free trade area is accompanied by active adjustment policies involving aided reconversion (*mise à niveau*) policies and significant foreign capital inflows. A surge in growth is expected and the labour market is expected to ease.

The first scenario allows us to illustrate the differential effects of the free trade area on social groups in the most explicit manner and three cases arise:

1. All other factors being equal, only changes caused by liberalisation of

the import regime and of the removal of tariff protection are significant.

Effects on Prices

- prices of imported goods could decline as a result of tariff reductions. This, in turn, either reduces input costs, because the goods involved are capital or intermediate goods, or labour costs decline because consumer goods are involved (provided salaries are price-indexed).

Social Groups Which Benefit

- importers
- consumers in general (increase in private consumption is anticipated at the macro-economic level)
- entrepreneurs in competitive export sector who depend heavily on imported inputs because of the anticipated improvement in profitability.

Social Groups Which Lose or Suffer Negative Consequences

- workers and employers in sectors unable to compete, particularly with goods that cannot be exchanged in the international market;
- senior administrative officials involved with external trade who experience a decline in their control of import networks and, to a degree, over general economic activity.

2. The state compensates for the fiscal deficit by increasing indirect taxation. The decline in imported goods is countered by an increase in indirect taxes (VAT) to compensate the fiscal deficit resulting from liberalisation. Since VAT is ultimately paid by the consumers, it is they (particularly those on fixed incomes) who suffer the negative consequences of the increase in fiscal pressure. A fall in purchasing power is likely which will affect society as a whole in view of the gradual erosion of the permanent purchasing power of employees in the wake of the introduction of structural adjustment policies.

3. The state compensates for the fiscal deficit by reducing public expenditure in terms of:

Current Expenditure which will have negative consequences on:
- public and parastatal employees who can anticipate salary freezes and redundancies
- graduates seeking public sector employment, because of the slow-down or blocking of recruitment.

Social Expenditure which will affect vulnerable groups.

The Likely Political Impact on South and East Mediterranean Countries

In view of differentiated redistributive effects, the political feasibility of the free trade area agreement may increase credibility which otherwise might erode away. However, wherever the deficit is high, there is a strong possibility that repression will increase, yet the path of outright repression is limited by:

The Potential Costs

- increase in police and army budgets accompanied by the risk of a military coup and the possibility of international political conditionality which might react through sanctions or boycotts.

The following scenario – which is flexible and opportunistic – could be imagined. In order to preserve power, the governing elite can adjust its policies by:

- repression (in the general sense of closing down political life)
- providing a limited degree of political liberalisation; and
- compensation.

Faced with apathy or latent resistance which it is prepared to acknowledge, the governing elite can take limited political liberalisation measures. However, if these newly acquired liberties are used to slow down or hinder the free trade agreement, repression will be called into play.

The governing elite can also make use of repression and compensation in tandem with one another for groups which suffer negative consequences. Compensation will be a price borne by the state in order to reconcile itself with groups socially disadvantaged by the free trade agreement. The price of the compensation should be compared with the cost of repression which might have to be exercised to impose 'sacrifices'. Opportunities for compensation depend on the ability to negotiate the degree of political conditionality linked to European financial assistance. It has to be admitted, of course, that the financial assistance for compensation (or reduction in the social cost of the free trade agreement) also involves the danger of delaying or slowing down the necessary political reforms since it will reduce the threshold of political acceptability of the social costs involved.

The proposed strategy, therefore, combines:

- an element of repression which is 'economically acceptable' in terms of costs and politically tolerable to the European partner;

- a component of limited political liberalisation which can be reversed and which in no way threatens the monopoly of the regime (formal pluralism);
- an element of compensation, as a cost absorbed also by the European partner or, as a political price to be paid to neutralise the domestic socio-political struggle, which restores the credibility of the governing elite and ensures continuity of power.

The effectiveness of such an 'adaptive strategy' depends on the ability of regimes to judge accurately the threshold of toleration of the social costs of adjustment by different social groups, beyond which confrontation can become violent destabilisation and undermine the strategy of the elite to remain in power. It also depends on an accurate assessment of the degree to which negotiation is possible with the European partner over political conditionality in terms of the level of repression which can be tolerated without threatening financial assistance. This must be seen against the background of a lack of pluralist institutional structure and along side a bundle of measures and practices which restrict fundamental liberties.

This scenario, which defines, in practice, a free trade agreement with little progress in institutional and political terms, is likely to occur, although it is not necessarily likely to succeed. Can it be sustained in the medium-term? Could it, as a result of economic growth, guarantee political stability? In view of what has already happened, medium-term sustainability seems questionable.

Should, therefore, another approach be adopted, so that the problem of the feasibility of the free trade agreement can be posed in different terms? Should not policies be defined which seek to maximise the economic benefits resulting from the free trade agreements – effective economic policies – and which minimise the social costs – more just social policies? Such policies would have an optimal degree of political feasibility since they would enjoy widespread support amongst the population and would genuinely contribute to the democratic transition process in the countries of the southern and eastern Mediterranean.

This optimal feasibility would require institutional reform which would allow executive authority enjoying wide popular support to emerge. The institutional mechanisms and structures required would be designed to minimise violence, social disturbance and political coercion. They would resolve social conflict in order to avoid the danger that any potential social tension would manifest itself by challenging the institutions of existing regimes.

In this context, it is important that the social and political dimensions of the issue are properly defined and that Euro-Mediterranean networks are developed which can:

- improve awareness of the interdependence and interaction between different elements of the free trade agreements, whether economic, social or political-institutional in nature;
- demonstrate the distributive consequences in terms of regional and social groups, so as to avoid potential risks of violent social and political confrontation; and
- recommend institutional reform which will optimize political feasibility.

In the immediate future, it is essential to engage in a large-scale and transparent public debate, involving the governing elite and civil society, over the social and political implications of the free trade agreement and of the consequent political and institutional reforms.

NOTES

1. Kebabdjan G., Mahjoub A., Zaafrane H. *et al.*, 'Etude prospective de l'impact sur l'économie tunisienne de la mise en place d'une zone de libre-échange avec l'Union européenne', COMETE, CEPEX, November 1994.
2. World Bank, 'République Tunisienne, Allégement de la pauvreté: bâtir sur les acquis pour préparer l'avenir', April 1996.

The Uses and Misuses of 'Culture' – A Comment

KEVIN DWYER

Introduction

To provide some groundwork for discussion, a few remarks of a general nature concerning our notions of culture are necessary for a number of reasons, not least being the fact that the term 'culture' has lately become a contentious one, a concept that, among its other uses, has been wielded to defend reactionary policies of exclusion and to excite xenophobic passions.

As one anthropologist has recently written, 'the standard anthropological definition of culture as constituting a way of life and a 'peoplehood' is now being used by reactionary political forces to justify social prejudice and nativism. Immigrants and their descendants are condemned as 'not belonging' by this opportunistic use of the concept of cultures and cultural relativism...'.[1] Another anthropologist has argued that, in the context of European attitudes toward Third World immigrants, '... a perceptible shift in the rhetoric of exclusion can now be detected. From what were once assertions of the differing endowment of human races there has risen since the seventies a rhetoric of inclusion and exclusion that emphasises the distinctiveness of cultural identity, traditions, and heritage among groups ...'.[2] This, she suggests, is different from racism because, although 'There may be occasional references to 'blood' or 'race', there is more to this culturalist discourse than the idea of insurmountable essential cultural differences or a kind of biological culturalism..., namely, [there is] the assumption that relations between different cultures are by 'nature' hostile and mutually destructive because it is in human nature to be ethnocentric; different cultures ought, therefore, to be kept apart for their own good.'[3] An extreme and extremely well-publicised formulation of this assumption is found in Samuel Huntington's *The Clash of Civilizations*, which argues that, in the foreseeable future, 'The great divisions among humankind and the dominating source of conflict will be cultural.'[4]

Dr. Kevin Dwyer is an anthropologist specialising in North Africa and the Middle East and is currently director of the Institut de Recherches Appliquées, Tunis.

As Edward Said (in a new afterword to his now classic *Orientalism*) recently asked, 'What is another culture? Is the notion of a distinct culture (or race, or religion, or civilisation) a useful one, or does it always get involved either in self-congratulation (when one discusses one's own) or hostility and aggression (when one discusses the 'other')?'[5]

The Notion of 'Culture'

I would like to look more closely at the notion of 'culture', in order to help us avoid the extremes that Said warns against. As Raymond Williams has pointed out, whereas '*culture,* in all its early uses was a noun of process: the tending *of* something, basically crops or animals ... a decisive change of use [occurred] in [Johann Gottfried] Herder ... [who argued that it was necessary] to speak of 'cultures' in the plural: the specific and variable cultures of different nations and periods, but also the specific and variable cultures of social and economic groups within a nation.' It is interesting to note, as Williams does, that Herder's innovative usage was closely tied to his attacks on both 'the assumption of the universal histories that 'civilization' or 'culture'... was what we would now call a unilinear process', and on 'what he called the European subjugation and domination of the four quarters of the globe...'. Williams goes on to say, 'This sense was widely developed, in the Romantic movement, as an alternative to the orthodox and dominant 'civilization.' It was first used to emphasize national and traditional cultures, including the new concept of folk-culture.'[6]

This view of culture gave pride of place to diversity but, at the same time, it tended to abstract a population's shared symbolic representations from material social relations and conditions, and helped to make the opposition between culture and material social relations a foundational principle of modern social consciousness.[7]

This foundational principle is in operation in many studies of the relationship between culture and economic behaviour – the unremarkable coupling of these terms suggests the pervasive nature of this principle – but perhaps the best known example lies in the work of the German sociologist Max Weber on *The Protestant Ethic and the Spirit of Capitalism*, during the first decades of this century. For better or worse, Weber's book set the terms for subsequent discussion of the issue.[8]

Weber focused on the relationship between attitudes towards work and profit on the one hand and doctrines of religious belief, particularly the Calvinist doctrine of predestination, on the other. He argued that this doctrine induced in believers deep anxiety over their personal salvation and that they came to view worldly success as a sign that God had predestined them for salvation in the afterlife. *The Protestant Ethic* dealt particularly with Christianity, but in other studies Weber examined why capitalism had not developed in China, India, within ancient Judaism or in the Muslim world.

In general, his work on this subject has often been criticised as somewhat too idealistic. As regards Islam, for example, Weber noted that early Islamic society had many of the preconditions for capitalist expansion, but he tended to offer what he saw as Islam's 'fatalism' as the decisive force to explain why capitalism remained stillborn. This interpretation has, of course, been challenged and one of the strongest refutations is that of Maxime Rodinson who argued, in *Islam et capitalisme*, that the crucial factors inhibiting capitalist development in the Islamic world had their source in the confrontation in the Middle Ages between Islam and Christianity. Whatever the case may be, the main point I want to make here is that this debate carried forward the German Romantic notions of 'culture', or '*Weltanschauung*' (world view), or 'spirit'.

To draw out some of the implications of this view of culture, let me take one of the standard anthropological formulations of the term as defined by Hatch: 'Culture is the way of life of a people. It consists of conventional patterns of thought and behaviour, including values, beliefs, rules of conduct, political organisation, economic activity, and the like, which are passed on from one generation to the next by learning – and not by biological inheritance.'[9]

Hatch notes that in this definition certain aspects are usually highlighted:

- 'the patterns which both guide and define thought and behaviour are learned...',
- 'a large component of culture is below the level of conscious awareness' – for example, language, and
- cultural patterns are not simply forms of behaviour but '... structure both thought and perception'.[10]

For a variety of reasons that there is not scope to address here this view, which had the clear merit of providing us with notions that did not lead inevitably to determining and ranking superior and inferior but encouraged us to look at societies and social groups on their own terms, led to the view that cultures were self-contained, relatively impermeable, and composed of comparatively stable entities like rules, values, and beliefs that persisted from one generation to another. This has been called, aptly, the 'billiard-ball' theory of culture.[11] However, among the many issues this view had difficulty treating was the question of cultural change: if culture is largely unconscious, transmitted from generation to generation, and cultures are incompatible and incommensurable, how then would cultures ever change?

Today this view may seem out of date to many of us, and no longer applicable to a world of significant population movements, growing global integration, glaring distinctions within societies, and where many people speak not only their native language but other dialects and languages and where 'by some calculations, more than 99 per cent of the world's peoples live in states containing more than one ethnic group'.[12] For these reasons among others, the billiard-ball view is no longer intellectually defensible, but this has not stopped its being used effectively to advance tactical political goals.

As a remedy for some of the paramount deficiencies of the billiard-ball view, a different vision has gained currency, a vision that sees cultures as *overlapping* (people of one culture find themselves situated in another), *interacting* (globalisation leads to growing influence and interchange across geographical boundaries), and *internally negotiated* (meanings and practices are not given once and for all, but are a product of the interplay of the various forces and constituencies both within and outside the unit).[13]

While undeniably an improvement on the previous formulation and constituting a more faithful representation of the world we live in, this more recent formulation leaves aside or does not sufficiently emphasise at least two crucial aspects: first, that the construction of the notion of 'culture' and of a particular culture as having certain characteristics is just that – a construction from a particular perspective. Secondly, as a *situated* construction, the notion becomes *self-reflexive* – it opens to question both the situation of the user and the relationship between this situation and the programmatic implications of the notion.

If we place a renewed emphasis on cultures as constructed or imagined entities, and insist on interpreting these reflexively, we might then see a culture (or a tradition) as constructed from the diverse actions and dispositions of 'individuals within social groups who inevitably have different perspectives, different psychological and physiological profiles, different points of view ... [a 'culture' is] a more or less coherent construction of these historically and geographically situated differences, a simplifying construction of course, but it too situated historically and geographically.'[14] To move in this direction helps us see competition between meanings as open-ended, reminding us of the unpredictability of the future and of the fact that any construction is inherently 'unstable, vulnerable to being called into question by other constructions, ... [and] its domination at any given moment and in any given place is not a forecast of its future domination.'[15] Also, viewing these terms as situationally constructed and self-reflexive pushes us to question not only particular boundaries and the processes behind their construction but, at the same time, the 'we' that works to construct them.

I hope that highlighting these principles helps draw attention to the dangers entailed by certain kinds of usage of the term 'culture' and also goes some way toward enabling us to avoid them. Let me list these principles here in summary form:

- 'cultures' overlap and interact,
- their meanings are negotiated;,
- these meanings and the very notion of 'culture' that these meanings presuppose are 'situated' or elaborated from particular perspectives, in particular situations, implying particular programmes, and
- use of these terms should encourage self-reflexivity – any particular interpretation calls for questioning the stance of the interpreter and the kinds of boundaries the interpretation constructs.

The effect of keeping these principles in mind when we deal with the notion of culture is not to provide a definition of culture but rather to encourage use of the concept in certain ways rather than in others. By holding these principles before us it also becomes more feasible, I believe, to approach complex questions like those of cultural change and the relationship between culture and economic behaviour with a recognition of the unpredictability of the phenomena we are addressing.

Globalisation, Culture and Management Systems

I would now like to turn to the paper by Professor Riadh Zghal, which examines the extent to which globalising trends impose constraints on one particular aspect of behaviour, human interaction within economic firms. She sees two major views: one, formulated by Mueller and others, which rejects the influence of local societal factors and argues that convergence is bound to occur; and a second which has many variants and sees these factors as having an important and sometimes positive influence on the management of firms. Zghal examines how these hypotheses have been formulated, what their differing relevance for developed and for developing countries might be, and then looks more closely at the case of Tunisia.

The questions with which I am most concerned in her paper are: what kinds of notions of culture do we find in it and what are the implications of these notions. I think there are three basic views presented – culture seen as composed of traits as composed of complexes, or as a guide. I think each view has some strengths and weaknesses, and each has certain practical implications and promotes certain policy initiatives.

By the view of cultures as traits, I mean the view that one can isolate a series of rather simple factors that:

- can be defined cross-culturally,
- can be described as either present or absent in a given society,
- are relatively independent of one another, and
- can be recombined in almost any conceivable way.

Mueller's study reflects this kind of approach: management style can be broken down into components, certain combinations of these components will lead to more efficient outcomes than others, and, under the pressures of global competition, these components will in fact recombine in the most efficient way, with all other combinations necessarily converging to it. I agree with Zghal's point here that this view may seem plausible when the phenomena are viewed from afar but that the similarity of traits quickly disappears when scrutinised more closely.

The view of culture as composed of complexes may be taken as a more sophisticated version of the trait view: here, traits come in bundles, each bundle coheres as a somewhat self-contained system. Unlike the trait view, these complexes are not strictly similar to one another across societies – it would not be easy to describe them as either present or absent since they may take on slightly or dramatically different forms from society to society. The studies on Western management practice that Prof. Zghal refers to seem to share this view; those she cites on Africa appear to convey elements of both the view of culture as traits and culture as complexes.

I think there are serious problems with these two views. They are rather mechanistic and perhaps too congruent with an 'engineering' approach to culture: one may pick and choose the traits that are desired and then by changing their utility functions (by exacting penalties through coercion, or offering benefits to encourage adherence) produce a new constellation of traits. In the view of culture as complexes, such engineering becomes, of course, more difficult, but the principle remains the same, only perhaps the investments made and penalties applied would need to be greater.

The third view – culture as guide – appears to be the one Zghal supports. It is formulated in her introduction to the section on Tunisia: 'to speak of culture as a determining factor in behaviour is to speak of an internal logic which members of a particular society share and which appears as customs – an unspoken agreement that everyone respects as if it were the pledge which determines social membership.'[16]

While I have some reservations regarding this third type – for example, it does not address some of the principles I mentioned earlier – I think it is important to note that this view presents values as a flexible system with many points of internal tension, imparting a dynamic character much less in evidence with the other approaches. The system of values is also assigned a potentially creative function in the subsequent elaboration of the kinds of management practices that would best satisfy the particular needs of an enterprise, a sector and a community.

Zghal's approach also has the advantage of not positing its own omniscience as the other views seem to do. It recognises, as Zghal says at the very end of her paper and consonant with what I have stressed above, the importance of allowing space for creativity in the conflict of interests, something that can only be achieved by maintaining a significant degree of diversity.

While I was asked to comment directly only on Professor Zghal's paper, it is worth emphasising that each of the three preceding papers raises in different ways, questions about the relationship between culture and economic activity: Professor Zghal's paper asks whether, in a 'globalising' context, the local character of behaviour within institutions can be maintained and whether losing this character would be a good thing; and Professor Mahjoub's paper asks, in the light of the economic and social pressures that the partnership accords between Tunisia and Europe are likely to produce, whether Tunisia has the political and cultural resources to respond positively. Each paper presents us with a more or less explicit vision of the relationship between culture and economic activity and each vision has certain policy implications that should not be overlooked.

These three papers, together with my comments, raise a series of questions that I hope we will be able to address in future discussion, among them being: what are the various views of culture that we see articulated around us, what are some of the benefits and disadvantages of these views, what are the programmes and policies that these views imply? As we proceed with this discussion, we would no doubt do well to advance our views tentatively, reflecting our deep-seated knowledge that an 'engineering' approach to human society is of very limited relevance, and that the future will no doubt sharply surprise us once again, as it has so often in the past.

NOTES

1. Fox, Richard Fox (1995), Editorial in *Current Anthropology*, 36/1, pp. i-ii.
2. Stolcke, Verena (1995), 'Talking Culture: New Boundaries, New Rhetorics of Exclusion in Europe', in *Current Anthropology* 36/1, pp. 1-13.
3. Ibid. p.5
4. Huntington, Samuel, (1996), *The Clash of Civilizations*, London, Simon and Schuster.
5. Said, Edward (1979), *Orientalism,* London, Random House.
6. Williams, Raymond (1983 [1976]), *Keywords*, London, Fontana p. 87-89. He is referring to Herder's *Ideas on the Philosophy of the History of Mankind* (1784-91).
7. For an anthropological example of this argument see Turner, Terence (1995), Comment in *Current Anthropology,* 36/1 pp.16-18.
8. Weber, Max (1985), *The Protestant Ethic and the Spirit of Capitalism*, London, Unwin Paperbacks.

9. Hatch, Elvin (1985), 'Culture', in *The Social Science Encyclopedia,* Adam and Jessica Kuper (eds.), London, Routledge, pp.178–9.

10. Ibid.

11. Tully, James (1995), *Strange Multiplicity: Constitutionalism in an Age of Diversity,* Cambridge, Cambridge University Press.

12. Zimmerman, W., 'Last chance for Bosnia?' in *New York Review of Books,* 19 December 1996, pp.10–13.

13. This formulation, as well as the term 'billiard-ball' theory of culture, comes from the political philosopher, James Tully (note 11), who adopts it from anthropologist Michael Carrithers. Carrithers, M., (1992), *Why Humans Have Cultures: Explaining Anthropology and Social History,* Oxford, Oxford University Press.

14. Dwyer, Kevin, (1996), 'Arguments moraux et projet universel', in *Prologues,* Casablanca, Morocco, 5 (Winter), pp.76–81.

15. Ibid, p.78.

16. Zghal, Riadh, *Globalisation,* 'Culture and Management Systems', paper presented in Workshop III of Europe and North Africa: Seeking an Economic Road to Security, Tozeur/RIIA and included in this journal.

Latin America's Path From Backwardness to Development

JOSEPH L. LOVE

Introduction

Although many Latin American countries underwent major structural transformations in the second half of the twentieth century, as evidenced by their rapid urbanisation and industrialisation, their per capita incomes remained low when compared to the advanced industrial nations, and with the possible exception of Chile, they have not been able to produce the decades-long dynamism of several East Asian countries. An additional characteristic of the region has been the very high concentration of income and wealth, which has persisted from colonial times to the present. Yet Latin America hardly stagnated; in 1991 only Haiti, Nicaragua, and Honduras ranked in the lowest of the World Bank's four tiers of per capita GNP, and five countries–in ascending order, Brazil, Venezuela, Uruguay, Mexico, and Argentina–were in the upper middle income group. Revised data for Chile place it in the same category.[1]

The Colonial Inheritance

Latin America did not share the relatively egalitarian frontier experience associated with the advance of Western settlement in the United States and the British Dominions. In Meso-America and the Andes sedentary and hierarchical indigenous societies were conquered by a patrimonial and legalistic regime in Spain. The latter easily imposed its own hierarchical structure on the former. With the early discovery of precious metals, the main interest of the Spanish Crown in administering the colonies was to maximise their exploitation; this aim was achieved through colonial-mercantilist policies which minimised investments in infrastructure and the development of human capital. For native-born individuals, including the offspring of Spaniards, access to the highest administrative positions during

Joseph L. Love is Director of the Center for Latin American and Caribbean Studies at the University of Illinois.

the colonial regime was sharply restricted, and the best positions in commerce were held by Spanish and peninsula-connected families. The creole elites (that is, native-born whites) therefore dedicated their efforts to exploiting agricultural labour by extra-economic means, and by the seventeenth century to acquiring large rural properties, which were not efficiently exploited. As domestic markets were small (given the low income of the rural masses), there was little incentive to invest in non-plantation agriculture. The rural elites, often being absentee-owners living in towns, used their influence and income to acquire more properties, and spent a considerable share of their resources on sumptuary consumption. They were commonly indebted to merchants, who provided the only credit available for agriculture, often at usurious rates.

Portuguese America (Brazil) had no significant sedentary native population, and Europeans initially found no precious metals there; Brazil was a backwater in an empire that had its most profitable colonies – most of them simply trading entrepots – in Asia. Brazil's lack of importance resulted in a loose administrative organisation of Portugal's New World colony. Sugar, the first major primary export product, was based on the direct entrepreneurial activities of landlords. This did not lead to long-term economic development, however, as sugar production was based on slave labour, using primitive technologies, which fell behind West Indian colonies by the seventeenth century. The discovery of gold in Minas Gerais at the end of that century led to a new export cycle and tended to shift economic activities to South-Central Brazil. But the gold boom had a negative developmental impact on Brazil, in that Portuguese authorities imposed strict mercantilistic controls over the newly-rich colony. Such controls were designed to make the colony as dependent as possible on the metropolis in the later eighteenth century; manufacturing was prohibited in 1785, shutting down a not inconsiderable wrought-iron industry. Meanwhile the 'accumulation' of human capital was presumably lower than that of Spanish America, as Portugal denied Brazil both universities and printing presses, both of which institutions Spain had established in Mexico and Peru in the sixteenth century.

Economic Setback in the First Decades of Independence

Conditions of most Latin American countries in the early years of independence were not propitious for economic growth. Much of Spanish America had suffered from the destruction caused by the wars of independence–parts of Mexico, Uruguay and Venezuela were devastated. On achieving independence in the 1820s, Latin American states found themselves heavily dependent on the British government for recognition and a guarantee of their independence, and on British merchants for overseas trade. These merchants took over the commodity trade by first extending credit to local producers in the early years of independence.[2] In Mexico per capita income, which had probably fallen in the years 1810-21 because of the civil wars and breakdown of the mining 'motor', did not recover the level of the 1830s for more than a generation, owing to continuing civil disturbances. In most of Spanish America the lack of agreement about the political rules of the game, the inability to pay armies and bureaucracies, and the breakdown of the mercantilist economies based on mining and plantation complexes resulted in a quarter-century or more of alternating moments of tyranny and anarchy. Unfortunately, Latin Americans had no experience in self-government, and the only colonial parliament ever to sit in the region occurred during the Dutch occupation of Pernambuco (1630-54). From an economic perspective, the first four or more decades after independence were *una larga espera*, a long wait.[3] Even in Brazil, where the legitimacy of the imperial regime, continuing the Braganza line, was less frequently challenged, per capita income tended to stagnate in the nineteenth century, as foreign trade disrupted handicraft industries and dislodged local merchants; growth in per capita income was not sustained from one decade to the next until after 1900.[4]

The incapacity to achieve a trade surplus which would have enabled the countries to service the debt contracted in the 1820s forced most to default. This gave the region a reputation as a major credit risk, which kept international investment from flowing in. The availability of foreign credit would only rise dramatically in the last decades of the nineteenth century.

As Britain was Latin America's major creditor and political guarantor of independence, it insisted on favoured access to its markets. The region was swamped by British manufactured products, which both destroyed the existing industrial artisan sector and delayed the appearance of domestic industries. The emergence of the region's specialisation in the export of primary products was in part imposed by Britain: if in the 1990s it is widely believed that growth and trade are closely linked, free trade and growth were not universally associated in the nineteenth century, when British and other European wares destroyed artisan industries in Latin America and elsewhere in the Third World. Before 1870-90, when several countries began to adopt policies of industrial protection, there was extensive de-industrialisation in Latin America, especially in the textile industry.[5] The pattern for the commercial treaties was set by Lord Strangford in 1810, when Britain imposed a treaty on the Portuguese court, then resident in Brazil, which allowed British goods to enter the colony at a *lower* customs rate than that for Portuguese goods – and this 12 years before Brazilian independence.

Most governments of newly independent Latin American countries were in the hands of the rural elites, which used their power to increase their landholdings at the expense of corporate bodies – first the Church and its constituent institutions, and subsequently, especially in the last quarter of the century, indigenous communities and other peasant populations. Thus the *latifundium* was a dynamic phenomenon, and land concentration occurred on economic frontiers as well as in areas of settled peasant populations. A continual rise in the concentration of property and income occurred, a process characteristic of most of the region's countries until the middle of the twentieth century or later. Given this concentration, the domestic market grew slowly, since there were few incentives to invest in sectors based on such a market.

Primary Export-Led Growth After 1850

The rapid expansion of world trade in the second half of the nineteenth century had a notable impact on Latin America. The economies of most countries in the region became geared to the export of a small number of primary products – cereals and meat in the case of Argentina; coffee in Brazil; nitrates, followed by copper, for Chile; silver and various minerals in the case of Mexico. As long as the industrialising countries of Europe, and later the United States, were growing rapidly, there was a strong world demand for the primary and food products that Latin American countries were exporting. The rapid growth of these export economies also attracted large capital inflows in the form of both direct investments and loans, at first mainly from Britain, but later also from France, Germany and the United States. The role of most of the capital inflows was to increase the efficiency of the economies' export orientation. It was directed at the construction of railroad networks designed to bring primary products from the interior more rapidly and efficiently to the ports; mining operations (in the Andean countries and Mexico); plantations (in Central America and the coasts of Colombia and Peru); and meat packing plants (in Argentina). Foreign capital was also invested in financial and commercial establishments to handle foreign trade and public utilities (such as power generation and distribution, telephone systems, and urban public transportation in the major cities).[6]

It was the last quarter of the century which witnessed a real transformation of the region's export economies: the so-called Second Industrial Revolution, associated with technological change in the production of capital goods and with the application of science to industry, brought unprecedented investment, technological innovations (steamships driven by screw propellers, railroads made of Bessemer steel, refrigeration, barbed-wire fencing), and above all a huge new demand for capital goods inputs (such as copper, rubber) and consumer goods (for example, sugar, wheat, beef, coffee).

The growth of this period, however, tended not to be developmental in nature. The benefits of the primary export economies accrued mainly to a small number of groups – large landowners, foreign owners of mines and plantations, the owners of public utilities, and a small professional class of government bureaucrats and lawyers. Much of the population continued to live on a subsistence level and little was spent on developing human capital through schooling, though Argentina was an exception: It had a rate of literacy roughly three times that of Brazil, for example, at the fall of the Brazilian monarchy in 1889.[7]

The export-led growth of the nineteenth century made the Latin American economies extremely 'dependent'. Imports consisted of foreign manufactured consumption and capital goods, while two or three primary products usually accounted for most export earnings. In an extreme case, Brazil in the latter 1920s, a country covering half the South American continent, earned three-fourths of its foreign exchange from a single export, coffee. Thus the Latin American economies became overly exposed to economic cycles emanating from the industrial countries, and were unable to counteract the impact of such cycles.

In the years from independence down to the Great Depression, Latin America was subject to three Kondratieff waves. The first was unfortunately timed, because the London stockmarket crash occurred in 1825, just as some Latin American governments were seeking foreign loans to rebuild their shattered mercantilist economies.[8] Others such as Argentina, however, had already contracted loans and were now defaulting. In fact, except for the years 1823-4, Spanish and Portuguese America received very modest amounts of European investment during the whole first half of the nineteenth century. The period 1825-50, when such investment might have occurred, roughly corresponds to the 'B' (downswing) phase of the Kondratieff wave. For a variety of reasons, of which the lack of foreign funding was probably second only to political disorder, Latin America experienced little economic growth in those years.[9]

Chile established a stable constitutional regime in 1833, and was widely admired in Spanish America for its stability. Brazil had done so earlier (1824), but only overcame the fissiparous tendencies of its agrarian elites after 1848. Mexico and Argentina would not know stable regimes until the 1860s. Many exports which helped to make stable polities possible had their origins in the colonial period, but new ones developed in the middle decades of the nineteenth century in response to Europe's industrial and consumer needs.

Yet it was the last quarter of the century, as indicated above, which witnessed a real transformation of the region's export economies, responding to the Second Industrial Revolution. In terms of sheer growth, the region benefitted immensely more from the second Kondratieff cycle, peaking in 1870-73, than from the first; in fact, Latin America continued to receive significant amounts of foreign investment through the long depression of 1873-96. The region apparently received its largest nineteenth-century investment by decade in the 1880s, partly as a result of a strong expansion of the primary goods trade.[10] Yet Latin America was integrated into the European economy at the price of consolidation of the *latifundium* and monocultural dependence on the world market.[11]

The transformation and dynamisation of the Latin American economies occurred at different times in the histories of the national states, depending on the export commodities involved and the relative success of state-building. State formation and consolidation, including the legitimation of the state for the relevant political actors, tended to secure property rights and limit transactions costs, and consequently was a necessary condition for foreign investment. Chile's oligarchic constitution of 1833 consolidated the power of a merchant-landlord elite, and Chile was affected by overseas demand as early as the 1850s (copper exports to Europe, wheat to California). Argentina and Brazil followed in the 1860s. But the period 1870-90 provided a much more rapid ascent. These three countries, plus Mexico, now felt the full impact of the combined effects of the European economic expansion, which, in the Argentine and Brazilian cases, brought in its train unprecedented levels of European immigration.

Argentina is the best exemplar of these processes; it was created as a nation – in the sense of definitively bringing the national territory under a single regime – in the third quarter of the nineteenth century. Formal political unity was achieved in 1859-61, with the accession of Buenos Aires Province to the Argentine Federation. But the governance issue was only resolved in the following two decades, with the closing of the Indian frontier in Patagonia; the suppression of the last regional revolt; and the creation of a Federal District, separating the city of Buenos Aires from the province of the same name (1880).

Argentina's economic growth was spectacular: On the average, exports increased five per cent a year between 1875 and 1914, both by quantum and by value. Profiting from the invention of refrigerated shipping, Argentina began to export frozen beef in 1894, sending abroad 328,000 tons in 1914, in which year chilled beef (a higher-grade commodity not produced in 1894) accounted for 41,000 tons. Overseas sales of canned meat in the same interval expanded ten times. Meanwhile wheat exports increased 23 times in value from 1880-84 to 1890-94. Transatlantic sales of both wheat and maize rose so rapidly that they had replaced beef as the chief exports by value on the eve of World War I. In the words of Carlos Díaz Alejandro, 'From 1860 to 1930 Argentina grew at a rate that has few parallels in economic history, perhaps comparable only to the performance during the same period of other countries of recent settlement.'[12]

Other countries were less completely transformed than was Argentina, with the debatable exception of its small neighbour, Uruguay; but the three others treated here – Brazil, Chile, and Mexico – were all profoundly affected by the forces we associate with the Second Industrial Revolution and the Age of Imperialism. Brazil's gross domestic product, for example, grew at a faster annual rate (2.5 per cent) than did those of developed countries between 1920 and 1929.[13]

Land tenure patterns changed in response to international demand, and it is abundantly clear that estate owners were generally responsive to price signals.[14] The first victim of estate-owners' land-hunger after 1850 was the Church, controlling as much as a third of the rural real estate in early nineteenth-century Mexico. One historian has remarked in this regard that the greatest service of the state to the landowning class was the forced sale of Church property – though this was much more important in Mexico than in the three other countries considered here.[15] Yet peasants suffered too: estate owners in Chile began to engross peasant lands in the 1850s and 1860s.[16] In Argentina, the *latifundium* arose in the nineteenth century, despite an open frontier stretching southward by the 1880s to Patagonia; likewise, the rise of the large plantation in São Paulo, Brazil, was a product of the nineteenth, and even the twentieth, centuries. In Brazil's census of 1920, only three per cent of the rural population owned land (although others were squatters), and of that landowning group, ten per cent owned three-fourths of the rural property.[17] In Mexico, the *hacienda* had its origins in the seventeenth century, but the Mexican Revolution of 1910 had as one principal source the vast and unprecedented alienation of community lands by *latifundistas* during the dictatorship of Porfirio Díaz (1876–1911). For Spanish America as a whole, Bauer remarks that the rural population '..probably underwent a greater change [in 1870-1930] than at any previous time.. except for the conquest'.[18]

Labour systems associated with the export boom varied widely, but often involved coercive elements. In the case of Brazil (led by the dynamic province of São Paulo), the coffee economy bid away thousands of slaves from other provinces in the 1860s and 1870s; in the 1880s slavery gave way to European immigrant labour based on a unique mix of wages, free housing, and usufruct. Elsewhere in Brazil the condition of rural labour was considerably worse, and lower classes resident on *latifundia* sometimes toiled in conditions resembling serfdom, rendering traditional services, including the corvee and the *cambao* (personal services in exchange for usufruct).[19] In Argentina, when the 'Mesopotamian' region north of Buenos Aires became one of the world's great wheat granaries, the land was subdivided and leased to Italian tenant farmers. In the Argentine case, and to a lesser extent in southern Brazil, there was a low labour-to-land ratio that resulted in relatively high rural wages.

In Chile, a rising demand for labour in the wheat farming area of the Central Valley coupled with the expansion of large estates led to a worsening of the peasants' lot in tenancy arrangements (*inquilinaje*) in wheat farming because of land monopolisation, and also increased proletarianisation of the *inquilinos* and other peasants.[20] Mexico had perhaps the largest variety of labour systems by the turn of the century, including illegal but *de facto* slavery for the Yaqui and Maya Indians, instances of debt servitude, sharecropping, and in some places rural wage labor and tenancy.[21] Vagrancy laws forced the proletarianisation of Indians and mestizo peasants in Central America and parts of Mexico.

Thus Latin American rural labour systems became much more highly differentiated as a result of the transformations after 1870. Whereas '...parts of Latin America, like Eastern Europe, experienced a sort of second enfeudation with the spread of a capitalist market...',[22] the immigrant-populated wheat regions of Argentina and the coffee regions of Brazil had modern labour and tenancy systems. A great contrast existed between the rural labour systems of Chile and Argentina, despite their common export booms in wheat (though the timing and markets were different), and despite Chile's impressive advances in manufacturing (see below). In Chile, the man-land ratio was considerably higher than in Argentina, the latifundist elite probably more unified, and land rents less differentiated.[23]

The nature of the process of production during and after this period is the subject of much controversy today. Those who defend a 'feudal' interpretation of the production system usually have in mind manorialism, which, as Marc Bloch pointed out, antedated feudalism and survived its demise.[24] The *hacienda* of this period is sometimes seen as poised between two worlds – the inner one of dependency and even extra-economic coercion of the labour force, while the outer one is recognisably capitalistic in its response to world markets.[25]

Why didn't the Latin American primary-exporting countries industrialise and diversify their economies the way the United States did, after having been a primary exporter? Most Latin American countries did not experience mass immigration, which in the case of the United States provided the manpower to settle the vast agricultural regions of the Midwest. The Homestead Act of 1862 resulted in a fairly equitable distribution of the income generated by agriculture. Such income flows provided a mass market, which set the stage for the industrialisation at the end of the nineteenth century and the first decades of the twentieth century.

In Latin America, the wealth created by the primary export sector was very unevenly distributed and, given the poverty of the rural masses and thus a limited market for manufactured products, the beneficiaries of these economies (foreign investors, local landowners, and the commercial-financial establishments related to the export sector) tended to invest their capital in rural estates, commerce, and foreign assets.[26] In rural areas, frontier expansion was not accompanied by enforceable Homestead Acts; rather, the *latifundium* continued to prosper. In the Brazilian case, ongoing land monopolisation was still observable in our own era.[27]

There were exceptions to this picture, especially in Argentina and Southern Brazil, which experienced a substantial amount of European immigration in the 1890s and the first three decades of the twentieth century. Industrial growth accompanied urbanisation and immigration from the 1890s in Argentina and Brazil, and sustained industrialisation seems to have begun in Chile in the 1870s.[28] In Argentina and Southern Brazil immigrants provided a local market which was attractive enough to invest in textiles and food products.[29] Immigrant income was heavily dependent on access to land – titles to small plots in Santa Catarina and Rio Grande do Sul, Brazil, and leases in Santa Fe, Argentina. Even in Mexico, which did not significantly benefit from immigration, urbanisation and export wealth laid the basis for a national market.[30]

Yet these developments were not weighty enough to counterbalance the structure of the primary export economies. In Argentina, landowners' preference for leasing rather than selling property to immigrant settlers, combined with the absence of credit for small farmers, led to the preservation of the *latifundium* in wheat-farming areas as well as poor conservation policies; such experience contrasted unfavorably with that of the prairie provinces of Canada.[31] In Brazil, a landowning peasantry had existed from the nineteenth century in parts of the three southernmost provinces, and the Great Depression brought about a new class of smallholders in São Paulo as coffee *fazendeiros* parcelled out their bankrupt estates.[32]

Generally speaking, however, international capital viewed late nineteenth- and early twentieth-century Latin America as one of the world's major suppliers of primary products, and its operations in the regions strengthened this specialisation and land monopolisation. The local oligarchies readily accepted the thesis of comparative advantage and acted accordingly, entering the 'commodity lottery' with enthusiasm.

The First World War, however, caused serious disruptions in the Latin American export economy. Grave problems followed the War in certain commodity markets, but the export boom continued in phase with the third Kondratieff wave. A major structural shift in the postwar era was the growing displacement of Britain by the United States as chief lender and investor. Britain exacerbated its problems in the region by overvaluing the pound through deliberate deflation. In any case, US advances resulting from the War were evident everywhere. For instance, the Americans sent three-and-a-half times as many exports (by value) to Mexico as the British did in 1913, and the ratio was ten to one by 1927. Great Britain led the United States in the other three countries considered here in 1913, but by 1927 the latter had dislodged Britain as the leading trading partner in Chile and Brazil; and in Argentina, Britain clung to its lead by a single percentage point.[33] Though Great Britain's overall capital investments in the region were still larger in 1929, the US had far outstripped Britain in its postwar lending, both direct and indirect.

Import Substitution Industrialisation (ISI)

The general absence of theoretical foundations for industrial development notwithstanding, Argentina, Brazil, and Chile had made rapid industrial advances during the 1920s, in part throught foreign investment in the peak years of the third Kondratieff wave. But after 1929 they faced a sustained crisis in export markets (the dollar value of Argentina's exports in 1933, for example, was one-third the 1929 figure); and despite the importance of industrialisation in the 1920s, the following decade can still be understood as a period of significant structural and institutional change. In Argentina, Brazil, Chile, and Mexico, convertibility and the gold standard were abandoned early in the Depression. The rise in the prices of importables, because of a fall in the terms of trade and exchange devaluation, encouraged the substitution of domestic manufactures for imported goods, as did expansionary fiscal and monetary policies. When war came in 1939, manufactures in international trade became scarce again, permitting further industrialisation to the extent that capital goods, fuel, and raw materials were available.

During the 1930s spokesmen for industry probably grew bolder, except perhaps those Brazilians who had initially followed the Romanian trade theorist Mihail Manoilescu.[34] Industrialists pointed to the vulnerability of export economies, which they more frequently dubbed 'colonial' than before. Gathering war clouds in Europe added another argument: domestic industries were necessary for an adequate national defense. A basic characteristic of the period 1930–45 was an intensification of state intervention in the economy, in Latin America as elsewhere, and industrialists like other economic groups sought state assistance; they asked for subsidies, credits and increased tariff protection.

In Argentina, Brazil, Chile, and Mexico governments began to heed the importuning of manufacturers. State aid to industry in the form of development loans tended to converge in the early years of the War. The establishment of industrial development banks was an important symbolic act, but changes in tariff structures, which have not so far been thoroughly analysed, may have been more important for growth.

The reasons for such a shift by governments are clear in retrospect: a decade of wrestling with the intractable problem of reviving traditional export markets; the relative unavailability of foreign industrial goods over virtually a 15-year period (1930-45); and the fact that states (and particularly the officer corps) as well as industrialists began to consider the relationship between manufacturing and national defence – a process that had already begun in Chile in the late 1920s. Governments, however, moved hesitantly and inconsistently towards addressing the problems of industry. As late as 1940, Finance Minister Pinedo's Plan for the economic development of Argentina still distinguished between 'natural' and 'artificial' industries, implying that industrial development would occur in concert with the needs of the agricultural and pastoral sectors. By the time of the colonels' coup in June 1943, intervention for industrial development had become state policy, and an industrial development bank was created in 1944. In the next few years, the Perón government would demonstrably put the interests of industrialists above those of ranchers and farmers.

In Brazil, Getúlio Vargas favoured industry but he had opposed 'artificial' industries (manufacturing) in his presidential campaign in 1930. Government loans to 'artificial' industries were still prohibited in 1937. Osvaldo Aranha, Vargas's Minister of Finance in 1933, even termed industries 'fictitious' if they did not use at least 70 per cent domestic raw materials. Vargas only became committed to rapid industrial expansion during his Estado Novo dictatorship (1937-45). In the 1940s the government showed a commitment to industrialisation by obtaining support from the Roosevelt administration for a state-operated steel complex at Volta Redonda, Rio de Janeiro. The mills opened in 1946 as Latin America's largest steel plant.

In Mexico, industrialisation in the 1930s made impressive advances even while agrarian reform was at the top of Lázaro Cárdenas' agenda. It was not, however, the result of government policy. Nacional Financiera, a partly government-owned development bank, had been established in 1934, but only became seriously committed to manufacturing after its reorganisation at the end of 1940, when the new pro-industry administration of Avila Camacho took office. In Chile, nominal government support for industrial development began with the creation of an Institute of Industrial

Credit in 1928. Ten years later the Popular Front government of Pedro Aguirre Cerda established CORFO, the government development corporation. But in 1940 the sum budgeted for the development of manufacturing was less than each of those for agriculture, mining, energy and public housing.

Thus ISI as a government policy began hesitantly in the later 1930s, *faute de mieux*, in the absence of sufficient foreign exchange to buy foreign manufactures. Explicit in the 1949 *Survey* by the UN Economic Commission for Latin America (ECLA) was the thesis that industrialisation in Latin America had historically occurred in periods of world crisis; that is, ECLA viewed development as occurring through the agency of 'external shocks', in Celso Furtado's phrase.[35] For the Brazilian case, Furtado pointed to rapid industrial growth in the Depression, partly due to 'the socialisation of losses' through exchange devaluation, which nonetheless helped maintain domestic demand.[36] In Brazil, Furtado viewed expansionary fiscal and monetary policies for the coffee industry during the Depression as a form of unwitting Keynesianism. Yet as a 'spontaneous' process ISI had already begun before the First World War. Industrialisation, it is now understood, was especially dynamic in the 1920s; so much so that the 1920s rather than the 1930s are now viewed as the critical moment of industrial development.[37] A now widely-held view is that investment in industry (capacity) grew in line with export earnings for the period 1900-1945, while output (but not capacity) tended to rise during the 'shocks', when imports had to be curtailed. Capacity could not grow appreciably during the Depression for lack of exchange credits to buy capital goods and inputs, nor during the World Wars because of the unavailability of capital goods and fuels from the belligerent powers.[38]

At any rate ISI accelerated in the 1930s, and foreign exchange earnings facilitated the process, contrary to the original 'external shocks' theory.[39] ISI, which intensified in the first two decades after World War II, for its defenders was supposed to provide a base for rapid economic development through the establishment of a diversified economic structure. In addition, it was supposed to arrest the transfer of resources from Latin America to advanced industrial countries by counteracting the decline in the terms of trade.[40]

The strategy consisted of protection, attraction of foreign investments to manufacturing, stimulation of local manufacturing enterprises, creation of complementary state enterprises, and the establishment of development banks. The immediate success of postwar ISI was found in its stimulation of periods of high rates of growth, in the changed structure of the economy – that is, the growing share of industry in GDP – and in the creation of a skilled labour force. In the initial decades of ISI (varying with the country at issue), manufacturing, industrial employment, and per capita income tended to expand briskly.

Yet the way ISI was actually implemented was censured by ECLA, which had originally championed ISI. In 1963, Raúl Prebisch, the outgoing Executive Secretary of ECLA, denounced the actual pattern of industrialisation in Latin America, pointing out that the exaggerated pattern of protection had allowed grossly inefficient industries to arise. Latin America had, on average, the highest tariffs in the world, depriving it of economies of scale and opportunities to specialise for export.[41] Given the small size of national markets, as early as 1959 ECLA had also championed the development of a Latin American common market, but such efforts at integration would only bear fruit in later decades. In retrospect, in articulating a theory and implicit ideology in favour of ISI and then pointing the way to correcting its excesses, ECLA may have had the right policies but an inadequate instrument for their execution: For ECLA, the national state was the vehicle of reform, and perhaps the agency put too great a faith in the capacity of the state to implement disinterested policies. The patrimonial residues in modern Latin American 'stateness' are significant, if we accept Gunnar Myrdal's notion of the 'soft state',[42] whose principal capacity is the employment of functionaries.

At any rate, the way in which ISI was carried out had serious negative consequences: the cost structure of most industries were high because of low labour productivity and, given the small market, the lack of economies of scale. In Argentina, Brazil, Chile, and Mexico, for two decades little attention was paid to diversifying exports and, given overvalued exchange rates, even traditional exports were placed at a disadvantage. Most disappointingly, ISI did not provide the jobs needed to employ the rapidly growing urban population effectively. The Latin American problem in recent decades was compounded not only by the world's highest regional rate of population growth in the 1950s and 1960s, but also by even higher rates of urbanisation. Most of the rural-urban migrants only found employment in marginal formal and informal service activities. In any event, one would expect industrial labour absorption to be considerably less than that of nineteenth-century, labour-intensive industrialisation.[43]

The relative capital intensity of the sectors affected by ISI also helps explain the continued skewedness and even worsening of the region's income distribution. Since industry was the country's most dynamic growth sector, its high capital-labour ratio resulted in much of the increment of the gross domestic product going to non-labour factors of production. Accompanying ISI were government policies to transfer income from the agricultural sector to industry through exchange rate discrimination and other controls; such policies in the 1950s and 1960s tended to shrink the sectors that produced the vital foreign exchange needed for the essential capital goods and fuels required for further industrial growth.

For economic policy in the late 1960s and 1970s, neoclassical orthodoxy, not structuralism or dependency, provided the signposts for most of Latin America. The neoclassical counterattack dismissed dependency and challenged structuralist interpretations of the capital-intensive bias in Latin American industry. Orthodox economists argued that the *actual* cost of labour was greater than that of capital (relative to respective shadow prices). Capital costs in Latin America were kept artificially low by liberal depreciation allowances, low or even negative real interest rates (in periods of inflation), low tariffs on capital imports, overvalued exchange rates, and institutionally-induced high wages. Therefore, according to this reasoning, choices of labour-saving techniques had been rational, in the face of distortions of relative prices. Furthermore, the neoclassical school argued that low productivity in agriculture was not necessarily caused by a lack of rural entrepreneurship (possibly owing to a traditional latifundist mentality) but derived in great measure from government programs of import-substitution. By this analysis, ISI, resulting in high-cost manufactured goods, had turned the domestic terms of trade against agriculture. Furthermore, exchange policies designed to assist industrialisation had given agricultural exporters less than the full value of their foreign sales, and thereby discouraged production.

In general, during the middle decades of the century, the state took over public utilities and natural resource exploitation, leaving foreign capital to develop the manufacturing sector, typically employing advanced technology with high capital densities. The Mexican government liberalised its rules on foreign investment in 1946, and Chile, Argentina and Brazil all took similar steps in 1955. The largest share of this direct investment was provided by the United States, half of which was in manufacturing by 1976.[44] In Brazil, the state's share of gross domestic product had risen dramatically in the 1960s and 1970s and by 1979, 28 of Brazil's 30 largest non-financial firms were publicly owned.[45]

In the post-ISI period remedies for the region's problems were of limited effect – for example, efforts to diversify exports by eliminating overvalued exchange rates and providing special incentives to non-traditional exports, such as steel subsidies in Argentina and Brazil. Although new exports began to appear in the late 1960s – soyabeans and footwear in the Brazilian case – there was insufficient attention to export innovation until the 1980s. The rate of total factory productivity growth declined from 2.3 per cent a year from 1950–73 to one per cent in 1973–80, and then fell to one per cent annually in 1980–89, compared to 1.2 per cent in the developed countries and four per cent in the Asian NICs for the 1980s.[46] Meanwhile, during much of the 1970s and 1980s, Latin American economic actors became involved in a distributional struggle, fuelling inflation, which further hampered and distorted growth and development. Nonetheless, Latin America's per capita income would probably have been much lower without ISI, and the growing share of industrial products in its export profile would have been impossible.

Following the 'lost decade' of the 1980s, in which Latin America's per capita income decreased by 0.8 per cent a year, it is still important to recall that Latin America's economy was anything but stagnant in the earlier years of the current half-century: From 1950 to 1981, the region's economy grew at 5.3 per cent per year, and income per capita – in a region with the world's highest population growth rates until the mid-1960s – expanded at 2.6 per cent a year; the real GDP of Latin America expanded five times in this period. From 1950 to 1981 industrialisation remained the chief transforming force: Brazil and Mexico in this period expanded their industrial output ten times, while Argentina and Chile tripled theirs.[47]

Of course this strong if not spectacular growth was closely associated with the growth of the world economy and international trade, and it seems that Latin America's great mistake was continued dependence on commodity trade. The developed countries' imports of manufactures grew at 12 per cent a year, whereas their imports of commodities grew at only 7 per cent a year from 1960 to 1973; in the 1980s, while the developed countries' imports of manufactures grew at 11 per cent per year, their imports of primary goods fell below 2 per cent.[48]

The problems of the 1980s had their roots in the previous decade, as declining rates of productivity growth in the United States led to an overvalued dollar, then floating exchange rates and inflation, compounded by the 1973 oil shock. The recycling of 'petrodollars' by overliquid private banks in the United States and elsewhere in the remainder of the decade proved irresistible to Latin American clients, as loans were made at negative real interest rates in the 1970s. Many countries of the region had decided to borrow in order to avoid having to curtail economic growth associated with higher energy prices. Brazil, for instance, engaged in 'debt-led growth' in the 1970s, using borrowed resources to invest in new import-substituting sectors (such as the capital goods industry) and in non-traditional exports. Mexico, which benefited from the oil shock, borrowed heavily in order to expand oil extraction and to establish a large petrochemical complex.[49] The interest rate shock of the early 1980s resulted in real rates which were more than three times as high as those of the 1950s and 1960s.[50] The Mexican debt moratorium of 1982 caused the closing of financial markets to most of Latin America and forced most countries into adjustment programmes. It was at this time that the IMF achieved a supremacy it had previously lacked over

Latin American fiscal and monetary policy, using a conditionality policy to approve debt rescheduling, and simultaneously IMF and World Bank policies tended to converge.[51] As a result, during the 1980s many Latin American countries made larger transfers as a share of GDP than the reparations payments of Germany after World War I.[52] In 1982–90, Latin America suffered a net outflow of capital amounting to 218 billion dollars.[53]

Although orthodox economists point to the 'high-performing' countries of East Asia – Japan, Korea, Malaysia, Indonesia, Singapore, Thailand and Taiwan – as successful examples of the application of liberal policies, a revisionist monographic literature has established that governments played important roles in development through market intervention in Japan, Korea and Taiwan.[54] Moreover, the same seven high-performing countries that achieved three times the growth rates of Latin America and South Asia between 1960 and 1985 – and five times those of Sub-Saharan Africa – also performed considerably better than the latter areas with regard to income distribution among social groups, partly because of state policy, including land reform in Japan, Korea and Taiwan. One of the themes development economists now stress is the importance of human, as opposed to physical capital, and the extension of primary education in the East Asian high-performers was, for the World Bank, 'by far the largest single contributor to...[their] predicted growth rates'.[55]

The long-term success of the Asian Tigers could hardly be ignored in Latin America, and though the generalised East Asian crisis of 1997-98 may make the model less attractive, the long-term achievement is still impressive. For the Brazilian economist Winston Fritsch, the recurrent external disequilibrium that concerned Raúl Prebisch in the 1940s and 1950s could be overcome in the 1990s not by less trade but by more, given the ever-rising share of manufactures in the world market, and the limits of a strategy of the compression of imports. Latin American nations should follow a policy of generalised liberalisation of trade combined with protection of nascent industries, especially manufactures, based on criteria of efficiency and competitiveness in the international market.[56] Here 'Neostructuralism' reconciles the structuralist tradition, emphasising industrialisation, with the mounting evidence linking economic growth with international trade.[57]

In fact, Latin American countries have been implementing the exports of industrial goods for some time. Exports of manufactures rose at 11.3 per cent a year from 1960 to 1973, and at 15 per cent a year between 1977 and 1990, so that the region's exports of manufactures are 25 times larger than in the early 1950s. Brazil diversified trade the most, so that the sale of manufactures accounted for 52 per cent of Brazilian exports by 1990.

Automobiles and related products surpassed the value of coffee sales in Brazil's export profile in the 1980s.[58]

A considerably different path was pursued by Chile, despite the fact that its guiding post-ISI policies, like Brazil's, were set by a military regime. For Chile in the 1970s, anti-Communist and anti-populist politics was accompanied by economic policies that would have as their top priorities the elimination of inflation and balance-of-payments deficits through monetarist stabilisation policies and export orientation, as recommended by the International Monetary Fund.

The new government of General Augusto Pinochet, like the new military dictatorships in Argentina and Uruguay, faced three-digit inflation, balance-of-payments crises, and social conflict. Furthermore, after 1973 the international economy was in recession: the volume of world trade from 1965 to 1973 grew at an average of nine per cent a year, but it fell to four per cent for the rest of the decade. In the earlier period, underdeveloped countries' share of world trade had been 6.4 per cent, but fell to 3.4 per cent in 1974, and protectionism was rising in the West.[59] To the extent that growth continued, it depended in large part on foreign borrowing, a policy only sustainable until the 1979 recession.

Nowhere was monetarism applied with greater determination than in Chile, where the Chicago School was dominant.[60] General Pinochet's government undertook the restructuring or even 'destructuring' of the Chilean economy, as it existed under the socialist government of Salvador Allende. Chile was to be opened to world trade, and protectionism ended; state agencies were to be disbanded or sold to the private sector; and wages were to be compressed. These goals were accomplished: By 1979, Chile's average level of protection was only ten per cent, as contrasted with 94 per cent in 1973, and with 41 per cent in the authoritarian Brazil of the later 1960s.[61] By 1980, the Chilean government had reduced the number of state entities from 50 per cent in 1973 to 15. By the late seventies, wages had dropped 25–35 per cent below those of 1970. Yet at the end of the 1970s or the early 1980s, the results were mixed, or even largely negative: Despite vigorous growth in the latter years of the decade, the creation of new exports, and the diminution of inflation, these achievements occurred at the expense of a fall in industry's share of GDP; high rates of unemployment; a reversal of agrarian reform; and a greater concentration of income distribution and of ownership of major enterprises.

In the 1980s, however, Chile achieved some real policy successes that were admired elsewhere. Although the orthodox stabilisation policy of 1978–82 resulted in lower wages and massive unemployment (up to 26 per cent), the Pinochet government's deficit of nine per cent of GDP moved to a three per cent surplus, while inflation remained moderate between 1984 and 1988. The GDP itself grew rapidly in the last years of the decade, though Chile's industrial sector did not grow at all in the years 1980-86, and income concentration, compared to the late 1960s, continued to increase into the 1980s. Chile achieved greater export competitiveness by lowering wages more than by technological innovation.[62]

By the 1990s the neoliberalism practiced by Chile had spread throughout the region. Although Brazil lagged behind the others until the mid-1990s,[63] the large majority of Latin American governments have engaged in orthodox stabilisation measures, and pursued programmes of privatisation and liberalisation. The lost decade of the 1980s seems to have been followed by a period of much lower rates of inflation (excepting Mexico and Venezuela), large inflows of foreign capital ($207 billion between 1991 and 1994), and a return to economic growth. Chile has achieved outstanding success, leading the Latin American nations with seven per cent growth of GDP for 1991-95. In a somewhat longer view, covering the oil shock in 1973 to 1994, Chile also did best of the four countries considered in detail above, in terms of GDP per capita. It posted a 2.1 per cent average annual growth rate, while Brazil averaged one per cent, Mexico followed with 0.9 per cent, and Argentina, with the highest per capita income, only grew at 0.2% over this period. Finally, Chile also led the Latin American countries in fiscal responsibility in a region notorious for hyperinflation in the 1980s: Chile achieved an overall surplus in its fiscal accounts from 1989 through 1995 and has handled its external adjustment successfully.[64]

The extent to which this fiscal discipline is attributable to the fact that Pinochet, despite his withdrawal from the presidency, was still commander-in-chief of the armed forces may be debated. But in any event the resumption of growth in Chile and elsewhere in Latin America 'has not brought any significant progress in terms of job creation or greater social equity,' according to ECLA. Over the years 1980 to 1992, there was a larger percentage of households living in poverty at the end of the period than at the beginning.[65]

Conclusion and Speculations

The fitful performance of the Latin American economies relative to the dynamism of the West has deep historical roots. I have shown how the organisation of the primary export economies of the region, which were inherited from colonial times and were vastly expanded in the nineteenth century, was responsible for a high degree of concentration of property and income. The great expansion of exports was not accompanied by institutions and practices to develop human capital, with the partial exception of Argentina; thus Latin America entered the twentieth century as an array of highly stratified societies, with small numbers emulating the lifestyles of the advanced West and the masses living at or near a state of subsistence. Between them lay a thin but growing stratum of middle sectors in the four Latin American countries considered here in some detail.

Import substitution industrialisation in this century occurred within a context of social backwardness and extremely rapid rural-urban migration. The new industrial sectors' technology did not permit a high absorption of labour, and thus the growth resulting from ISI was unevenly distributed, at times even worsening the income distribution in the region.

Latin America's income inequality has tended to rise over the second half of the century, in a world region where income inequality in 1970 was 'far higher than in the developed countries at a comparable stage of their development' and where the rich have consumed a larger share of their income than in Europe. Though the state provided the additional investment required to increase per capita income after World War II, 'the process collapsed in the 1980s'.[66] The sale of state property currently underway almost everywhere tends, naturally enough, to divest the state of the most productive and efficient enterprises. In its reinforcement of the skewing of income and wealth, this process of transferring assets to the upper classes which can invest in newly alienated property has been compared by one student with the Liberal parties' alienation of Church property in the nineteenth century. Unfortunately as well, the privatisation tends to replace public monopoly with private ones, not to increase competition.[67]

Although most of Latin America's population is presently urbanised, and industry's contribution to the national product is over three times greater than that of agriculture, the region is still relatively underdeveloped; this state of affairs reflects the continuing concentration of property and income, combined with severely limited educational opportunities for the majority of the population. The recent policy shifts in the region, emphasising privatisation of state enterprises, have the potential of expanding the tax base available to states with more focused mandates to improve health and education. True, the 'lessons' of East Asia may be limited in their applicability elsewhere, and the corruption attendant to South East Asian development could scarcely be recommended for emulation. Yet the longer-term East Asian experience, which frequently included government intervention in economy and society, seems to show that vigorous growth can be combined with a more equitable sharing of the fruits of economic progress. 'Growth by concentration', as Celso Furtado styles the Latin American experience, is not the only way.

If education and know-how are the larger part of the unexplained residual in total factor productivity, it is clear that Latin American governments spend too little. During the 'lost decade' of the 1980s, real per capita educational expenditure fell in the region, but this trend was reversed in the 1990s. Yet even now, investment in the physical infrastructure is inadequate, and regional real per capita expenditure on education in 1994-95 was an appalling $58, with Argentina leading the field at $146 per person.[68] Perhaps the IMF can be a help in this regard: Pursuant to a new agreement linking credit approval (and lower interest rates) to governance, in July 1997 the IMF began negotiating with Argentina, currently growing at seven to eight per cent annually, to fund improvements in education and health. If successful, this experiment may bring the IMF more extensively into the area of human capital development.[69]

Education is of course only one of the state's multiple responsibilities. Despite the current tide of privatisation, directed at the waste and mismanagement of state bureaucracies, it seems unlikely that a basic appeal of structuralism in Latin America – the state's role as economic actor to correct imbalances and distortions – will soon disappear. Certainly it will have its defenders in those who believe in population and environmental policies. The power of the modern state has advanced symbiotically with the development of capitalism over the last five centuries. More concretely, it is notable that the most developed countries have governments, on the average, with much greater extractive powers than those of Third World countries, which fact seems to indicate the large government is inherent in 'mature' development. Of 24 industrialised countries in 1990, government tax collections ranged from 30 per cent of the national product in the United States and Japan, to 37 per cent in Germany, to 43 per cent in France, to 58 per cent in Sweden.[70]

In Latin America, the privatisations and state-shrinkage processes now underway can have many positive effects, though the theme of swollen bureaucracies may be exaggerated: In 1980, probably the height of public employment, the state employed only about four per cent of the Latin American population as opposed to nine per cent in the public sector in OECD countries. Though the states of Latin America were significant producers of goods and services, even at their high-water mark in the 1970s, the public enterprises' contribution to GDP in the region was below the average for developing countries. These states had developed extractive and law enforcement capabilities rapidly in the postwar era, so that by the 1980s '...almost all Latin American states...possessed a capacity for centralised territorial control quite beyond comparison' with their counterparts in the Great Depression.[71] But power to regulate and control admittedly have been too great a temptation for some states, and the larger Latin American countries had some of the most heavily regulated markets by 1980, leading to serious market distortions and misallocation of resources. Hernando de Soto even argues that in the Peruvian case, government red tape has driven a huge if unmeasurable portion of economic activity into the informal (underground) economy.[72] State-related transactions costs are doubtless, on the average, too high. But only an efficient state can set and enforce the rules whereby markets function efficiently. And in a critical phase of the 1930s through the 1960s, the state developed essential social overhead capital and promoted import substitution. The states' failure was missing opportunities for niche-based specialisation in manufactured and other nontraditional exports based on modern technology and market-efficient production.

The Dependency school of the 1960s and 1970s was pessimistic about closing the technology gap between developed countries and Latin America, but Jorge Katz and his associates have undertaken a variety of case studies showing how innovation occurs in manufacturing industries in Latin American milieux, making use of comparative advantage, and holding out the possibility that, if Latin Americans cannot operate on the technological frontier because of capital costs, they may operate not too far from that frontier by taking advantage of lower labour costs in specific and well-defined niches, as the East Asians did.[73] Another student has emphasised the importance of institutions and coalition-based politics in building state-assisted technological research programmes in Argentina and Brazil.[74]

States are necessarily the key actors in regional integration. Whether regional markets within Latin America and ultimately a hemispheric market can play the dynamising role of the historical development of the European Union is still an open question. In part such schemes are a response to First World protectionism, especially from the mid-1960s through the 1970s. Efforts at Latin American integration go back to the Latin American Free Trade Association in 1960, but LAFTA's goal was to extend selective bilateral preferences to protected markets in ISI-oriented economies. Although the first 30 months of NAFTA have been something of a disappointment, owing principally to the fiscal and economic crises in Mexico, Mercosur (Argentina, Brazil, Paraguay, and Uruguay) holds the promise of a single market of one trillion dollars in the year of its full integration, 2001; it will have a common external tariff, which NAFTA lacks. At that time Mercosur will be the world's fourth largest market, after NAFTA, the European Union, and Japan.

Specifying the proper role of the state in development is difficult enough, but much more so is assessing the role of culture in the process. This is almost purely a speculative enterprise, but we may infer that Hispanic culture is not an impediment to high levels of economic development from the very fact that Spain has become a developed country in the last two generations, with a per capita income presently about equidistant from those of Ireland and the UK. A recent synthetic study by Gabriel Tortella[75] demonstrates that Spain's economic development in the last two centuries has tended to move in line with trends in the Mediterranean countries of Europe, separating it from the Latin American experience, where nineteenth-century political history has striking Spanish parallels. Even more fundamentally, perhaps, Spain's demography includes a secularly falling rate of natality across the twentieth century, so that now the birth rate is below the replacement level, while the Latin American population is still growing above two per cent per year.

If a diminution of Spain's birth rate was one fundamental element in raising per capita income, another was the rapid industrial growth in the 1960s and beyond. Still another element was an agricultural revolution, sharply raising productivities from 1950 through 1980, especially in the 1970s. Both of these phenomena depended heavily on European investment, a process which accelerated as Spain was phased into the European Union. Still, the fact that Spain did not have a land reform (as Taiwan, Japan and Korea did) perhaps shows that Latin America, with its large frontiers, may not be fundamentally blocked by its current land tenure concentration.[76]

How well regional economists predicted the course of Latin American economic performance is difficult to assess, but the Structuralists of the mid-1960s were surprised, and admitted their perplexity, when external dependency increased with advancing industrialisation. (In fact, this unwelcome realisation led Celso Furtado and Osvaldo Sunkel to pioneer Dependency Theory.) Chilean orthodox economists were likewise surprised during the first decade of their dominance (1973–82) by the much greater difficulty of restructuring than they had anticipated. No one can be blamed for failing to predict the complex results of exogenous shocks, such as the spikes in oil prices and the spread effects of the Mexican moratorium of 1982. Even today, when most economies are booming, a sharp rise in United States interest rates could make a shambles of the currency reform programmes of Argentina and Brazil, and induce massive capital flight. History, as the economic historian David Landes once remarked, is full of surprises.

NOTES

This paper is partly derived from the author's essay with Werner Baer, 'The Roots of Latin America's Backwardness,' in Derek H. Aldcroft and Ross E. Catterall, eds., *Rich Nations – Poor Nations: The Long-Run Perspective* (Cheltenham, Eng.: Edward Elgar, 1996), pp. 39-64.

1. The US dependency Puerto Rico and the West Indian island-state, Trinidad and Tobago are also included in this group. World Bank, *World Development Report: 1994*, 163, note c.). New York, Oxford University Press.

2. Halperin-Donghi, Tulio (1973), *The Aftermath of Revolution in Latin America*, New York, Harper and Row, p.49.

3. Halperin-Donghi, Tulio (1970), *Historia contemporanea de América Latina*, 2d ed., Madrid, Alianza Editorial, p. 134.

4. Coatsworth, John (1978), 'Obstacles to Economic Growth in Nineteenth-Century Mexico', in *American Historical Review*, 83/1, p. 82; and Contador, Cláudio R., and Haddad, Claudio L. (1975). 'Produto real, moeda e precos: A experiência brasileira no período 1861–1970', in *Revista Brasileira de Estatística*, 36, 143. 82; p.412.

5. See Bairoch, Paul (1993), *Economics and World History: Myths and Paradoxes*, Chicago, University of Chicago Press. Bairoch generalizes that '...in the nineteenth century, the liberal trade experience in the Third World was a complete failure' (p.171). On Latin America, see Glade, William P. (1969), *The Latin American Economies: A Study of their Institutional Evolution*, New York, American Book, pp. 196-197.

6. For some details, see Rippy, J. Fred (1959), *British Investments in Latin America, 1822-1949*, Minneapolis, University of Minnesota Press; and Marichal, Carlos (1989), *A Century of Latin American Debt Crises in Latin America*, Princeton, N.J., Princeton University Press.

7. Brazil's rate of literacy was 15 per cent in 1890, and Argentina's, 46 per cent in 1895. See Ludwig, Armin K. (1985), *Brazil: A Handbook of Historical Statistics*, Boston, G.K. Hall, p.132; and Vázquez-Presedo, Vicente (1971), *Estadísticas históricas argentinas (comparadas)*, Buenos Aires, Macchi, p.27. However, the Brazilian figure is for all ages, including 0-4, and that of Argentina, for those aged six and older.

8. Hernández y Sánchez-Barba, Mario (1971), 'Ciclos Kondratieff y modelos de frustración económica Ibero-americana (Siglo XIX)', in *Revista da la Universidad de Madrid*, 20/78. Nonetheless, these estates were highly differentiated across the region as to the modernity of their technology, business practices, and labour relations.

9. Halperin-Donghi, Tulio (1985), 'Economy and Society in Post-Independence Latin America', in Bethell, Leslie (ed.), *Cambridge History of Latin America (CHLA)*, vol. 3, Cambridge UK, Cambridge University Press, p.304.

10. Morner, Magnus (1977), 'Latin American 'Landlords' and 'Peasants' and the Outer World during the National Period', in Duncan, Kenneth and Rutledge, Ian, eds., *Land and Labour in Latin America*, Cambridge, UK, Cambridge University Press, pp.459–60; Also see Suter, Christian (1994), 'Cyclical Fluctuations in Foreign Investment 1850–1930: The Historical Debate and the Latin American Case' in Marichal, Carlos, ed., *Foreign Investment in Latin America: Impact on Economic Development, 1850–1930*, [Proceedings: Eleventh International Economic History Congress], Milan, Universitá Bocconi, p.14.

11. Hernández y Sánchez-Barba (note 8) pp.230–l.

12. Díaz Alejandro, Carlos F. (1970), *Essays on the Economic History of the Argentine Republic*. New Haven, CT, Yale University Press, p.2.

13. Dean, Warren (1986), 'The Brazilian Economy, 1870–1930', in Bethell, Leslie, ed., *CHLA*, vol. 5. Cambridge, UK, Cambridge University Press, p.685.

14. Leff, Nathaniel (1982), *Underdevelopment and Development in Brazil*, London, Allen Unwin, pp.43–51. and Jacobsen, Nils (1984), 'Cycles and Booms in Latin American Export Agriculture' in *Review* [of the Fernand Braudel Center], 7/3, pp.488–9.

15. Bauer, Arnold J. (1986), 'Rural Spanish America, 1870–1930', in Bethell, Leslie, ed., *CHLA*, vol. 4. Cambridge, UK, Cambridge University Press, p.177.

16. Inferred from Bauer, Arnold J., and Johnson, Ann Hagerman (1977). 'Land and Labour in Rural Chile, 1850–1935', in Duncan and Rutledge eds., *Land and Labour in Latin America*, Cambridge, UK, Cambridge University Press, pp.88–9.

17. Dean (note 13), p.702.

18. Bauer (note 15), p.185.

19. Extra-economic coercion in Brazilian agriculture was still widely observable in 1993. See 'Forced Labour in Brazil Re-visited: On-site Investigations Document That Practice Continues.' (30 Nov. 1993), *Americas Watch: A Division of Human Rights Watch* 5/12.

20. Kay, Cristóbal (1980), *El sistema señorial europeo y la hacienda latinoamericana*, México, D.F., Ediciones Era, p.76.

21. Katz, Friedrich (1974), 'Labour Conditions on Haciendas in Porfirian Mexico', in *Hispanic American Historical Review*, 54/1, pp.1–47.
22. Glade (note 5), p.38.
23. Laclau, Ernest (1969), 'Modos de producción, sistemas económicos y población excedente: Aproximacion historica a los casos argentino y chileno,' *Revista Latinoamericana de Sociologia* 5/2, pp.300-308.
24. Bloch, Marc (1961), *Feudal Society*, Chicago, University of Chicago Press, p.442.
25. Bartra, Roger, et al. (1976), *Modos de produccion en America Latina*, Lima, Delva, p.81.
26. For Argentina: Inferred from Díaz Alejandro (note 12), p.6; Oddone, Jacinto (1967), *La burguesia terrateniente argentina*, 3d ed, Buenos Aires, Ediciones Populares Argentinas. For Chile, see Mamalakis, Markos J. (1976), *The Growth and Structure of the Chilean Economy*, New Haven, CT, Yale University Press, pp.79–80. For Mexico, Haber notes the preponderant role of foreigners in industrial development in Haber, Stephen J. (1989), *Industrialization and Underdevelopment: The Industrialization of Mexico, 1890–1940*, Stanford, CA., Stanford University Press, pp.80–2. For Brazil, Dean credits Paulista coffee planters with investments in railroads, but views immigrant importers as more important in developing early manufacturing in Dean, Warren (1969), *The Industrialization of Sao Paulo, 1880–1945*, Austin, TX, University of Texas Press.
27. See Souza Martins, José de (1981), *Os camponeses e a política no Brasil*. Petrópolis, Vozes and Foweraker, Joe (1980), *The Struggle for Land: A Political Economy of the Pioneer Frontier in Brazil from 1930 to the Present Day*, Cambridge, UK, Cambridge University Press.
28. Palma has shown that industrial development was extensive between 1875 and 1900, despite a literature that emphasizes lost opportunities for modernization under the regime of a traditional landed oligarchy. He found that import substitution industrialization was already well underway in Chile by 1914, and was reaching its limits by 1934, much earlier than in other countries. He also found a correlation between export growth and the growth of manufacturing before World War I, but not later. Palma for Chile, like Dean for Brazil, argues that export expansion was a precondition for industrialization. Palma, José Gabriel (1979), 'Growth and Structure of Chilean Manufacturing Industry from 1830 to 1935'. PhD. diss., Oxford University.
29. Gallo, Ezequiel (1970), 'Agrarian Expansion and Industrial Development in Argentina, 1880–1930', in Raymond Carr (ed.), *Latin American Affairs*, London, Oxford University Press, pp.49, 50, 53, 60; and Dean (note 26), p.52.
30. '[D]uring the twenty years between 1890 and 1920 Mexican manufacturing was transformed. Large, vertically integrated firms replaced the small shops and artisan producers...,' using new technology and machinery. Haber (note 26).
31. Solberg, Carl (1987), *The Prairie and the Pampas: Agrarian Policy in Canada and Argentina, 1880–1930*, Stanford, CA, Stanford University Press, pp.142–3.
32. Holloway, Thomas H. (1980), *Immigrants on the Land: Coffee and Society in Sao Paulo, 1886–1934*, Chapel Hill, NC, University of North Carolina Press, chap. 6.
33. Thorp Rosemary (ed.) (1984), *Latin America in the 1930s: The Role of the Periphery in World Crisis*. London, Macmillan. (1984), p.66 and Suter (note 13), p.15.
34. Manoilescu, Mihail (1929), *Théorie du protectionnisme et de l'echange international*, Paris, Felix Alcan. His leading champion in Brazil was the industrialist and economic historian Roberto Simonsen. See Simonsen, Roberto (1931), *Crises, Finances and Industry*, Sao Paulo, Limitada, p.91. On Manoilescu's influence in the Ibero-American world, see Love, Joseph L. (1996), *Crafting the Third World: Theorizing Underdevelopment in Rumania and Brazil*. Stanford, CA, Stanford University Press, chaps. 7 and 9.
35. See United Nations: Economic Commission for Latin America (1950 [Sp. orig., 1949]), *The Economic Development of Latin America and Its Principal Problems*. Santiago, Chile, United Nations,. p.97, citing the case of Argentina; and Furtado, Celso (1950), 'Características gerais da economia brasileira', *Revista Brasileira de Economia*, 4/1, p.28.
36. See Furtado Ibid. For a similar thesis about the socialization of losses through exchange depreciation and government maintenance of aggregate demand, see United Nations: Economic Commission for Latin America (1951 [Sp. orig., 1950]), *Economic Survey of*

Latin America: 1949, Santiago, Chile, United Nations pp.171–2.
37. For a summary of Furtado's arguments and the subsequent debate in Brazil, see Suzigan, Wilson (1986), *Indústria brasileira: Origem e desenvolvimento*, São Paulo, Brasiliense pp.21–73. Also see Cardoso, Ciro F.S., and Brignoli, Hector Perez (1979), *Historia económica de América Latina*, vol. 2,. Barcelona, Critica, p.197, summarizing literature on México, Argentina, Brazil, and Chile, and p.199; see also the essays in Thorp, (note 33) and Lewis, C., (1986), 'Industry in Latin America before 1930', in Bethell (ed.), *CHLA*, v. 5 (note 13) p.287, p.320.
38. On Brazil, see Baer, Werner, and Villela, Annibal V. (1973), 'Industrial Growth and Industrialization: Revisions in the Stages of Brazil's Economic Development', *Journal of Developing Areas*, 7/2 pp.217–34.
39. Bulmer-Thomas, Victor (1994), ' The Latin American Economies, 1929–1939', in Bethell (ed.), *CHLA*, v. 6. Cambridge, UK, Cambridge University Press, pp. 101-102. Argentina, the author notes, was the exception.
40. See United Nations (note 35), Raúl Prebisch was the author of this essay-manifesto that began the 'structuralist' school. According to Prebisch (and Hans Singer), at the international level, unequal exchange derived from differential productivities between industrial Center and agricultural Periphery in the world market, combined with different institutional arrangements in capital and labour markets. Technological progress in manufacturing, in any case, was shown in a rise in incomes in developed countries, while that in the production of food and raw materials in underdeveloped countries was expressed in a fall in prices. The explanation of contrasting effects of technological progress was found in the disparate income elasticities of demand for primary and industrial goods. Since consumers of manufactured goods in world trade tended to live in underdeveloped countries, and the contrary was true for consumers of raw materials, the latter group had the best of both worlds, while the former had the worst. On the origins of Prebisch's theories, see Love 1996 (note 34), Chap. 8.
41. Prebisch, Raúl (1963), *Towards a Dynamic Development Policy for Latin America*, New York, United Nations: Economic Commission for Latin America, p.71.
42. Myrdal, G. (1970), *Asian Drama*, London, Allen Lane, pp.208–52.
43. Relevant for the 'classical' experience as well is the fact that much of Europe's surplus labour did not have to be absorbed because of emigration.
44. Calcagno, Alfredo Eric (1980), *Informe sobre las inversiones directas extranjeras en América Latina*. Santiago de Chile, Naciones Unidas: Comisión Económica para América Latina, p.35.
45. Trebat, Thomas J. (1983), *Brazil's State-Owned Enterprises: A Case Study of the State as Entrepreneur*. Cambridge, UK, Cambridge University Press, p. 59.
46. United Nations: Economic Commission for Latin America and the Caribbean (ECLAC), 1996, p.68.
47. Ffrench-Davis, Ricardo, Muñoz, Oscar, and Palma, José Gabriel (1994), 'The Latin American Economies, 1950-1990', in *CHLA*, vol. 6 (note 39), pp.159–60, 165, 197, 247.
48. Ibid, pp.165, 167.
49. See Baer, Werner (1989), *The Brazilian Economy: Growth and Development*, New York, Praeger, chap. 6; and Ramírez, Miguel D. (1989), *Mexico's Economic Crisis: Its Origins and Consequences*, New York, Praeger, chap. 5.
50. As an index, the London Inter-Bank Offer Rate averaged 5 per cent in 1950-71; it fell to -5.3 per cent in 1972-80, and then rose to 14.6 per cent in 1981–87. See Ffrench-Davis (note 46), pp.165, 167, 231.
51. Bulmer-Thomas, Victor (1994), *The Economic History of Latin America since Independence*, Cambridge, UK, Cambridge University Press, p.371.
52. Ffrench-Davis (note 46), p.246.
53. ECLAC (note 45), p.25.
54. World Bank (1993), *The East Asian Miracle: Economic Growth and Public Policy*, New York, Oxford University Press, p.83. On the same page the Bank takes a middle position, arguing for a limited 'market-friendly' interventionism 'to ensure adequate investment in people, provision of a competitive climate for enterprise, openness to international trade, and

stable macroeconomic management'.
55. Ibid, p.52.
56. Fritsch, Winston (1991), 'El nuevo marco internacional: Desafíos y oportunidades', in Osvaldo Sunkel, ed., *El desarrollo desde dentro: Un enfoque neoestructuralista para la América Latina*. Mexico, D.F., Fondo de Cultura Económica, pp. 407, 414.
57. On the linkage, see, for example, Levine, Ross, and Renelt, David (1992), 'A Sensitivity Analysis of Cross-Country Growth Regressions', in *American Economic Review*, 82, pp.42–63 and Esfahani, Hadi Salehi (1991), 'Exports, Imports, and Economic Growth in Semi-Industrialized Countries', in *Journal of Development Economics*, p.35. Levine and Renelt examined data for 119 countries, and Esfahani considered data for 31 semi-industrialized countries. Esfahani emphasizes that the correlation between export and GDP performance has mainly to do with exports' mitigation of import 'shortages', which restrict the growth of output in these countries.
58. Ffrench-Davis (note 46), p.205.
59. Foxley, Alejandro (1983), *Latin American Experiments in Neo-Conservative Economics*, Berkeley, CA, University of California Press, pp.33–5.
60. Valdés, Juan Gabriel (1989), *La escuela de Chicago: Operación Chile*. Buenos Aires, Grupo Editorial Zeta, offers a full study.
61. Foxley (note 58), pp.2, 16, 58, 71. Figures exclude duties on automobiles.
62. See Corbo, Vittorio, and Solimano, Andrés (1991), 'Chile's Experience with Stabilization Revisited', in Michael Bruno *et al.*, *Lessons of Economic Stabilization and its Aftermath*, Cambridge, MA, MIT Press, p.78; Ffrench-Davis, Ricardo, and Muñoz, Oscar (1991), 'Latin American Economic Development and the International Environment', in Patricio Meller (ed.), *The Latin America Development Debate*. Boulder, Colo., Westview p.13 and Meller, Patricio (1991), 'Adjustment and Social Costs in Chile during the 1980s', *World Development*, 19/11, pp.1545–7, 1555).
63. If the man with the best claim as the chief theorist of the Dependency school, Fernando Henrique Cardoso, currently the President of the Brazilian Republic, now believes that the 'principal priority' of the state is 'to provide basic services, in particular, education and health', and that the state's role is no longer, as he once imagined, 'to shape progress', the framers of the Washington Consensus could scarcely object. Cardoso, Fernando Henrique (1995), 'Ainda a 'teoria' da dependência', *Folha de S. Paulo*, 28 May 1995.
64. ECLAC p. 14,18,44 (note 45) and Maddison, Angus (1995), *Monitoring the World Economy: 1820-1992*. Paris, Development Centre of the Organization for Economic Cooperation and Development, p.63.
65. Ibid, pp. 44-45.
66. Bulmer-Thomas (note 50), p.313, 423.
67. Ibid p.425, 428 and Fishlow, Albert (1990), 'The Latin American State', in *Journal of Economic Perspectives*, 4, 3, pp.61–74.
68. United Nations: Economic Commission for Latin America and the Caribbean (1996), *Social Panorama of Latin America: 1996*. Santiago, Chile, United Nations, pp.94, 96.
69. 'I.M.F. Seeks Argentine Deal Linking Credit to Governing', *New York Times*, 15 July 1997, C1.
70. OECD figures. Obviously, gauged from the expenditure side, the role of governments is even larger, to the extent that expenditure is chronically greater than income.
71. Whitehead, Lawrence (1994), 'State Organization in Latin American since 1930' in *CHLA*, vol. 6, part 2. pp.34, 56 (note 39).
72. De Soto chose one of the region's most disorganized and least effective states at the time of his research, the early 1980s. de Soto, Hernando (1989), *The Other Path: The Invisible Revolution in the Third World*, London, Tauris. See also Balassa, Bela, *et al.* (1986), *Toward Renewed Economic Growth in Latin America*, Washington, Institute for International Economics.
73. Katz, Jorge M. (ed.) (1987), *Technology Generation in Latin American Manufacturing Industries: Theory and Case-Studies concerning its Nature, Magnitude, and Consequences*, London, Macmillan.
74. Adler, Emanuel (1987), *The Power of Ideology: The Quest for Technological Autonomy in*

Argentina and Brazil. Berkeley, University of California Press.

75. On these matters, see Tortella, Gabriel (1995), *El desarrollo de la España contemporánea: Historia económica de los siglos XIX y XX,* Madrid, Alianza Editorial, 2d (rev.) ed.

76. Spain was furthermore dependent on Europe in the 1960s for jobs, as emigrant workers eased agricultural unemployment and remitted hard currencies. Thus, in the well-known model of Arthur Lewis, agricultural wages rose at home, just as new investments were made and new markets opened up for agriculture. Finally, from the 1960s, Spain gained large revenues from tourism, which, as a share of national income, only Mexico could hope to match in Latin America. See also Ibid.

The Lessons of South East Asia's Miraculous Growth and Fall From Growth

JONATHAN RIGG

Introduction

At the beginning of 1997, notwithstanding one or two areas of concern, the growth economies of South East Asia – Indonesia, Malaysia, Singapore and Thailand – still appeared to deserve their World Bank-bestowed appellation 'High Performing Asian Economies' (HPAEs) or, more popularly, 'miracle' economies. Nor was this view held only by the World Bank. From academic papers to popular journalism, South East Asia, usually in tandem with East Asia, was depicted as a developmental success story. Few would have guessed that within the space of a few months the Asian miracle would have evaporated and some of the Tiger economies at least would be turning to the IMF to bail them out. This extreme economic turbulence makes it difficult to identify the South East Asian 'lessons' that might apply to the experience of North Africa, and given the turn-about from miracle to crisis, some of the lessons may be at odds. Indeed there are doubts whether there were ever any clearly identifiable lessons. Nonetheless, while it is far from obvious how the economic crisis in Asia will, ultimately, be played out, it does seem that the accepted wisdom is in the process of being either overturned, or at the very least substantially refined.

The Miracle in Outline

The Asian miracle thesis was most clearly – and influentially – stated in the World Bank's *The East Asian Miracle: Economic Growth and Public Policy*.[1] This book identified a group of HPAEs spanning the East and South East Asian regions: Japan, South Korea, Hong Kong, Taiwan, Singapore, Indonesia, Thailand and Malaysia. This paper is concerned largely with the South East Asian quartet – the latter four.

Dr Jonathan Rigg is a South East Asian specialist in the Geography Department of Durham University.

While the authors of *The East Asian Miracle* express caution about selecting and then generalising from such disparate national experiences, they nonetheless arrive at what they term the 'essence of the miracle'. In doing this the study identifies a set of apparently shared economic characteristics that set the HPAEs apart from other developing countries.[2] The essence and the recipe are familiar: a combination of sustained economic growth, highly equal income distributions, rapid demographic transitions, strong and dynamic agricultural sectors, and unusually rapid export growth underpinned by sound, market-based, foreign investment-friendly, export-oriented, and generally equitable policies. Hal Hill in his survey published in the same year identifies a very similar recipe of economic success (Table 1).

For some economists it was not merely a case of different countries embarking on similar paths to development. There were also important interdependencies between the growth economies of the East and South East Asian regions. This idea is most famously associated with Yamazawa's work in which he likened the countries of Asia to a flock of geese, with

TABLE 1
THE 'ESSENCE OF THE MIRACLE'

Characteristics of the miracle
Rapid economic growth
Equitable distribution of income
Dramatic improvement in human welfare, including
    increased access to basic services
    declining poverty
    better nutrition
    rising life expectancy
    improving education

Roots of the miracle

World Bank (1993)	Hill (1993)
'Getting the basics right'	'Getting the fundamentals right'
High levels of domestic saving and investment	High savings and investment rate
Declining population growth rates	-
Efficient public administration	A stable and predictable policy environment
Fundamentally sound macro-economic policy	Conservative macro-economic management
Disciplined government intervention	Pragmatic and effective role for the state
Investment in building human capital	Sustained investment in social services, especially education
Investment in physical capital	Sustained investment in physical
Openness to foreign technology and investment	infrastructure
Export-orientation	Outward orientation
	-
	A generally benign and accommodating international environment

Sources: adapted from World Bank 1993 and Hill 1993.[3]

Japan in the lead, followed by the four Tigers (Taiwan, South Korea, Hong Kong and Singapore), and they in turn by a group of emerging industrial economies (including Indonesia, Malaysia and Thailand, and possibly the Philippines). Yamazawa argued that not only were these economies enjoying similar developmental experiences but that they were also becoming increasingly interdependent as industries transferred from 'early starters to late comers'.[4] Thus the success of the countries 'ahead' enabled those following to emulate that success.

The Cultural Basis of Asian Development: Asian Values and the Asian Way

A noticeable thread in discussions of Asia's successful modernisation – particularly among commentators and officials within the region – is what might be termed the cultural pre-determinant. Governments have been at the forefront of espousing what has become popularly known as the Asian Way. This interest in a distinctly Asian approach to development has come about because of the apparent ability of the countries of Asia to achieve high rates of economic growth while avoiding many of the perceived social costs of progress such as rising crime and rampant individualism. In accounting for Singapore's economic success, for example, former prime minister Lee Kuan Yew explained: 'We were fortunate we had this cultural backdrop, the belief in thrift, hard work, filial piety and loyalty in the extended family, and, most of all, the respect for scholarship and learning'.[5] In Singapore, the National Ideology is based on a number of so-styled Asian core values.

These are:
1. nation before community and society above self,
2. family as the basic unit of society,
3. community support and respect for the individual,
4. consensus not conflict, and
5. racial and religious harmony.
   Source: Tremewan 1994[6]

Significantly, Lee observed shortly after *The East Asian Miracle* was published that one of its shortcomings was its failure to address the issue of culture in economic development. It is the unique cultural context of East Asia which makes, he argued, the transferability of the miracle to other developing countries so difficult.[7] This view echoes the insistence of some scholars, and particularly the post-developmentalists, that development must be contextually defined.[8] So far as this paper is concerned, the importance of the Asian Values argument is that it seems to put non-Asian cultures off limits.

Perhaps inevitably, with its underlying theme of cultural determinism, the Asian Values thesis has been vigorously contested – usually by scholars and commentators in the West. In particular critics like Buruma and Tremewan[9] have pointed to the difficulty of ascribing a single set of values to such a culturally varied region. It is also worth considering the irony of Asian Values theorists using Confucianism (or something close to it) to account for the region's recent economic success, when not very long ago Max Weber was using Confucianism to explain China's failure to modernise.[10] With something as nebulous and malleable as culture it is seemingly possible to bend it to sustain just about any argument. Indeed, the tables have turned once more and some commentators are highlighting Asian values to explain Asia's economic crisis.

Challenging the Miracle

Before addressing the possible 'lessons' of South East Asian development it is worth reviewing the primary critiques that have been presented to challenge the miracle thesis. These critiques, it should be noted, predate the economic crisis of 1997-98. In broad terms they fall into two categories, with some overlap between them. First there are those critiques which stress the very real developmental challenges and tensions which have arisen as a direct result of the economic policies that have been pursued. These range from widening inter-personal and regional inequalities to the environmental costs of modernisation. And second there are those which raised doubts about the sustainability of the miracle and questioned whether there was anything particularly miraculous about Asia's economic success.

Miracles and Mal-Development

> There is reason...to question the use of the term 'development' at all when applied to this pattern of economic growth [in Thailand] as it violates important values of equity, economic democracy, ecological balance, and human decency.[11]

The main challenge to the miracle thesis comes from scholars who have tried to look below the aggregate statistics to highlight what are perceived to be the very real tensions of development. More to the point, these tensions are seen to be a *strategic result* of the policies that have been pursued. For the more radical among these scholars[12] the development trajectory is fundamentally flawed, resulting in mal-development 'with strongly negative socio-economic consequences in terms of inequality, unevenness, cultural fragmentation, and a negative impact on women and the environment'.[13] For other scholars[14] it is a case of qualifying the miracle thesis by recognising the problems have arisen as a result of the policies that have been pursued, and attempting to ameliorate them.

The Miracle, Poverty and Inequality

A key criticism levelled at South East Asia's development is that it has tended to perpetuate poverty. As Amsden has written, playing on the World Bank's admonition to embrace 'market friendly' policies, the results have often been 'not so friendly to labour'.[15] The argument is a comparatively simple one: in order to remain attractive to footloose foreign investors operating in a global market, wages must be kept competitive. This is reflected in the response of government ministers in the region to outbreaks of labour unrest or the contravention of existing labour and employment laws. For example, following unrest at foreign invested companies in Vietnam[16] during 1993–96 Minister of Labour Tran Dinh Hoan, while sympathetic to demands that the minimum wage be increased, explained that 'Vietnam can not set its minimum wage higher than other regional countries...otherwise foreign investment will not come to Vietnam but will go elsewhere'.[17] Similarly, in Cambodia, the director of the Ministry of Social Welfare, Labour and Veterans' Affairs' labour inspectorate, Haing Sitha, warned against prosecuting foreign companies that had possibly contravened existing labour laws, stating that 'before we take action, we must think carefully about the possible consequences. If we punish them too severely we risk losing these investors...'.[18] In Schmidt's view, Transnational Corporations 'play nations and communities off against one another' in their efforts to maximise profits.[19] For their part, governments in the region, trapped by the inescapable logic of the global economy, restrain wages and institutionalise unions in order to maintain competitiveness and, therefore, attractiveness. This results in what has been termed competitive austerity.

While the operation of the global market may exert a downward pressure on wages in certain sectors and skills groups, it is difficult to take this a step further to sustain the argument that development in Asia has perpetuated poverty. The evidence consistently shows that well-being improved on a broad front for the great majority of the population of the HPAEs during the period of rapid economic growth and that 'the relationship between growth and poverty alleviation is strong and positive'.[20] Ahuja et al. suggest that 'the general picture presented...is unambiguously positive: poverty has been declining in every East Asian economy for which we have data except Papua New Guinea'.[21] With respect to Thailand, Ji Ungphakorn takes issue with those who argue that development there has perpetuated poverty, writing:

FIGURE 1
INCIDENCE OF POVERTY IN SOUTH EAST ASIA

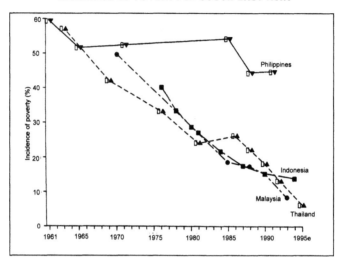

Source: Rigg (1997) see endnote 33.

We do the poor no service by not starting out with the facts. Numerous studies have been made as to the effects of economic growth on the well-being of the Thai population and there is every reason to believe that the standard of living of the majority of Thais has improved over the last 20 years. ... The real question...is why have the rich taken a much larger share of this new wealth than the rest of the population?[22]

A key element of the Asian miracle has been the extent to which the grail of 'growth with equity' has been achieved. As the World Bank puts it: the HPAEs while sustaining high rates of economic growth 'have also achieved unusually low and declining levels of inequality, contrary to historical experience and contemporary evidence in other regions'.[23] This, though, is not necessarily borne out when individual HPAEs are examined in detail. Thailand, for example, has experienced a significant widening of inter-personal inequality in recent years – coinciding with the period of fastest economic growth. While in the cases of both Indonesia and Thailand there has been a significant widening of regional (spatial) disparities.

In Thailand, the poorest quintile of the population saw its share of income more than halve between 1962 and 1995, declining from just 7.9 per cent to 3.4 per cent (Table 2). Furthermore, scholars of the Thai economy have argued that there has been a trade-off between growth and equity in the Kingdom.[25] While the preliminary figures for 1996 do indicate a

TABLE 2
PER CAPITA INCOME DISTRIBUTION, INDONESIA AND THAILAND

INDONESIA

	Lowest	Middle	Highest
	40%	40%	20%
1976	19.6	38.0	42.5
1980	19.5	38.2	42.3
1981	20.4	37.5	42.1
1984	20.7	37.3	42.0
1987	20.9	37.5	41.6
1990	21	37	41
1996	19	35	45

THAILAND

	Lowest	Lowest	Lowest	Middle	Highest
	10%	20%	40%	40%	20%
1962/63	-	7.9	16.5	33.7	49.8
1975/76	2.4	6.1	15.8	35.0	49.3
1980/81	2.1	5.4	14.5	34.0	51.5
1985/86	1.8	4.6	12.4	32.0	55.6
1988/89	1.8	4.5	12.5	32.5	55.0
1990		4.2	11.6	30.8	57.7
1992		3.9	11.0	30.0	59.0
1994		4.0	11.3	31.2	57.5
1995e		3.4	9.5	27.4	63.1
1996e		4.5	12.4	32.2	55.4

Sources: Tjondronegoro *et al.* 1992 p.71 (Indonesia); Akin Rabibhadana 1993 p.62, Suganya Hutaserani 1990, Medhi Krongkaew 1995 and Nanak Kakwani and Medhi Krongkaew 1996 (Thailand). Note that the 1995 and 1996 figures for Thailand were separately estimated on the basis of linear trends from previous years.[24]

(temporary?) reversal of the trend, Thailand can scarcely be characterised as a country where growth with equity has been achieved. In Indonesia the pattern of income distribution appears to have remained relatively stable, with no obvious widening or narrowing between income groups (Table 2). This, though, has been contested on the grounds that the data collected by the Biro Pusat Statistik (BPS) are unreliable.[26] In addition, recently released figures for 1996 do offer some support for the view that disparities widened during Indonesia's period of rapid growth from 1990 (Table 2). There are certainly numerous village studies which indicate that inequalities are widening and there is also a wealth of anecdotal evidence to indicate as much.

The different experiences of Thailand and Indonesia have been linked to the policies pursued by each country. In Indonesia the revenue generated by the oil boom was relatively widely distributed. There was a sustained effort to raise rice productivity and considerable investment also went into the provision of rural roads, health centres and primary schools.[27] In Thailand, by contrast, 'rural areas, particularly in the 1960s and 1970s, were neglected by a state élite which systematically allocated resources to urban areas, particularly Bangkok...'.[28] Ahuja *et al.* also identify a trend towards greater inequalities emerging among the Asian economies. They link this to two mechanisms: a widening in the returns to work between the better and the less well-educated; and a concentration of economic activity and prosperity in certain geographical regions.[29]

This latter point – that inequalities have widened in both inter-provincial/regional and rural-urban terms – has been recognised for some time (Table 3).

There seems little reason to doubt that economic activity has been geographically concentrated and that certain 'lagging' regions have been left even further behind. Indonesia's four poorest provinces are East and West Nusa Tenggara, East Timor and Maluku. In 1993-94, these four

TABLE 3
THE POOR IN INDONESIA AND THAILAND: RURAL/URBAN DISTRIBUTION
(PERCENTAGE OF THE POPULATION DEFINED AS POOR)

THAILAND

	Rural (All villages)	Urban (All municipal areas)
1976	36	13
1981	27	8
1986	36	6
1988	26	6
1990	21	5
1992	16	2
1994	11	2

Sources: National Economic and Social Development Board (NESDB) figures quoted in Warr 1993 p.46, Medhi Krongkaew 1995, Nanak Kakwani and Medhi Krongkaew 1996.[30]

INDONESIA

	Total	BPS Urban	Rural	World Bank Urban	Rural
1970				50.7	58.5
1976	40.1	38.8	40.4	31.5	54.5
1978	33.3	30.8	33.9	25.7	54.0
1980	28.6	29.0	28.4	19.7	44.6
1981	26.9	28.1	26.5	-	-
1984	21.6	23.1	21.2	14.0	32.6
1987	17.4	20.1	16.4	8.3	18.5
1990	15.1	16.8	14.3	-	-

Sources: Biro Pusat Statistik (BPS) and World Bank figures quoted in Booth 1993 pp.65-66; updated from Firdausy 1994 and Cohen 1995.[31]

provinces received some 11 per cent of INPRES development grants, yet they supported five per cent of the country's population and nine per cent of its poor population (Table 4).

TABLE 4
REGIONAL WEALTH AND POVERTY IN INDONESIA

	Population (% of total)	Poor Pop'n (% of total)	Incidence of Poverty (%)	INPRES Grants 1993-1994
Jakarta	4.7	1.9	5.6	2.3
Java/Bali	56.2	55.3	13.4	31.1
Mining 4 [1]	6.0	6.4	14.5	14.5
Sumatra	16.9	16.0	13.0	20.1
Kalimantan	4.1	6.6	21.9	9.5
Sulawesi	7.0	5.1	9.9	11.5
Eastern Islands [2]	5.1	8.6	22.6	10.9
Total	100	100	100	100

[1] Aceh, East Kalimantan, Irian Jaya and Riau
[2] West and East Nusa Tenggara, East Timor and Maluku
Source: Booth 1995.[32]

TABLE 5
REGIONAL AND INCIDENCES OF POVERTY IN THAILAND
(1975/76, 1988/89 AND 1992)

	1975	1988	1990	1992	1994
North	33	20.7	16.6	13.6	8.5
Northeast	44	34.5	28.3	22.3	15.7
Central	13	16	12.9	6	5.2
South	31	21.5	17.6	11.8	11.7
Bangkok (BMR [1])	8	2.9	2	1.1	0.5
Whole country	**30**	**22.2**	**18**	**13.1**	**9.6**

[1] BMR = Bangkok Metropolitan Region

Note that there is some discrepancy between the figures here and those quoted in Table 3.1.

Sources: Suganya Hutaserani 1990 p.16, Medhi Krongkaew 1995; Nanak Kakwani and Medhi Krongkaew 1996.[30]

It seems that while the Indonesian government may have allotted comparatively generous development grants to the country's lagging regions, the character that development has taken in the country has meant that they are poorly placed to benefit from the modernisation process. As Booth points out, the three pillars of Indonesian economic development during the New Order period (from 1967) – import substitution industrialisation, labour-intensive export-oriented industrialisation, and resource-based industrialisation – have all been centred elsewhere in the Archipelago.[31] The same argument could be applied to Thailand's lagging north-eastern region which has seen its share of GDP decline markedly over time while the incomes of its population relative to the rest of the country have not improved significantly despite years of regional development.

To some extent the rural-urban and regional income figures can be challenged on the grounds that they do not sufficiently take account of the presence of 'rural' people in urban settings and the flows of wealth back to rural locales that result.[33] In other words, using static spatial units as a basis to measure the relative wealth/poverty of people who move between rural and urban areas and across provincial divides is problematic.

These concerns about inequality are important, both for reasons of human decency and for persuasive political and security reasons. Notwithstanding the fact that the data are somewhat mixed with respect to whether inequalities are widening, there is a widespread perception that the development cake is being apportioned unfairly. Koppel, for example, writes of the 'Other Asia' – the Asia that was hidden by the froth of the miracle.[34] A challenge before the crisis was to make Asian growth more inclusive: to draw people in and make them partners and players in the development game, not just watching, powerless, from the touchlines. Further there are also worries, which have not been touched on here, about the environmentally destructive nature of development in the region and the deleterious effect that it is having on local cultures.[35]

Notwithstanding the need to make Asian growth fairer, there seems little reason to question the central conclusion that during the period of rapid economic growth in the region – and this applies to Indonesia, Malaysia, Singapore and Thailand – the well-being of the majority of people substantially improved. This applies even to Koppel's Other Asia. As the economist Arndt put it:

> 'It was not caprice that made economic growth central to thinking about development, that put GNP on the throne and has, in the face of all the onslaughts and pinpricks, firmly kept it there. ... Economic growth...was the only effective way of making the people of the Third World materially better off, of raising consumption standards'.[36]

Sustainability of the Miracle

Given the economic crisis that swept through South East and East Asia in 1997 and 1998 the question of the sustainability of the economic miracle has become particularly pertinent. Indeed, it might be argued that from the perspective of early 1998 the question is not whether the miracle can be sustained, but whether it can be resurrected. Nonetheless, this issue of sustainability pre-dates the crisis and it is valuable to look at the arguments that were being presented 'before the fall'.

A central area of debate concerned whether the type of development pursued in South East Asia, based on foreign investment-led, export-driven industrialisation, had created dependency and vulnerability. Rodan, writing of Singapore, warned that 'there is an externally-imposed precariousness about participation in this [global economic] structure over which even the most astute policy-makers...have very little control'.[37] Chant and McIlwaine, in their examination of the Mactan EPZ in the Philippines, write of 'the inherent vulnerability of multinational export manufacturing...'.[38] Even some scholars of transitional economies like Vietnam have highlighted the dependency and vulnerability which flow from reliance on export-oriented, foreign investment-funded industrialisation.[39]

In writing of the 'precariousness' of this type of development authors are alluding to a set of overlapping fears. One area of concern focuses on perturbations in the global economy. For example, Singapore's recession of 1985 was partly due to a simultaneous decline in its key export sectors.[40] A second area of concern is linked to the possibility of a rise in global protectionism. The motivation behind Asean's attempts to create a free trade zone by 2003 – AFTA (the Asean Free Trade Area) – is partly informed by this fear of emerging inward-looking trading blocs in Europe and North America. A third issue is linked to the commitment of foreign companies to the countries they invest in, especially when the industries are footloose. It has been noted, for example, that garment and footwear industries have continually shifted their operations to those countries with the lowest wage rates – from Taiwan, South Korea and Hong Kong to Malaysia; from Malaysia to Thailand; from Thailand to Indonesia; and from Indonesia to Vietnam and China. Thailand has seen its textile and garment sector suffer as orders have been placed in other, cheaper wage locations and the share of garments in total exports has declined from a peak of 12.1 per cent in 1987 to less than half that figure by the end of 1997 (Table 6). Even in Vietnam, the government is concerned that rising wages could price them out of the market.[41] It is on these grounds that Dean Forbes has stated that '[t]he longer-term viability of...dynamic Pacific Asian growth must be critically questioned'.[42]

However perhaps the single most influential – and contentious – recent piece of work challenging the sustainability of the Asian miracle is Paul Krugman's paper 'The myth of Asia's miracle'. Simply put, Krugman argues that East and South East Asia's growth was based on a remarkable mobilisation of resources. In Singapore, for example, the economically active proportion of the population rose from 27 per cent in 1966 to 51 per

TABLE 6
THE RISE (AND DEMISE?) OF THAILAND'S GARMENT INDUSTRY

	Value of garment (bn baht)	Total value of exports total exports (%)	Share of garments in exports (bn baht)	
1980		133.2		
1981		153.0		
1982		159.7		
1983	8.8	146.5	6.0	
1984	12.2	175.2	7.0	
1985	14.7	193.4	7.6	GROWTH
1986	20.2	233.4	8.7	
1987	36.3	299.9	12.1	
1988	45.6	403.6	11.3	
1989	57.9	516.4	11.2	
1990	65.8	589.8	11.1	STAGNATION
1991	86.7	725.5	11.9	
1992	86.8	824.6	10.5	
1993	89.6	940.9	9.5	
1994	100.7	1,137.6	8.9	
1995	102.0	1,404.5	7.3	DECLINE
1996	79.6	1,412	5.6	
1997*	55.2	1,024	5.4	

* = January-August
For much of the above period US$1 = 25 baht

Sources: National Statistical Office data, *Bangkok Post Economic Review* (various), Tasker and Handley 1993.[43]

cent in 1990. There was also a massive investment in physical infrastructure and an upgrading of human resources as increasing numbers of young people received secondary education. 'These numbers', Krugman writes, 'should make it obvious that Singapore's growth has been largely based on one-time changes in behaviour that cannot be repeated'. He asserts that there is little evidence that the NICs' (Newly Industrialised Countries) growth included any great increases in efficiency. The primary impetus behind growth was the mobilisation of resources on a grand scale.[44] Not only does Krugman's thesis raise questions about whether growth can be sustained now that human resource mobilisation has peaked; it also challenges whether there was anything particularly 'miraculous' in Asia's economic achievements before 1997.

Although the findings of Krugman's paper were vehemently refuted in South East Asia when it was published, governments in the region were already grappling with at least some of its practical implications even before the paper was published. Thailand's and Indonesia's governments have been concerned with raising secondary school enrolment rates for some time, so that their economies are in a position to make the transition to high skill,

TABLE 7
SCHOOLING IN SOUTH EAST ASIA
ENROLMENT RATES (1993, %)

		Indonesia	Malaysia	Philippines	Thailand
Primary	*male*	116	93		98
	female	112	93	110*	97
Secondary	*male*	48	56		38
	female	39	61	74*	37
Tertiary		10	7*	26	19

* = 1991, male and female.

Sources: Hill 1996, World Bank 1997[45]

high value added, high wage industries (Table 7). While in Singapore there has been concern that although the country's education system may turn out well qualified workers there is a notable absence of innovators with the creative skills to lead the Republic into its much vaunted 'intelligent island' future. To this end, in 1996, Prime Minister Goh Chok Tong announced the creation of a 'thinking skills programme' while the Economic Development Board has established an 'innovation development scheme'.

Interpreting the Miracle and the Question of Replicability

The first point to stress is that because there is more than one interpretation of the Asian miracle, the lessons that can be drawn are also at variance. At the risk of over-generalising, scholars embrace four broad perspectives of the Asian miracle. Firstly, there is the neo-classical, 'free-market' view. This holds that economic growth has been based on distinctly limited government intervention beyond providing a stable macro-economic environment within which business can operate. Second, there is the World Bank view – most clearly enunciated in the *The East Asian Miracle* – which also emphasises the critical place of a 'market friendly' strategy but accepts a rather broader role for 'effective but carefully delimited government activism' in economic management.[46] Third, there are the 'revisionists' who argue that the World Bank and its supporters have underestimated the role of government in stage managing growth, encapsulated in the term 'developmental state'. And fourth and last there are those who subscribe to the Asian values thesis and emphasise the central role of culture in understanding the region's economic success. The consensus opinion tends to gravitate towards the second and third of these perspectives.

The World Bank suggests that when Asian states have intervened in economic affairs they have done so ineffectively and that the promotion of specific industries, in the main, did not work. It is on this basis that that the authors of *The East Asian Miracle* reject the 'revisionist' view that the East Asian economies represent developmental states where states have governed markets.[47] The revisionists, on the other hand, tend to emphasise the degree to which the World Bank has tried to shoe-horn Asia's experience into an ideological box of their own.[48] Jenkins, for example, suggests that 'many of the lessons that have been drawn [from the East Asian experience] are false lessons, because they have been based on a number of myths concerning the East Asian NICs'.[49] He then goes on, as he puts it, to 'explode' the myths that East Asian growth has been based on outward orientation, getting prices right, and de-emphasising the role of the state in development.

A key area of debate concerning the 'lessons' of Asia's economic success centres on the issue of replicability. Simply put, if there are lessons to be learnt, are they transferable, and is the experience of Asia therefore replicable? There is a body of opinion – which dates back some years – that suggests that Asia's economic success was historically specific. For example, in the late 1980s Rodan was arguing that Singapore's strategy of foreign investment-driven, export-oriented industrialisation 'was feasible because of opportune historical conditions, not because this strategy made universal sense'.[50] The assumption seemed to be that as other developing countries embarked upon the same strategy they would not find the global economic climate so conducive to growth. As the experience of the Thai, Malaysian and Indonesian economies between the late 1980s and the 1997 economic crisis showed, countries could, and did, successfully embrace export-oriented growth strategies. This is not to say, however, that historical conditions do not create unique opportunities. Rather, it is in making the leap from this self-evident statement to pronouncing that given constantly changing and unique historical conditions one country's strategy of development offers no lessons to learn and no framework to emulate.

A second reason which is sometimes highlighted to promote the non-replicability argument is that other developing countries lack the 'institutional capacity' to repeat the success of East Asia.[51] This perspective suffers from many of the problems that bedevil the historical specificity argument. For merely looking at the institutional bases of the eight HPAEs – from the tightly structured and highly efficient bureaucratic regimes of Singapore and Korea to the far looser system of control in Thailand – highlights that even here variety is more obvious that commonality.

A third and related issue concerns the cultural bases of East Asia's success and, in particular, the Asian values thesis. As Singapore's Senior Minister Lee Kuan Yew observed when he visited Vietnam – widely perceived to be a 'dragon in waiting' or 'tiger cub' – it had that 'vital intangible' necessary for rapid growth. This argument does not convince because of Asia's varied cultural mosaic. Taiwan, South Korea, Japan and Singapore might be broadly defined as 'Confucian' – and even this, as Kim[52] argues, entails a fairly courageous leap of faith – but it is hard to see Thailand, Indonesia and Malaysia fitting easily within the same cultural formulation. Further, cultures are not set in stone but undergo constant and often deep change. There is a distinct sense in which the cultural explanation for East Asia's rapid growth is an *ex post* rationalisation.[53]

Key Policy Lessons of the Miracle

In their study *Everyone's Miracle: Revisiting Poverty and Inequality in East Asia,* the authors account for the region's unprecedented economic growth in the following terms:

> The evidence favors the following explanation: East Asian savings and investment rates are exceptionally high by international standards. By and large, investment has been put to good use: any rise in capital-output ratios has been a consequence of a natural process of capital deepening. Both technological change and product upgrading have taken place throughout economies and in all sectors...'.[54]

The emphasis here, and in the earlier World Bank *East Asian Miracle*, is on the degree to which governments in the region have allocated resources efficiently and effectively. The focus on providing basic social services also particularly helped the poor and near poor. The provision of universal primary level education, for example, was a key element driving the process of movement of rural workers into non-farm employment.[55] This, in turn, provided the workers for the region's export-orientated industrialisation. But a possible side effect has been that in providing universal primary level education governments in the region have also created conditions of labour surplus at the lower end of the skills spectrum. This has tended to exert a downward pressure on wages while also widening the income gap between skilled and un-/semi-skilled workers. The outcome of this process is similar to that outlined by Amsden and others noted above – that the policies of Asian governments have been 'not so friendly to labour', creating conditions of competitive austerity. But importantly the interpretation of the outcome is different.

Reflections on the Crisis

If the above had been written at the beginning of 1997 it would have been phrased largely in the present tense. A year later, the past tense had become more appropriate. Inevitably, given the speed of the collapse of the Asian economies, the longer term implications are far from clear. It should also be emphasised that while some scholars were predicting that there might be a slow-down in Asian economic growth there was scarcely anyone who predicted such a deep and rapid collapse. We are also a little wiser after the event.

The roots of the Asian economic crisis lie in the close links that evolved in the region between government and business. In its extreme form this was 'crony capitalism'. But more generally it led to investment decisions being based on implicit government guarantees that encouraged financial institutions to overlook the business risks of their actions. As Krugman argues, the Asian crisis 'was mainly about bad banking and its consequences'.[56] In Indonesia private overseas corporate debt amounted to an estimated US$65 bn by the beginning of 1998.[57] The size of the debt – and the same was true in Thailand, South Korea and Malaysia – was shielded from scrutiny by financial systems which lacked transparency and by excessively lax reporting and supervision rules. Nayan Chanda summarises the widely held view of the roots of the region's economic crisis in the following terms:

> In country after country the story was remarkably similar. Corruption and crony capitalism had weakened solid economies built on years of hard work and prudent investment. Lax, outdated banking rules had left nations unprepared to handle a flood of foreign funds. In short, a potent mix of globalisation, poor governance and greed brought about the crisis that now engulfs the region'.[58]

There are three important, and wider, implications of this interpretation of the crisis. First it suggests that the developmental state may be to blame. While during the heady years of growth in the 1980s and 1990s the ability of 'strong' or 'autonomous' states carefully to craft the policy landscape of modernisation was highlighted as a key reason explaining growth, it is now the state that takes the blame – implicitly – for the profligacy underpinning the crash. While states *may* be efficient economic managers, the concentration of power and the close links that evolve between government and well-connected individuals is inherently risky. This is particularly true when investors – financial intermediaries as Krugman classes them – receive implicit guarantees from the government and are therefore not exposed to the full consequences of their investment decisions. The important point is that it is not that states *per se* were being profligate but that they created the investment climate in which financial institutions could engage in excessively risky lending practices. While the explicit problem may lie largely with the private sector, this can only be understood by looking at the wider political and economic structures which encouraged the problem to grow to crisis proportions.[59] Therefore, addressing what may appear to be a private sector problem must begin and end with extensive reform to public institutions. In Thailand this may involve reforms to banking regulations; in Indonesia it may require a more fundamental dismantling of the system of state-orchestrated patronage. It is notable that Ammar Siamwalla in his analysis of the economic crisis in Thailand believes, like Krugman, that the problem lies primarily in private debt and that 'In the end, a financially, institutionally [referring to the loss of confidence in the central Bank of Thailand] and politically bankrupt Thailand had to go cap in hand to the IMF.'[60]

A second associated implication links with the Asian values thesis. For it can be argued that the Confucian capitalism which some suggested was a particular ingredient of the miracle is also a critical factor in the crisis. For it was this that permitted authority and power to become so concentrated, thereby creating the environment in which the conditions leading to crisis could evolve. There may also be a case that South East Asia's family-dominated firms – mostly controlled by families of Chinese ethnic origin – need to reform their methods in the light of the crisis. As Ammar Siamwalla writes with reference to family firms in Thailand: 'families displayed little willingness to relinquish control over their firms [and] consequently... borrowed heavily to meet their need for capital'.[61] Their debt dependence grew and this made many highly vulnerable in conditions of economic crisis.

The third point concerns the role of savings in development. For years a central pillar in the Asian miracle edifice was the region's high rate of savings (see Table 1). This provided the funds to finance the industrial boom. However, with the benefit of hindsight it is possible to argue that banks were so awash with funds that they were under pressure to invest in projects which had considerable risk attached. In Thailand much went to finance companies and from there into speculative real estate investment creating an asset bubble waiting to be pricked. Foreign investors, attracted by Asia's miracle, were also drawn into the process. Why banks and finance companies should have felt it safe to use funds in this way links back to Krugman's argument that they were protected by implicit government guarantees. It is significant that the one country in South East Asia which weathered the storm best (so far) is the 'sick man' of Asia – the Philippines. The Philippines never 'enjoyed' the flows of funds nor the high rate of savings of other countries in the region.

So, What are the Lessons?

Until 1997, the growth economies of Asia had achieved impressive and sustained economic progress. However even with respect to the period of growth it is hard to identify a single development 'trajectory'. The World Bank may have tried to tease out the commonalities that apparently linked the eight HPAEs, but even in the early 1990s there were at least as many reasons to treat each economy as distinct and unique as there were to link them. Even before the Asian economic crisis there were several competing interpretations of the miracle. The lessons that each drew, as outlined above, were different – sometimes fundamentally so. To make matters still more confused, the economic crisis has provided a reason to add yet further qualifications. It may be tempting to see the current crisis as a reason to reject all that has happened to date and to conclude that Asia's miracle was a mirage. Not only is this view overdone, but it also ignores the important possibility that 'Asia's economic transformation is entering its second generation'.[62]

While it is attractive to be able to arrive at some slate of policies which can magically induce rapid growth à la East Asia before the Fall, the tedious reality is less clear cut. It is best, perhaps, to articulate it in general terms: consistently good government. Jenkins argues:

> The key to the superior industrial performance of the East Asian NICs does not lie in the general superiority of export-oriented industrialisation strategies over import substitution, or of market-oriented policies over state intervention... It is rather the ability of the state to direct the accumulation process in the direction which is required by capitalist development at particular points in time which is crucial. This in turn has to be located in the existence of a developmental state with a high degree of relative autonomy from local classes and class factions'.[63]

Leftwich argues much the same in writing that developmental states are those '...whose policies have concentrated sufficient power, autonomy and capacity at the centre to shape, pursue and encourage the achievement of explicit developmental objectives...'.[64] The issue though, in the light of the 1997 economic crisis, is whether this concentration of power and autonomy is wise. Proponents of the developmental state perspective emphasise the intimacy of the relationship of the state with the private sector. Yet it is also this intimacy which underlies the economic conditions which led to crisis. Again we come back to the quality of government intervention. Singapore's economy has been well-managed; those of Korea, Malaysia, Indonesia and Thailand have not. Yet all have been characterised as developmental states. The criticisms that can be laid at the door of the World Bank – of building broad generalisations on the basis of varied experiences – can also be applied to developmental state theorists.

It could be argued that ultimately the lessons that can be learned from Asia are independent of the interpretation we attach to the miracle. Broad lessons like investment in physical and human infrastructure, and effective economic management have resonance and relevance beyond this corner of Asia. There has been a tendency to malign the World Bank's admonition to 'get the basics right' but perhaps this is about as far as we can go. The 'basics' will clearly vary from place to place given each country's unique historical, cultural, political and geographical milieu. Countries may attain rapid growth by focusing on the basics, but the specifics will inevitably vary. There is perhaps one final lesson to be learnt from Asia – or at least to be re-learned: that there is always the potential for rapid and unexpected change in economic fortunes. And in the light of those changes the formerly perceived foundations of growth can be transformed into the quicksand of crisis.

NOTES

1. World Bank (1993), *The East Asian Miracle: Economic Growth and Public Policy*, Oxford: Oxford University Press. The label HPAE is associated with this publication.
2. Ibid p.2.
3. Adapted from The World Bank (note 1) and Hill, Hal (1993), *Southeast Asian Economic Development: An Analytical Survey*. Australian National University , Research School of Pacific Studies, Economics Division Working Papers 93/4, p.1.
4. Yamazawa, Ippei (1992), 'On Pacific Economic Integration', in *Economic Journal* 102 (November), pp.1519–29.
5. Zakaria, Fareed (1994), 'Culture is destiny: a conversation with Lee Kuan Yew', in *Foreign Affairs*, 73/2, pp.109–26.
6. Tremewan, Christopher (1994), *The Political Economy of Social Control in Singapore*, Basingstoke, St Martin's Press, p.146.
7. Oddly, many academic critics of *The East Asian Miracle* argue just the reverse.
8. See Brohman, John (1995), 'Universalism, Eurocentrism, and Ideological Bias in Development Studies: From Modernisation to Neoliberalism', in *Third World Quarterly*, 16/1, pp.121–40; and Escobar, Arturo (1995), *Encountering Development: the Making and Unmaking of the Third World*, Princeton: Princeton University Press.
9. Buruma, Ian, 'The Singapore way', *The New York Review*, 19 October 1995 , pp.66–71 and Tremewan (note 6).
10. McVey, Ruth (1992), 'The Materialisation of the South East Asian entrepreneur', in Ruth McVey (ed) *South East Asian Capitalists*, Studies on South East Asia, Ithaca: Cornell University Press, pp.7–33, 9.
11. Bell, Peter F. (1992), 'Gender and Economic Development in Thailand', in: Penny van Esterik and John van Esterik (ed.) *Gender and Development in South East Asia*, Toronto. Canadian Council for South East Asian Studies, pp.61–81.
12. See Bell 1992, ibid and Bell, Peter F. (1996), 'Development or Maldevelopment? The Contradictions of Thailand's Economic Growth', in Michael J.G. Parnwell (ed.) *Thailand: Uneven Development*, Aldershot: Avebury, pp.49–62; and Schmidt, Johannes Dragsbaek (1997), 'The Challenge from South East Asia: Between Equity and Growth', in Chris Dixon and David Drakakis-Smith (ed.) *Uneven Development in South East Asia*, Aldershot: Avebury, pp.21–44.
13. Bell, 1996, ibid p.49.
14. See Parnwell, Michael and Arghiros, Daniel A. (1996) 'Uneven development in Thailand', in Parnwell (ed.) (note 12), pp.1–27.
15. Amsden, Alice H. (1994), 'Why isn't the Whole World Experimenting with the East Asian

Model to Develop?: Review of The East Asian miracle', *World Development* 22/4, pp.627–33. See also Jenkins, Rhys (1994), 'Capitalist Development in the NICs', in: Leslie Sklair (ed.) *Capitalism and Development*, London: Routledge, pp.72-86, Bell (note 13) pp.54–5 and Hewison, Kevin and Brown, Andrew (1994) 'Labour and unions in an industrialising Thailand', in *Journal of Contemporary Asia*, 24/4, pp.483–514.

16. Vietnam is not a 'miracle' economy but it has been characterised as a 'Tiger cub'.
17. Quoted in Schwarz, Adam, 'Proletarian Blues', in *Far Eastern Economic Review*, 25 January 1996, pp.21–2.
18. Quoted in Vittachi, Imran (1996), 'Cambodian Dilemma: Labor Rights or Investors', *Phnom Penh Post*, 14–27 June, p.15.
19. Schmidt (note 12), p.32.
20. The evidence is, admittedly, largely economic and some critics would wish to look at well-being in much broader terms, embracing various non-economic quality of life indicators. Hill, 1993 (note 3) p.63.
21. Ahuja, V., Bidani, B., Ferreira, F. and Walton, M. (1997) *Everyone's Miracle? Revisiting Poverty and Inequality in East Asia*, Washington DC: World Bank. p.25.
22. Ungphakorn, Ji (1995), 'Time For a Rethink on the Fight Against Poverty in Thailand', *Thai Development Newsletter* no. 29: pp.54–5.
23. World Bank (note 1), p.29.
24. Tjondronegoro, Sedonio M.P. Soejono, Irlan and Hardjono, Joan (1992), 'Rural Poverty in Indonesia: Trends Issues and Policies' in *Asian Development Review* 10/1 pp.67–90; Rebibhadana , Akin (1993) *Social Inequity: A Source of Conflict for the Future?*, Bangkok, Thai Development Research Institute, p.62; Hutaserani, Suganya (1990), 'The Trends of Income Inequality and Poverty and Profile of the Urban Poor in Thailand', in *TDRI Quarterly Review*. 5/4, pp.14–19; Krongkaew, Medhi, 'Growth Hides Rising Poverty' *Bangkok Post* 29 December 1995; Krongkaew, Medhi, Tinakorn, Pranee and Suphachalasai, Suphat (1992) 'Rural Poverty in Thailand: Poverty Issues and Responses', in *Asian Development Review*, 10/1, pp.199–225.
25. Medhi Krongkaew *et al.* 1992, ibid, p.199.
26. See Booth, Anne (1992), 'The World Bank and Indonesian Poverty', in *Journal of International Development* 4/6: pp.633–42; and Booth, Anne (1992) 'Income Distribution and Poverty', in: Anne Booth (ed.) *The Oil Boom and After: Indonesian Economic Policy and Performance in the Soeharto Era*, Singapore, OUP, pp.323–62.
27. Bresnan, John (1993), *Managing Indonesia: The Modern Political Economy*, New York: Columbia University Press.
28. Parnwell, and Arghiros (note 14), p.15.
29. Ahuja (note 21). p.26
30. Warr, Carl G. (1993), Thailand's Economic Miracle, Thai Information Paper No. 1, Australian National University, Canberra, p.46; Nanak Kakwani and Medhi Krongkaew (1996) 'Big Reduction in Poverty in Thailand', *Poverty Alleviation Initiatives* 6/4, pp.7–12.
31. Booth, Anne (1993), 'Counting the Poor in Indonesia'. *Bulletin of Indonesian Economic Studies*, 29/1, pp.65–6; Also Firdausy Carunia (1994) 'Urban Poverty in Indonesia, Issues and Policies' in *Asian Development Review*, 12/1, pp.68–89, and Cohen, Margot, 'Seed Money Poverty Scheme Fuels Both Enterprise and Red Tape' *Far Eastern Economic Review*, 9 February 1995, pp.24–6.
32. Booth, Anne (1995), 'Regional Disparities and Inter-Governmental Fiscal Relations in Indonesia', in: Ian G. Cook, Marcus A. Doel and Rex Li (ed.), *Fragmented Asia: Regional Integration and National Disintegration in Pacific Asia*, Aldershot: Avebury, pp.102–36.
33. See Rigg, Jonathan (1997), *South East Asia: The Human Landscape of Modernisation and Development*, London: Routledge, and Booth 1992b (note 26) p.340.
34. Koppel, Bruce (1997), 'Is Asia Emerging or Submerging?', *Nordic Newsletter of Asian Studies*, no. 4, December, pp.5–10.
35. See Bryant, Raymond L. and Parnwell, Michael J.G. (1996), 'Politics, Sustainable Development and Environmental Change in South-East Asia', in Raymond Bryant and Michael Parnwell (ed.) *Environmental Change in South East Asia: People, Politics and Sustainable Development*, London, Routledge, pp.1–20.

36. Arndt, H.W. (1987), *Economic Development: The History of an Idea,* Chicago, Chicago University Press, p.173.
37. Rodan, Garry (1989), *The Political Economy of Singapore's Industrialisation: National State and International Capital,* London, Macmillan, p.113
38. Chant, Sylvia and McIlwaine, Cathy (1995), 'Gender and Export Manufacturing in the Philippines: Continuity or Change in Female Employment? The Case of the Mactan Export Processing Zone', in *Gender, Place and Culture,* 2/2, pp.147–76.
39. For example see Kolko, Gabriel (1995), 'Vietnam Since 1975: Winning a War and Losing the Peace', in *Journal of Contemporary Asia,* 25/1, pp.3–49.
40. See Rigg, Jonathan (1988), 'Singapore and the Recession of 1985', *Asian Survey* 28/3, pp.340–52.
41. Schwarz (note 17).
42. Forbes, Dean (1993), 'What's in it For us? Images of Pacific Asian Development', in Chris Dixon and David Drakakis-Smith (edits.) *Economic and Social Development in Pacific Asia,* London, Routledge, p.60.
43. Tasker, Rodney and Handley, Paul (1993) 'Economic Hit List' in *Far Eastern Economic Review,* 5, pp.38-44.
44. Krugman, Paul (1994), 'The myth of Asia's miracle', in *Foreign Affairs* 73/6 pp. 62-78. Krugman's thesis has links with the earlier work of Kunio Yoshihara (1988), *The Rise of Ersatz Capitalism in South-East Asia,* Singapore: Oxford University Press, who suggests that South East Asia's development is based on 'technologyless' industrialisation. He uses the technical weakness of industrial capitalism in the region, and the absence of indigenous innovators, to suggest that growth will not be sustained. Like Krugman, he also highlights the inefficiencies in many industrial activities.
45. Hill, Hal (1996), *The Indonesian Economy Since 1966,* Cambridge, Cambridge University Press and World Bank.
46. See Auty, R.M. (1997) 'The East Asian Growth Model: South Korean Experience', in R.F. Watters and T.G. McGee (eds.) *Asia-Pacific: New Geographies of the Pacific Rim,* London, Hurst, pp.161–9.
47. Reflected, for example, in Linda Lim's claim, that Singapore's 'spectacular' success is 'the result more of the Long Arm of state intervention than it is of the Invisible Hand of the free market' would be rejected. Lim, Linda (1983), 'Singapore's Success: The Myth of the Free Market Economy', in *Asian Survey,* 23/6, pp.752–64.
48. Wade, Robert (1997), 'Effectiveness and Replicability of East Asian Industrial Policies', in R.F. Watters and T.G. McGee (eds.) *Asia-Pacific: New Geographies of the Pacific Rim,* London, Hurst, pp. 133-139 and the papers in the special issue of *World Development,* 22/4, (1994) including Amsden 1994, Lall 1994 and Perkins 1994.
49. Jenkins, Rhys (1991), 'Learning from the Gang: Are There Lessons for Latin America From East Asia', *Bulletin of Latin American Research* 10/1, pp.37–54.
50. Rodan (note 37), p.208, see also Harris, Nigel (1986), *The End of the Third World: Newly Industrialising Countries and the Decline of an Ideology,* Harmondsworth. Penguin.
51. See Wade (note 48).
52. Kim, Kyong-Dong (1994), 'Confucianism and Capitalist Development in East Asia', in Sklair (note 15), pp.87–106.
53. See Jenkins (note 49), p.39.
54. Ahuja *et al.* (note 21), p.48.
55. Ibid p.49.
56. As Paul Krugman emphasises, unlike currency crises in other countries, on the 'eve of crisis all of the governments [of countries affected by the crisis] were more or less in fiscal balance; nor were they engaged in irresponsible credit creation or runaway monetary expansion' (1998: 2). The roots of the crisis lay elsewhere.
57. Chanda, Nayan, 'Rebuilding Asia', *Far Eastern Economic Review,* 12 February 1998, pp. 46-50.
58. Ibid. pp. 46-7.
59. Ammar Siamwalla writes of the Thai experience: '...to say that the crisis had its origins in private borrowing is not to absolve the government from blame for the resulting problems'

Ammar Siamwalla (1997) 'Can a Developing Democracy Manage its Macroeconomy? The Case of Thailand', *TDRI Quarterly Review* 12/4, pp.3–10.

60. Ibid. p.9.
61. Ibid. p.4.
62. Koppel (note 34) p.5.
63. Jenkins, Rhys (1991), 'The Political Economy of Industrialisation: A Comparison of Latin American and East Asian Newly Industrialising Countries', in *Development and Change* 22, pp.197-231. Also Jenkins, 1991, p.37 (note 49).
64. Leftwich, Adrian (1995), 'Bringing Politics Back In: Towards a Model of the Developmental State', in *The Journal of Development Studies* 31/3, p.401.

Lessons to be Learned by the Mediterranean: Jordanian Development, the MENA Process, Water and Value Systems

JOHN ROBERTS

Image and Substance: Jordan and the Development Conundrum Confronting the EU's Arab Partner Countries

The image of a country carries a tremendous weight. The Asian Tigers have been identified as fast growing economies for more than two decades which should serve them well in the event of an economic downturn. For the EU's partner countries in the Mediterranean, however, images shaped by decades of low growth accompanied by impressions of national or regional instability make it much harder for both their governments and entrepreneurs to convince the outside world that they are indeed growing steadily and regularly.

It will not be easy to change such perceptions. There is a very real conflict which, in the case of some of the EU's Arab partner countries, touches on their very identity. At some point in the late 1970s or early 1980s, it became clear that the Communist states of Indochina were not in a position to push any further forward but were both politically and economically on the defensive. With the Malayan emergency over, and with the main islands of Indonesia stable following the failure of the 1965 Communist coup, there was no overwhelming external enemy or internal source of fundamental destabilisation to cause the kind of persistent instability that has characterised the Middle East as a result of Israel's emergence by force in 1948/9 and its post-1967 subjection of a major Arab community, the Palestinians.

Many of the Asian Tigers and their cubs–notably the original ASEAN countries: Singapore, Malaysia, Thailand, Indonesia and the Philippines – have thus been able to develop their economies in an atmosphere of regional

John Roberts is Senior Partner, Methinks Ltd, an Edinburgh-based consultancy specialising in the inter-relationship between energy and economic development. He is also co-editor of *Global Water Report*.

stability, although internal instability certainly delayed economic take-off in the Philippines.[1] For the last two decades, the political background to whatever economic miracle may have occurred in Asia has been one of overall regional stability, despite occasional bilateral friction between ASEAN member states. In contrast, even though the last full-scale Arab-Israeli war was in 1973, the Middle East has been the location of several major cross-border military operations.[2]

Jordan offers a good example of the problems of trying to secure sustainable economic development in such a hostile political climate. In the last several years the country has experienced a major economic turnaround. Since 1992, when the economy grew by a striking 16.1 per cent, GDP has routinely grown by an average of close to six per cent a year (Table 1).

This makes Jordan one of the few countries to conform with the principle enunciated in 1995 by Caio Koch-Weser, the World Bank's Vice President for the Middle East and North Africa, that sustainable economic development required real economic growth of some three per cent above population growth.[3]

TABLE 1
JORDAN: ECONOMIC GROWTH & POPULATION

	Economic Growth		Population Growth	
	('000)	(%)	('000)	(%)
1990	1.0	n/a	3.468	4.260
1991	1.8	n/a	3.701	4.440
1992	16.8	16.1	3.844	4.670
1993	5.8	5.6	3.993	4.940
1994	5.8	8.1	4.139	5.200
1995	6.2	6.9	4.291	5.440
1996	n/a	5.2	4.441	c.5.700*

* Author's extrapolation
World Bank, cited by *Business and Investment in Jordan* (1996)
Central Bank of Jordan (market prices).

In the last decade, Jordan has pursued a path of sustained economic reform, characterised by such actions as:

- the 1989 structural adjustment programme effectively imposed on the Kingdom by the IMF, the World Bank and Jordan's principal development partners,
- the government's revenue enhancement programme introduced in 1993,
- the trade liberalisation programme epitomised by moves to accede to GATT and to become a member of the WTO, and
- the 1995 Investment Law.

Yet Jordan is still walking a knife-edge. In practice, its prospects are still viewed in an essentially political light, so that its economic development currently remains hostage to politics and international relations and, in particular, to the future of whatever peace process may still be said to exist between Israel and the Palestinians. Furthermore, perhaps the most important determinant of all, concerning external perceptions of its ability to gain recognition as a successful developing economy, is its 1994 peace treaty with Israel.

Ironically, the initial spurt of economic growth in 1992 was essentially political in origin since much of the increase in GDP that year is directly attributable to the influx of some 350,000 Jordanian passport-holders (usually a euphemism for Palestinians) evicted from Kuwait and the Gulf states in 1990 and 1991 as a result of Gulf Arab perceptions that the Jordanian government favoured Iraq in the Kuwait crisis. Since they were able to bring all or most of their savings with them, and since they were homeless in a world which does not look kindly on Palestinian refugees, it was natural for them to invest in Jordanian real estate. This triggered the original 1992 boom, and it is on the back of that boom that the Jordanian government has been able to introduce the bulk of its economic liberalisation programme.

But perceptions that Jordan's future will essentially be determined by political events beyond its control make it quite possible that even if the Kingdom is able to secure economic growth of around six per cent per year for some years to come, it may still not be generally viewed as a successfully developing economy in its own right. The intimate nature of Jordan's relationship with the Israeli-Palestinian issue (since more than half of all the estimated 5.7 m people living in Jordan are of Palestinian identity or origin) will continue to cloud external commercial perceptions.

Jordan is, admittedly, an extreme example of the way in which a country's development can be retarded by impressions of national or regional instability. But it is impressions which count. There is still an impression that the Middle East – however broadly or narrowly it is defined – remains unstable and, perhaps, that it is chronically and unchangeably unstable.[4] If the EU's partner countries are to convince the rest of the world that they are not subject either to national or regional instability then they will have to divorce themselves from such terms as 'the Middle East.'

To a certain extent this is already happening. Despite a range of alternative ideological options – Pan-Arab nationalism, Maghrib or Mashrik unity, socialism and even Islamism–the most potent driving force is still nationalism, and often a somewhat old-fashioned form of nationalism. Even the Islamist movements have quite distinct national characteristics, so that there is no uniform manner of analysing them, although this does not, of course, stop their critics from lumping them all together. A policy which bluntly stresses the need to put the nation's individual interests before those of any group to which it may belong seems no more than a restatement of the basic rationale driving most governments. The point here is that for the EU's partner states, they have to speak twice as loudly to silence the echoes of past generations used to hearing the clamour of war and unrest.

In particular – and however immoral or amoral this may seem–it implies keeping a distance from the Arab-Israeli conflict, and this is a very difficult issue to face. For decades many Arab governments have virtually based their popular legitimacy as much (or more) on their opposition to Israel as on the benefits they have brought to their own peoples. For many of those leaders old enough to remember the actual creation of the Jewish state in a land which at that time still possessed an Arab majority, the issue is personal. Of current non-combatants (amongst the EU partner countries), this applies in particular to King Hussein of Jordan and King Hassan of Morocco; the former because of the origins of his own state and its people, as well as because of his personal connections with Jerusalem, and the latter in his capacity as a chairman of the Jerusalem Committee. The importance of Jerusalem in the Arab-Israeli context does not need restating, though the Islamic context of the two monarchs' descent from the Prophet should also be noted.

In this political, economic and indeed moral dilemma, the conundrum facing governments in Arab EU partner countries is how they can portray their own countries as stable, safe places for investment, whilst remaining involved in one of the world's most intractable problems. The best example to follow may be that of Egypt, on the grounds that Egyptian economic development in recent years has gone hand-in-hand with its perceived role as a moderating force in the peace process. Yet at the same time it is far from clear that even the US economic love-affair with Egypt (still the second biggest recipient of US aid funds) could hope to survive a complete collapse in the peace process even if there was a general consensus (outside the US) that the collapse was essentially due to Israeli intransigence. In the case of a clear breakdown in the Palestinian-Israeli peace process – and, as of mid-1998 it would appear that there is no real prospect of peace so long as the Netanyahu government rules Israel – the prospects for Egypt's recovery (let alone Jordan's) are questionable.

What aids the Arab partner countries in this respect is, paradoxically, their very lack of considerable institutionalised inter-Arab trade. Economically, the EU's Arab partner countries gain politically from the way in which their trade is essentially focused towards non-Arab external trading partners, notably the EU itself. Pending the clear end to the Arab-Israeli conflict, the partner countries could make a positive virtue of their bilateral trading patterns and their isolation from each other. If Arab partner countries are to succeed in securing sustained economic growth in a climate which is heavily dependent on investment from the industrialised world (and in the anticipated continued dearth of substantial aid from the former surplus nations of the Gulf), they will have to do so by marketing themselves individually, and not as a group.

In a world which regards external investment as one of the key motors for sustainable development, much depends on just how much they can convince prospective investors that they are stable internally, can also play a constructive role in overall Arab-Israeli peace efforts and are not vulnerable to either domestic or international fallout from the conflict. Morocco and Tunisia have to divorce themselves from Algeria, less they be considered vulnerable to the kind of Islamist pressures in Algeria that so frighten western onlookers, particularly those in industry (energy excepted). The same applies to relations with Libya. These have to be handled discreetly, even though Libya does play an important role in economic relations between regional Arab states as an employer of hundreds of thousands of workers from Egypt and Tunisia. This may be grossly unfair on Algeria, but it is potentially a life-and-death matter for its immediate neighbours.

The MENA Process and Arab Reactions

In this context it is worth considering the role of the Middle East and North Africa summits and conferences. The first summit, at Casablanca in 1994, spelled out the message that the road to sustainable development in the Middle East would be based on investment, not aid. At the end of the conference, when one local journalist asked the organisers whether there would be '..a new Marshall Plan' to pay for the grandiose projects outlined, one of the organisers, Leslie Gelb of the US Council on Foreign Relations, replied: 'You don't understand; this is the new Marshall Plan'.[5]

Gelb was right, many of those present did not understand. In Casablanca, more than $30bn worth of potential projects were put on display, but while they routinely carried price-tags, only a few came with prepared payment mechanisms – and those tended to be extensions of existing aid-funded schemes. Morocco clearly (and sensibly) used Casablanca as a showcase for its own commercial and economic prospects, as Jordan was to do at the Amman summit in 1995 and Egypt at the Cairo conference in 1996. But in Casablanca the focus was essentially on regional, cooperative projects. In Amman, the Jordanians placed a much greater emphasis on their own projects, but framed most of them in a regional context. In Cairo (where the event was downgraded from a summit to a conference in the wake of cool Israeli-Egyptian relations following Netanyahu's electoral victory in Israel), the Egyptians blatantly sought to ensure that the overwhelming focus of the conference was the prospect of doing business in Egypt, regardless of whether there would be peace between Israel and the Palestinians.

Given the uncertain state of the peace process, this was a healthy development. It showed that the MENA conference process was taking on a life of its own. However, the decision of a number of Arab states to suspend or reduce their involvement in the MENA process, epitomised by Rabat's move to terminate the Morocco-based secretariat, was MENA's death-knell. The fourth, and final, MENA summit was held in the Qatari capital of Doha in November 1997. From a strictly Qatari perspective, it was a great success, enabling the emirate to show off its emergence as one of the world's great gas producers to a much wider range of foreign entrepreneurs than would normally visit the country. But in terms of its role as a major economic component of the peace process, MENA IV was a decided failure; not only was it attended by a mere seven Arab countries, with the rest actively boycotting or displaying a profound lack of interest, but its most controversial participant, Israeli Trade Minister Natan Sharansky, knew (or cared) so little about MENA's origins that he sought to challenge the inclusion in the final declaration of any reference to such key principles of Middle East peacemaking as reaffirmation of UN Security Council Resolutions 242 and 338 and the exchange of land for peace.[6]

The collapse of the MENA process[7] will not necessarily reverse perceptions of Morocco, Jordan, Egypt and Qatar gained by entrepreneurs who attended the first three gatherings. However, it will prevent other countries from gaining in a like manner, notably Tunisia, which was favoured to be the venue for the fifth MENA Summit. While it is not yet possible to really assess how effective these jamborees have been in terms of promoting regional economic development, they did at least succeed in bringing well over a thousand international businessmen to the region, including CEOs from some of the world's largest companies. This gave the host countries a chance to convince an essentially commercial audience of their commitment to economic liberalisation and the achievement of sustained economic development on essentially market lines.

A bitter irony of the MENA process is that it was not so much destroyed by Arab concern about Israel as by inter-Arab bickering. Qatar, for example, had ceded to Cairo the right to host the third MENA summit, which behoved Egypt to support Doha for the fourth. Egypt, awakening somewhat late to the possibilities offered by MENA, completely failed to understand this and poured scorn on the fourth MENA gathering, arguing that the peace process with Israel was so poorly there was no point in participating in an economic conference designed *inter alia* to bolster Arab-Israeli commercial connections.

It would have been better, by far, had Egypt and the 14 other Arab states which boycotted MENA IV in Doha remembered the precedent set by MENA III (in Cairo in 1996) when Arab participants quite capably used the process to further their own development whilst pointedly ignoring Israel. In Cairo, the Israeli ministerial team, accompanied by many of the substantial Israeli commercial team, returned home barely half-way through the conference when they found that relatively few Arab entrepreneurs and merchants actually wanted to do much business with them. Far from disrupting a conference which was, after all, an offshoot of US efforts to promote Arab-Israeli peace, it positively contributed to a feeling of relaxation amongst Arab delegations. Moreover, there was no sign of US or European businessmen leaving as a result of the decision of Israeli Deputy Prime Minister David Levy's decision to quit the conference early.

The MENA failure, and its origins in inter-Arab wrangling and negativism, demonstrates that the EU's Arab partner states have to work doubly hard to show that their political as well as their economic programmes are based on positive, rather than negative, principles. The Arab frontline states – including Syria and Lebanon – generally do try to adopt such an approach to the role in the Arab-Israeli dispute but they are still haunted by the three 'Noes' of the Khartoum declaration of September 1967 – no direct negotiations with Israel, no recognition of Israel and no peace treaty with Israel. If sustainable economic development is their priority (and it should be noted that political imperatives often outweigh economic aspirations) then they will need to work with rather than against the grain of those industrial powers most engaged in the Middle East peace process.

Hurdling the Price Barrier: Jordan's Water Reforms

In one area, water, Jordan is testing to the limit the issue of whether a thoroughly commercial pricing system – albeit one with protection for the poorer and thrifty can replace a regional norm: the provision of a highly subsidised, and usually highly inefficient, basic service.

The need for substantial investment in fresh utilities infrastructure is prompting the steady privatisation of utilities in most partner countries. In theory, since utilities come with a revenue stream from customers, funding for fresh investment should be available to either public or private utility operators, since they can either use the revenue stream itself for investment or as collateral for loans. In practice, however, the issue of investment requires that utilities be run on a largely – though not necessarily wholly commercial basis – and this favours private companies for various reasons. One is that they are more familiar with commercial operations; another concerns the problem of raising prices following years of subsidised supply.

Even though it should logically make no difference whether it is a private or state company which raises prices sufficiently place the utility's operations on a sound financial basis, in practice it makes a lot of difference indeed. A public utility, is, after all, a state concern and thus it is the state which would be the direct target of any unrest which might accompany substantial price increases. If a private company is held responsible for the price increases then anger may be diffused, being partly directed at the private company running the utility and partly at the state authorities. The level of anger may also be reduced on the basis that popular expectations of the behaviour of private companies are commonly different from views of public corporate behaviour.

In 1997 Jordan announced it was completely overhauling both the management and structure of the utility providing water for Amman and its suburbs which serves roughly one-third of the country's population. As of mid-1998, Jordan was about to award a leading French company a four-year management contract to run Amman's water services. But in order to ensure that the successful bidder was able to operate on a basis which would allow for much needed investment, the Jordan Water Authority (JWA) began by overhauling the pricing structure. Moreover, just to make sure that everyone got the idea that the government was in earnest, Water Minister Munther Haddaddin demonstrated his commitment to these reforms in October and November 1997 by physically cutting off the water supplies to such notorious bad payers as the Ministry of Justice, the municipality headquarters and even the army barracks at Zarqa. They paid up.

The radical new pricing structure introduced in October 1997 was aimed at ensuring that consumer payments covered 125 per cent of operation and maintenance costs and would thus generate a surplus to be used for much needed capital improvements. The first of the new bills, which raised the price of water to JD0.85 ($1.20) for every cubic metre of water used by households which failed to limit their consumption to just 48 cubic metres a quarter, went out at the start of 1998. Jordanian officials acknowledged there were problems in securing full payment of the new charges with one official commenting: 'They pay, but really there is some trouble. They complain that the price is very high.'[8]

Some customers responded by simply cutting consumption to less than 48 cubic metres of water per quarter, thus entitling them to a much lower tariff of just JD0.15 (about 21.5 US cents). The JWA considers this a quite acceptable response, with one official saying: 'We didn't increase prices just because of finance, but to control demand.'

Under the old system, consumers were charged on a sliding scale in which low initial prices intended to ensure affordable water for the poorest ensured subsidised water for everybody. But the new system allows only those households which restrict their water consumption to 48 cubic metres a quarter to receive their water at the lowest rate. Those who use even a drop more (and the water supplies are all metered) will have to pay the higher rate for every cubic metre of water used, whether it is 49 or 149.

The JWA has calculated that if consumption patterns remain essentially unchanged, then as much as 73 per cent of all consumers could fall into the lowest price category, contributing some 36 per cent of all revenue under the new system. Jordanian economist Fahed al-Fanek has estimated that those restricting their use to the minimum will pay much the same as they do at present. 'There's no real change, if anything it's a little down.'[9]

The increased income is sorely needed, with Haddaddin saying that 'if the Water Department was a company, then, under our Companies' Law, it would have to file and announce bankruptcy'. The JWA needs to overhaul its finances if it is to embark on its planned extensive renovation of Amman's overstretched infrastructure. Leakage rates in the Jordanian capital are thought to have reached 50 per cent, which means that the municipality was only selling half of the water it was actually pumping into the system in 1997. Reducing such leakage rates is vital since Jordan is already operating at close to subsistence level in terms of its ability to harness a strictly limited resource to serve the needs of its rapidly growing population. The Ministry of Water and Irrigation has estimated that Jordan needs to spend some $5bn on water projects over the 14-year period 1997-2011. This amounts to roughly $350m a year, a large sum, though not an impossible one, for a small country with a GDP of around $8bn a year.

The subsidy/cash shortage problems which the JWA is seeking to confront in Amman are found in many other parts of the Middle East and North Africa. The World Bank – which considers the MENA region to extend from Iran and the Gulf to Morocco and Mauritania – estimates that spending on water collection, treatment and delivery is costing the region some $12.5bn a year. Much of this is attributable to the heavily subsidised provision of desalinated water in the Gulf states.[10] But the rest of the Islamic world also contributes its share to this enormous subsidy. The gap between actual costs and revenues is shown in Table 2.

The charges recorded in the table are comparable with prices paid by such countries as Indonesia and the Philippines a decade ago. Yet today both Jakarta and Manila are implementing contracts which essentially require the private sector operators to fund investment in the system directly from revenues and also to cover the running costs and profit margins from those revenues. In the case of Jakarta, average charges will be around 66 cents per

TABLE 2
WATER SUBSIDIES IN SELECTED MENA COUNTRIES

	Cost to supplier (Long-run marginal cost) (US $)	Cost to consumer (Average charges) (US $)
Algeria		
- Urban	0.52	0.12
- Rural	0.32	0.02
Wastewater Treatment		
Egypt		
- Urban	0.25	0.03
- Rural	0.03	>0.03
Wastewater Treatment		
Morocco		
- Urban	c0.50	c0.30
- Rural	c0.45	c0.4
- Wastewater Treatment	0.12	
Jordan		
- Urban	1.10	c75
- Rural	c0.23	
0.03		
- Wastewater Treatment	0.37	

Sources: A Strategy for Managing Water in the Middle East and North Africa, World Bank, 1994.
Middle East and North Africa Environmental Strategy, World Bank, 1995.

cubic metre.[11] Morocco has taken a similar decision, with the award of the Casablanca water supply management contract to Lyonnaise des Eaux, although this raised concerns when it was feared that prices would rise by some 30 per cent as a result of private sector management. If this was to occur it would take charges to around 40 cents per cubic metre for a capital city (and its environs) of a country with a per capita GDP of around $1,300. By comparison, residents of the Indonesian capital of Jakarta (and its environs) will be paying a rate which is at least 50 per cent more than this, yet the country's per capita GDP is much the same as Morocco's.[12]

There is a natural humanitarian concern that the populations of poor countries, or poor communities in countries making progress in economic development, cannot afford to pay for basic commodities. UN agencies argue that one unintended consequence of inefficient and heavily subsidised systems is that it is very often the poorest people who have to pay the highest cost for their water when public utilities operate an essentially subsidised system.

To date, the poor have commonly fared worst in countries where high subsidies have reduced efficiency (and availability) of actual delivery. High leakage rates have contibuted to vast wastage, with as much as 50 per cent of water supplies recorded as entering some systems in the MENA region having no identifiable end-user. With governments running low on cash for fresh investment, it is routinely the poorest sections of sprawling cities which are connected to municipal supplies. Residents of these districts, whether villages or suburbs, may thus find that in order to secure a basic volume of water for personal use (most will have some access to public supplies) they will have to top up their regular supply with purchases from street vendors or in bottled form (when water commonly costs as much as gasoline, if not more). According to one study by the UN Economic and Social Commission for Asia and the Pacific: 'Experience in the region, as in the case of the UNICEF-assisted project in the slum of Begbari in Dhaka, Bangladesh, shows that the urban poor can and do pay for safe water and usually at a rate ten times higher' than that paid by better off residents in receipt of subsidised water from public utilities.[13] A similar report could be made on many villages in the West Bank of Palestine.

It should be noted that there is an upper limit to the cost of water, which is the cost of desalinating water and its distribution to the consumer. For coastal communities, the limit is defined by Malta, which relies on desalinated water to meet 70 per cent of its supply, and which charges an average of $1.70 per cubic metre in order to ensure that fresh investment for water projects is covered by actual revenues.

Costs for countries with populations living farther from the sea would, of course, be higher because of increased distribution costs. By comparison, Malta's per capita income is currently around $7,000, although it began its policy of providing desalinated water on a commercial basis more than ten years ago, when per capita income was around $5,000.

Singapore, which relies for more than half its total water consumption on supplies imported from Malaysia and Indonesia, currently charges rates close to actual desalination costs for the bulk of its water supplies. In 1993, delivery costs for more than 40 cubic metres per month amounted to $1.17 per cubic metre; with basic charges levied at a lower rate of $0.56 for the first 20 cubic metres and $0.80 for the next 20. Shipping charges were set as high as $2.07 per cubic metre.

The generally higher level of prices which consumers in Asian countries of comparable per capita GDP to the EU's Arab partner countries are prepared to pay would appear to indicate that price liberalisation is necessary to remove the burden of developing this important sector of public infrastructure from the public purse. However, what is worrying about the Middle East (and the same may also obtain in the Far East) is the lack of debate on the subject in terms of consciousness ranging amongst the general population. In Jordan, which faces one of the most extreme contrasts between the charges currently levied for water use and the replacement cost of water which is actually supplied, the government has an ingrained fear of the consequences of each and every price rise that effects a basic commodity, whether it be bread, fuel or water.[14] Thus it is not prepared to debate the issue in advance in order to reduce the impact of subsequent opposition.

It is one thing to pursue a policy of conscious subsidies for the poor or disadvantaged: it is quite another to subsidise those who do not need any subsidy since they are already engaged in fully commercial activities. The provision of subsidised utilities, such as power, telecommunications and water, to entrepreneurs in the tourist industry constitutes a hidden subsidy of this kind when the ultimate consumer, the tourist, can well afford to pay the full commercial cost.

Whether or not governments are already pursuing a policy of eliminating such hidden subsidies, proof of the successful development of commercial utilities for the tourist sector can be found in a number of locations. Backup generators, which in practice may have to be used virtually round the clock, are a routine feature of hotels in countries where blackouts and brownouts are common, but commercial water and telecoms services also play their part. Mobile phone systems have enabled some hotels in the FSU and elsewhere to bypass the state telecoms system, with charges passed on to the guest. In Egypt, the hotels at Sharm el-Sheikh, a rapidly developing tourist destination, secure their water from a commercially-run desalination plant.

The need to provide such services on a commercial basis is the key issue at stake: whether these can most efficiently be provided by the public or private sector is quite another matter.

Value Systems in the Middle East and Elsewhere

What kind of value system must a society have if it is to progress? The argument that the Asian Tigers have succeeded because of their adherence to an essentially Confucian value system may indeed prove that such values are – or can be made – conducive to development. But while one could argue that Germany's post war economic miracle might in part be due to a value system embracing at least some Confucian ideals – defined by Rigg as respect for elders and the law; hard work; and recognition that the interests of society may transcend those of the individual[15] – can one as easily apply such a judgment to Europe's more modern Tigers, such as Finland and the Irish Republic?

Indeed, judging by the US and the current UK bid for sustained growth on a free market basis, corner-cutting rather than respect for rules and regulations, shedding of experienced but high paid labour for cheaper younger labour and rampant individualism rather than respect for the interests of society (who was it who said 'there's no such thing as society'?) would seem to be the order of the day as these established industrial societies seek to compete with the Asian Tigers.

Rigg asks the question of whether the Asian states can described as homogeneously Confucian anyway, when clearly they are not. One concern amongst Japanese educationalists is that their students are still being taught by rote rather than being taught how to think for themselves, but were Japanese educational practices to change dramatically would this herald a downturn or a recovery in its work ethic and work performance?

Societies can and do change their views and their values. And the more open they are to diverse internal and external influences the more likely they are to change, by and large, their own value systems and even their way of life. How much has the Asian miracle been prompted, and how much changed by aspirations to live life in the McDonald's era? Moreover, it is worth remembering that whilst 'McJobs' can be considered a term of opprobrium in industrialised nations, in developing societies they may be highly prized. In addition, cheap exploitative jobs, whether in East Asia, Western Europe, North America or the Middle East, scarcely sit comfortably with either Confucian, Islamic or Western/Christian ideals of respect.

As elsewhere, Middle East and North African societies are in a state of flux. For some women, Islam can actually be a form of emancipation; for others it means repression and oppression and often hampers their participation in the workforce. The same might be expected in Malaysia or Indonesia, and yet such trades as garment making and computer assembly are, in these countries, carried out by women effectively integrated into the workforce.[16]

This is not to decry social or motivational factors, merely to serve as a reminder that social values and stresses may vary not only between societies but within societies. Whilst some workers produce their best under pressure, others produce their best when stress is reduced to a minimum. Hard work and an emphasis on savings/investment makes sense in any economy, but it seems useful to remember that it also makes sense to work with society, rather than against it, and that means respect by external investors for the society in which they seek to invest.

For the largely Islamic societies which comprise the bulk of the EU's partner countries, the obvious models to follow would appear to be those of Malaysia and Indonesia. Malaysia – admittedly blessed by one of the world's greatest balances of mineral and agricultural wealth in still relatively under-populated terrain – appears to have overcome what is perhaps Islam's greatest flaw when it comes to issues of economic development: its essentially fatalistic attitude of what will be, will be regardless.

Yet even here there are elements with which society can be motivated. If Calvinist faith in predestination can be transformed into the Protestant work ethic (as Weber suggests) then perhaps what is needed is a Islamic Weber, or better still, a Tawney for the EU's Arab partners. In similar manner one can ask whether systems of economic liberalism should use *laissez-faire* ideals to impress on both entrepreneurs and workforces in the EU partner countries the advantages of market-led development.

In the end, what is required is the right language in which to address the existing concerns of a society, so that practical examples of what works in one country or society can be adapted for use by another. Societies do have value systems, but societies also learn from each other. What matters for the EU's partner countries in the Mediterranean is that they are addressed in a language which they understand. It is translating values and value systems which is important, and not any putative stress which may be placed on the (allegedly) unique nature of any one society's breakthrough to long-term economic development.

NOTES

1. It is also perhaps worth pondering the irony that the US military presence in the region did much to boost the economies of two of the ASEAN states – Thailand and Singapore – in the early stages of their respective economic success stories. Whether it performed the same function in the Philippines is more debatable. The parallels with the Middle East are uncomfortable. Israel clearly benefited from the massive $3–4 billion a year programmes of the last two decades. Egypt has also gained, though to a much lesser extent and with much less freedom to use US aid as it saw fit, whilst the impact of foreign aid in Turkey, the region's third biggest recipient of US assistance, was far outweighed by the internal economic reform forced upon the country by the oil price crises of 1973/4 and 1978/9 and by the IMF.
2. For example: Israel's invasions of Lebanon in 1978 and 1982, and its still-continuing de facto occupation of parts of South Lebanon as part of its unilaterally-proclaimed security zone; the Israeli occupation of the West Bank and Gaza since 1967, which prompted the Palestinian Intifada of 1987-93; Morocco's war in the Western Sahara; the proximity of many EU partners to Iraq and their involvement in military actions concerning Iraq (including the participation of Egypt and Syria in the Second Gulf War in 1990-91); Turkey's repeated cross-border operations in northern Iraq; and the current civil war in Algeria.
3. Briefing at MENA Summit, Amman, November 1995.
4. Samuel Huntingdon's *The Clash of Civilisations* makes much of the instability of Islamic societies in the Middle East; yet his argument that Islamic societies will come into conflict with western societies does not appear to be taken as a sign of incipient instability in those western societies
5. Author's notes from MENA Summit, (I) Casablanca, 1994.
6. Author's notes from talks with diplomats at MENA Summit (IV) in Doha, 1997.
7. The principal organisers of MENA – the World Economic Forum – announced after Doha that they would not be organising any further MENA gatherings for the time being.
8. For a fuller account of the introduction of Jordan's new water laws see the Financial Times' *Global Water Report*, Issue 35, 20 December 1997 and Issue 44, 2 April 1998. The articles

on Jordan were based on interviews conducted by the author with Jordanian officials.

9. From interview with author. See FT *Global Water Report*, Issue 35, 20 November 1997.

10. Charges for desalinated water in Saudi Arabia are commonly as low as 5 cents per cubic metre, yet the actual production cost exceeds one dollar, and may well exceed two dollars.

11. The downfall of the Suharto government in Indonesia in May 1998 prompted the authorities to take a fresh look at the water management contract. However, while the situation remains unclear at time of writing in June 1998, it appears the main focus is on the removal of any Suharto family members from involvement in the project rather than a fundamental reworking of the management contract itself.

12. Indonesia's GDP in 1996 was $221.9 billion and its population was 196.7 million giving it a per capita GDP of $1,128; in 1995, Morocco's GDP was $31.45 billion and its population was 27.62 million, making per capita GDP $1,138.

13. United Nations, Economic and Social Commission for Asia and the Pacific, 1996.

14. During a discussion on the 1995 bread riots in the Jordanian town of Kerak, the senior civil servant responsible for water management and pricing (a market-oriented technocrat) asserted that there had indeed been dialogue on the news of bread price increases which had triggered the unrest. The Prime Minister had gone to parliament to announce the government's plans, which would be put into effect at the end of the debate, and had then debated the issue for three hours in parliament, as well as making a major public announcement explaining the logic behind the price increases. This is what is held to constitute debate in much of the region. The official flatly rejected any suggestion that Jordan's policy of moving towards the full commercialisation of water prices for customers in the Greater Amman region should be considered a subject for legitimate and general public discussion in order to prepare the population for what might otherwise prove – should it be implemented – a traumatic event (author's notes of December 1996 from discussions with the official concerned).

15. Rigg, Jonathan, 'The lessons of Southeast Asia's miraculous growth and fall from growth'; paper presented to Workshop IV of 'Europe and North Africa: Seeking an Economic Road to Security', RIIA, July 1997, and included in this journal.

16. The Indonesian factories in the free zone on Batam island are a case in point, though whether the girls working at the plants there are integrated into any kind of general society during their working stints of two years or so (when they live in dormitory accommodation) is quite another matter.

Security Implications of the EMPI
for Europe

CLAIRE SPENCER

The EU and Security

It is the main contention of this paper that the EU still has a long way to go to address both the external and internal implications of the type of co-ordination required for the EMPI to succeed. One of the premises for this assertion is that the EU is still less than comfortable with tackling military issues already addressed elsewhere. In fact, the channels for implementing policies which reflect the kind of connections envisaged by the global approach of the EMPI are still not in place, for a number of reasons pertinent to the current project.

Firstly, although most of the framers and signatories of the Barcelona Declaration are in agreement over tackling the causes as well as effects of instability in the region, both current and projected, the way security policies continue to be formed on both shores of the Mediterranean have lagged behind the need to prioritise non-military aspects of security. Since security questions have arguably motivated much of the common purposes underlying the European Union's conception and design of the EMPI, one might expect most of the work of inter-linking these issues to have taken place on the European side.

It remains, the case, however, that in European foreign ministries, security questions tend to be dealt with apart from questions of economic and commercial interest and overseas development. Within the British Foreign and Commonwealth Office, for example, the division of labour between the Policy Planning Staff and the Security Department reflects only a shallow interaction between security policy – conceived primarily in terms of policy coordination with Western security institutions such as the North Atlantic Treaty Organisation (NATO) and the Western European Union (WEU) – and broader commercial and development policy, also dealt

Dr Claire Spencer is Deputy Director of the Centre for Defence Studies, King's College, University of London.

with by the newly renamed Department for International Development (DfID) and the Department of Trade and Industry (DTI).

Secondly, for the purposes of policy-making, security is at one and the same time extremely broadly and narrowly defined, if indeed it is defined at all. With the exception of calculating military force strengths and the proliferation of arms, there are few equivalents in the security field for measurements of the growing distance between GDP per capita, unemployment rates and levels of demographic growth on either shore of the Mediterranean, however imprecise these may be. Security thrives, in fact, on imprecision and future scenarios, the prevention or containment of which constitute the most complex equations of 'high-state' policy-making. At best, the management of security issues in their broadest sense constitutes the essence of good diplomacy; at worst, their mismanagement gives rise to all-but imagined demons, whose ferocity is accentuated by their level of abstraction and hence inherent unmanageability.

Recent examples of this include debates about the security consequences of civilisations destined to clash with one another, or of the destabilising effects of much Islamic expression, both of which detain academics engaged in polemics more than policy-makers of a more pragmatic turn of mind. The influence of these debates nevertheless lurks behind much of European policy-making towards the Muslim world, and is not entirely absent from the security provisions of the EMPI.

Thirdly, and despite the motivating force of security concerns behind the EMPI, in the overall concerns of European security in general the Mediterranean is not a priority. Any perusal of the detail of mainstream European security discussions over last few years will demonstrate infrequent references to the Mediterranean, often included as an afterthought. The mainstream agenda of European security continues to be largely with the management of Russia in the post-Cold War period and with institutional arrangements to integrate or cooperate with the EU's neighbours in eastern and central Europe over security issues. Initiatives in this respect have included extending invitations to new members, such as Poland, Hungary and the Czech Republic at the NATO summit of July 1997, or through closer operational cooperation, as in NATO's Partnership for Peace (PfP) initiative launched in January 1994.

Of almost equal importance have been debates about the role, functions and inter-relationship of the main Western security institutions and their adaptation to new challenges. This has included defining the so-called Petersberg tasks of the Western European Union (WEU) in the sphere of peace-keeping and humanitarian intervention, as well as adaptations in command structures, such as NATO's Combined Joint Task Force (CJTF) concept. Except in disputes over commands themselves – most notably between France and the US over the control of NATO's southern command, AFSOUTH, the Mediterranean has barely featured in these discussions at all. This is not least because until the mid-1990s there was little pressure from within Europe to create a balance between the so-called 'east-west' focus of European security and its more neglected 'north-south' dimension.

The activity of the main security institutions to rectify this imbalance has reflected a reticence to commit resources or engage too closely in what is still considered in NATO terms as 'out-of-area' for the purposes of European defence. The launching of exploratory and explanatory dialogues - such as the WEU's bilateral dialogue with Morocco, Algeria, Tunisia, and later Israel and Egypt from 1992 and NATO's similar exercise from 1995 with Morocco, Tunisia, Israel, Mauritania and Egypt, followed by Jordan – has sought to reassure Europe's southern neighbours of the benign intent of developments in Western security arrangements, even where these institutions are still planning for the defence of Europe from attacks which might arise in the Mediterranean.

Most analysts agree that the Mediterranean does not present Europe with major military threats.[1] The collapse of the Soviet Union, and the replacement of its global military scope by the more regionalised reach of Russia in its 'near abroad', has in fact de-emphasised the strategic importance of the Mediterranean. Military activity nevertheless remains a concern in the eastern Mediterranean, particularly in the recurrent tensions between Greece and Turkey, in the recent outbreaks of violence in Cyprus and in the regional manifestations of the chequered Middle East peace process.

The proliferation of weapons of mass destruction in the region is also a preoccupation, but their use against Europe is a matter of debate among analysts.[2] In general, the most frequently cited risks and challenges in the Mediterranean are non-military in nature, arising from increasing development gaps between southern Europe and northern Africa, and the volatility of states and societies yet to achieve the social and political balance of European democracies. In other words, conflicts and violence in the Mediterranean are perceived to arise as much from economic deprivation and socio-political inequalities as from arms build-ups or conventional intra-state tensions. For Europe itself, the main fears derive from the potential overspill effects of domestic as much as regional conflicts, the dangers most frequently cited being uncontrolled flows of migrants northwards, an export of terrorism (such as the bomb attacks in France in 1995 and 1996 linked to the Algerian conflict) and the contaminatory effects of Islamism on migrant populations resident within Europe or on inflaming inter-racial tensions (as in Germany and France).

None of these fears have directly measurable or quantifiable causes and effects. The most Europe can aspire to do is to alleviate the worst perceived privations of its Mediterranean Partners, not least through encouraging regional governments to engage in economic reform and development, assisted by foreign direct investment. There has also been pressure to explore ways of increasing trans-Mediterranean cooperation over shared threats or challenges, particularly where, as in the case of illegal migration, these are of a human and social rather than military character. Given that the defence and military alliances of the West are not the best equipped to deal with this type of issue, from the mid-1990s the EU has assumed a more proactive role in evolving a new Mediterranean security agenda.

The EMPI – What is on the Security Agenda?

The aspirations of the EMPI in the security field are perhaps best addressed through an examination of the Barcelona Declaration and the follow-up conclusions of the Malta Summit in April 1997. Since less than two years have separated the two inter-governmental conferences, the first thing to observe is that the ambitions of the Barcelona Declaration have been little modified by the Malta Summit.

There is, however, one key distinction in the context of the two meetings, which is that the Barcelona Conference of November 1995 took place prior to the revision of the Maastricht Treaty's defence and security provisions during the 1996-97 Inter-Governmental Conference (IGC), and fully within the expectation that advances would be made in defining the EU's competencies as regards evolving a European Common Foreign and Security Policy (CFSP). The fact that little progress was in fact made in this sphere – as will be discussed below – has compounded the difficulties of implementing and expanding upon the objectives of the EMPI. In some respects, the Barcelona process might be considered a pre-emptive expression of the CFSP, left, two years on, as an instrument without much effective muscle in the security sphere.

In the preamble of the Barcelona Declaration, the signatory parties stressed that 'the Euro-Mediterranean initiative is not intended to replace the other activities and initiatives undertaken in the interests of the peace, stability and development of the region', but rather 'to contribute to their success'.[3] Against this background, the Chapter on Political and Security Cooperation reiterates in its opening declaration of principles the signatory parties' support for a number of existing international instruments, such as the United Nations Charter and the Universal Declaration of Human Rights, as well as established international principles, such as the peaceful settlement of conflicts, the equal rights of peoples and their right to self-determination. More detailed provisions seek to strengthen the cooperative actions of all parties in preventing and combatting terrorism, drugs and organised crime, as well as promoting measures to limit the regional proliferation of arms of mass destruction and limit the size of regional armies to what is required for 'legitimate defence requirements'.[4]

In addition to promoting regional security through the adherence to and compliance with existing non-proliferation and arms control regimes, such as the Non-Proliferation Treaty (NPT) or the chemical and biological conventions, the crowning aspiration of the Chapter is 'to consider any confidence and security-building measures' that could lead to the creation of 'an area of peace and stability in the Mediterranean' including 'the long-term possibility of establishing a Euro-Mediterranean pact to that end'.[5] As the only concrete measure proposed at the multilateral level, this provision has given rise to speculation about the possible creation of a more institutionalised arrangement for coordinating Mediterranean security issues of concern to all 27 signatories of the Barcelona declaration. By the time of the Malta follow-up summit, however, the word 'pact' was exchanged for 'Charter', and the list of measures destined to form the basis of this Euro-Mediterranean Charter reflected the reiterated intention of the Summit's Conclusions not to duplicate or supplant initiatives undertaken elsewhere.

Additionally, the list of measures outlined at Malta, loosely referred to as 'confidence-building measures', concentrates more on the political or diplomatic aspects of the first chapter of the Barcelona Declaration than on measures which directly address the resolution of existing conflicts. They include the setting up 'of a network of contact points for political and security matters', and exchange of information on adherence to international human rights instruments, 'of information on adherence to international legal instruments in the field of disarmament and arms control' as well as in 'the prevention of and fight against terrorism'. Also included in the list are EU-sponsored diplomatic seminars convened in Malta and Egypt, together with the establishment of the 'EuroMeSCo' network of foreign policy institutes.[6]

Most of what is new is the emphasis on cooperation, rather than on novel ways of approaching these issues. Missing from the agenda are the means to address specific issues, such as the Middle East peace process and the question of Cyprus as mentioned above. The EMPI supports the resolution of these issues, but in deferring to existing processes or other fora to deal with them, it imposes a potential ceiling on its own on its own success. On the one hand, this means that the key security concerns of many of the EU's twelve Partners are not directly addressed, most notably the resolution of the Middle East peace process. In the longer term the dependence on other initiatives to promote peace is likely to outweigh the benefits of ensuring that all parties to the Middle East peace process (including Lebanon and

Syria, alongside Israel and the Palestinian Authority) continue to attend follow-up meetings precisely because the details of the peace process are not mentioned. On the other hand, it means that security questions of concern to all 27 signatories are reduced to questions at the lowest level of convergence and controversy. This amounts, in effect, to a kind of 'lowest common denominator' policy-making. The main result is that the substance of the envisaged Charter for Peace and Stability is likely to remain devoid of content, beyond the reiteration of principles to which, at least in theory, all EMPI signatories already adhere.

If advances on specific security issues have thus been left in abeyance, pending resolution elsewhere, it is equally the case that the global approach espoused by the EMPI is not reflected in any direct connections across its three chapters. In both theory and practice, the EMPI's political and security chapter is functionally separate from the chapters dedicated to the envisaged Economic and Financial Partnership and the Partnership in Social and Cultural and Human Affairs. A growth in mutual understanding and cooperation in these spheres is nevertheless implicit to the success of ventures in the sphere of cooperative security, as it has been in Europe, as well as in founding the bedrock of the 'Western' security community of Europe and North America represented in NATO.

Rather than enlightening or reassuring its Mediterranean Partners, however, the fact that the necessity of these connections is not more clearly spelt out casts doubt on the sincerity of the EU in promoting and acknowledging the security interests of the south with the same cooperative vigour as their own. In other words, analysts to the south of the Mediterranean may continue to suspect that the EU's commitment to economic development in the Mediterranean is only as strong as its commitment to its own security, conceived more in terms of the traditional defence of Europe than in the innovative and inter-dependent ways aspired to on paper.[7] The issue goes beyond the satisfaction of the EU's Mediterranean Partners to the development of Europe's own security identity, and the EU's place within it: questions which still need to be fully addressed.

Implications for European Security Cooperation

The EMPI approach is in keeping with moves in the broader context of European security policy to look beyond the collective defence of the Cold War era to more cooperative or joint security ventures within and beyond European borders. It has long been the aspiration of the European partners of NATO to evolve a European security and defence identity (ESDI) through which to articulate, and act upon, issues most directly related to their collective security and defence. Plans to reinvigorate the almost moribund WEU were nurtured in some European capitals (most notably Paris and Bonn) as providing the most appropriate institutional expression of this aspiration in the post-Cold War era: a vision which was accepted, at least on paper, in the EU's Maastricht Treaty of 1991. During the course of the EU's Inter-Governmental Conference (IGC) of 1996-97 to revise Maastricht, however, it became clear that measures to integrate the WEU as the acknowledged defence and security wing of the EU were resisted in other capitals, most notably London. At the Amsterdam Summit of June 1997, this question remained unresolved, along with the development and articulation of the EU's broader aspiration towards elaborating a Common Foreign and Security Policy (CFSP).

The relevance of this for the EMPI lies largely in the fact that EU member-states continue to define and coordinate their collective defence and security policies at the inter-governmental level. Without the express consent of ministerial summits, the European Commission has little discretionary power to define policy initiatives beyond what has already been agreed at the Barcelona and Malta summits. Above all, in the sphere of 'hard' security issues, the EU has no defence wing nor military capabilities at its disposal, nor is it inclined to address concerns which fall more naturally within the competences of the WEU and NATO. The fact that many, but not all EU-member states are also members of these alliances tends to complicate rather than simplify the coordination of European security questions, especially where the division between their 'hard' and 'soft' components becomes blurred.

There are also substantial differences – and difficulties – associated with attempts to replicate in the Mediterranean what has been undertaken with respect to east and central Europe and Russia. The first major difference is that the expansion of NATO and the EU itself towards the east has been undertaken within a vision of an expanding and developing Europe. In this vision, security and defence issues largely overlap with one another, and are implicitly treated as synonymous. Only in respect of Russia has an inherent ambivalence become more apparent between maintaining a defensive posture while introducing more cooperative elements of joint security, such as the NATO joint commission with Russia of May 1997. As far as initiatives towards the Mediterranean are concerned, only Cyprus, Malta and Turkey have any claim (however weak) to being European. Of the EU's largely Arab and/or Muslim Mediterranean Partners, they are therefore the only states which can aspire to membership, and hence the common European defence guarantees, of any of the key Western security institutions.

A second difficulty stems from this effective exclusion of most Mediterranean Partner states from European defence guarantees, namely, that European defence planning may in fact undermine the cooperative intentions of initiatives such as the WEU and NATO dialogues, as well as the EMPI. As Pedro Moya writes: '(i) initiating a dialogue assumes creating a minimum of confidence between the participants, which is inconceivable if one party brands the other a threat.'[8] In planning for emergencies in the Mediterranean, the imprecision with which potential missions are drawn up for the newly formed call-up forces of the WEU, EUROFOR or EUROMARFOR, has not inspired confidence in several of Europe's southern neighbours, where they are not expressly included or subject to prior notification of any envisaged regional intervention. In this specific case, reassurances have been forthcoming, but not without raising question about how defence policy (which excludes the Mediterranean) and cooperative security policy (which by definition includes them) are to interact in future. The further incorporation of units from non-NATO non-European states in joint missions in other areas, such as the troop contributions of Morocco, Jordan and Egypt to the NATO-led IFOR and SFOR in the Former Yugoslavia, might in practice do more to diminish apprehensions about Europe's military intentions in the Mediterranean.

A third major difference is that the EU's supporting role in the sphere of security is to some extent taken for granted in the east-west context, where its strengths in the 'soft' security sphere of economic cooperation complement existing initiatives in the 'hard' security sphere of the traditional military or defence alliances. In the Mediterranean, the complementarity of the EU's security focus with pre-existing initiatives, such as those of NATO and the WEU, is not so clear, even if the same assumptions prevail in policy-making circles. In this respect, one of the possible sources of tension might arise where European priorities in the Mediterranean do not coincide with those of NATO, which enjoys broader objectives than the security of southern Europe, or of Europe vis-à-vis the Mediterranean alone. This touches primarily on the role of the US, as the key player in the NATO alliance, in providing not only the cement of the NATO alliance, but also Europe's foremost defence guarantee, as will be discussed at greater length in a later paper. The key question centres on the extent to which European states are willing, able and prepared to take primary responsibility for security in the Mediterranean, where the US provides important logistical support for any foreseeable operation in the region.

The discussion over these issues continues to take place in the context of the future of NATO. Most recently, the French government announced that France would not be rejoining NATO's integrated command structure as envisaged over the past two years because of US reluctance to cede AFSOUTH to a European rather than American commander. It remains symptomatic of much of European security discussions, however, that the focus is on the structural and operational nature of the various security organisations which have continued to exist in the post-Cold War era rather more than on the question of why, and to what end, these organisations need to coordinate their activities against threats and eventualities, often defined in only the vaguest and most unspecific of fashions.

Conclusions

The security implications of the EMPI for Europe itself cannot be examined outside the context of the wider European security debate. In many ways, the EMPI is seeking to fill a number of 'security gaps', in acting to integrate a number of cross-cutting security concerns. This, at least, is the vision on paper.

In reality, much of the EMPI focuses on maintaining current stability in the Mediterranean, while looking ahead to prevent the emergence of unforeseen crises or threats to stability through opening channels to discuss and exchange views over issues of common concern. However, where some of the 27 signatories have a more direct interest or more direct involvement in an existing crisis or security dilemma, the EMPI excludes itself as a forum in which to discuss more than the general principles governing its potential resolution. In the short-term, this contributes to maintaining the cohesion of the follow-up meetings to the Barcelona and Malta ministerial summits. In the longer-term, however, it runs the danger of raising expectations that the elaboration of confidence-building measures will eventually be used to apply to real crises or issues, not the hypothetical ones to which they currently apply. Equally, the raising of security issues in a general sense might lead to the creation of tensions where they do not already exist, by dint of exploring areas where hypothetical security problems might arise in future.

The EMPI promises much, on paper, in terms of innovative approaches to cross-sectoral policy-making in the field of security. In elaborating the EMPI, the EU has certainly recognised the need to address the structural impediments to peaceful change in the non-European Mediterranean region, as well as building on the willingness of regional governments to engage or accelerate their processes of reform towards this end. However, the EU itself still lacks the capacity to coordinate policies across the board, thus keeping the economic and cultural provisions of the EMPI largely separate from their security dimensions. This incapacity is a problem of a more general nature in Europe's security policy-making, which will need to be addressed as much in the structure of domestic governments and bureaucracies in future as at the inter-governmental or European Commission level.

Of more particular significance to North Africa, however, it means that the whole EMPI process ignores immediate crises – such as the violence and high number of deaths in Algeria – as being beyond its immediate sphere of competence. This lends a surrealistic quality to bilateral negotiations over Algeria's Association Agreement with the EU, which incorporates clauses concerning the respect of human rights but no mention of the daily death toll, nor any means for seeking to implement the international principles – such as the peaceful settlement of conflicts – outlined elsewhere. As in Europe, the sovereignty of states in the sphere of internal and external security policy remains paramount in North Africa, and it is perhaps this which presents the greatest obstacle to any real achievement or progress towards more integrated and cooperative approaches to security in the Mediterranean in general.

NOTES

1. Moya, P., *Frameworks for Cooperation in the Mediterranean* North Atlantic Assembly, Civilian Affairs Committee, Sub-Committee on the Mediterranean Basin, AM 259 CC/MB (95) 7 October 1995, p.12.
2. de Rato, R., *Cooperation and Security in the Mediterranean* NAA, Political Committee, Sub-Committee on the Southern Region, AM PC/SR (95) 2, October 1995, p.7. Lesser, Ian O. and Tellis, Ashley J (1996), *Strategic Exposure: Proliferation around the Mediterranean*, Arroyo Center, RAND Corporation; and Lipkowski (1996*, Security in the Mediterranean region: Report Submitted on Behalf of the Political Committee*, Proceedings of the Assembly of the WEU, 42nd Session, Document 1543, WEU, Paris, 4 November 1996, p.172.
3. Barcelona Declaration (EC, November 1995): p.2. Malta (1996) 'Second Euro-Mediterranean Ministerial Conference, Malta 15–16 April 1997, Summit Conclusions, p.3.
4. Barcelona Declaration, ibid, p.3.
5. Barcelona Declaration, ibid, p.3.
6. Malta (1996) (note 3), p.10.
7. Tozy, *El Pais*, 23 November 1995.
8. Moya, 1995 (note 1), p.17.

The Changing Mediterranean Security Environment : A Transatlantic Perspective

IAN O. LESSER

The Mediterranean security environment is changing in important ways. This analysis discusses the evolving significance of the region from an American perspective, and decribes three different models for conceptualising Mediterranean security, each of which highlights important dimensions of change as well as differences in perspective among Europe, US and southern Mediterranean observers.

Origins of the US Approach

Only very recently have Mediterranean questions become a fashionable part of the American foreign policy debate, and their importance remains limited. This is not because the US lacks interests in the region – far from it. Nor is it because Washington has no tradition of engagement there – the presence in the Mediterranean long pre-dates the US involvement in continental Europe. The US is actively engaged in and around the post-Cold War Mediterranean, partly as a consequence of being both a European and a Middle Eastern power, and partly because the Mediterranean is the scene of crises, potential crises and initiatives of concern to policymakers. From Algeria to the Aegean, and from the Balkans to the Middle East peace process, the region's problems place important, perhaps even disproportionate demands on America's foreign policy leadership.

Nonetheless, one will search in vain for any explicit, official US reference to a 'Mediterranean policy' as the term has come to be used in Europe. US officials and most American observers do not speak of policy toward the Mediterranean as a whole because the US lacks the specific intellectual tradition (largely a product of France Italy and Spain even within the EU) for doing so. Intellectually, and not least bureaucratically, American foreign policy decisionmakers and analysts, as well as scholars, have tended to think rigidly in terms of 'European' and 'Middle Eastern'

Ian Lesser is a Senior Analyst at RAND, Santa Monica, CA and a former member of the Policy Planning Staff, US Department of State. The views expressed here are the author's and do not necessarily reflect those of RAND or its research sponsors.

affairs, with North Africa as a minor subset of the latter. In sum, there is little consciousness of the Mediterranean as a coherent geostrategic space.

Indeed, the notion of Mediterranean policy and Mediterranean initiatives has had negative connotations in some quarters. During the Cold War Mediterranean initiatives, especially in the security sphere, came to be associated in the American view with Gaullist and Non-Aligned concepts of the 'Mediterranean for the Mediterraneans', or even naval arms control, all of which implied limitations on American freedom of action. Some of this uneasiness remains, and may be seen in the preference for security approaches in the region to be organised from NATO southward, rather than on a global CSCM-like basis.[1] This may also reflect a more general US intellectual preference for the concrete over the theoretical.

The compartmentalisation of American policymaking into quite separate European and Middle Eastern spheres (the Middle East peace process is further isolated as an activity of its own) has also made Europe's Mediterranean initiatives, above all the Barcelona process, difficult to digest and difficult for US diplomacy to support with enthusiasm. The European bureau of the State Department and others concerned with European policy remain firmly fixed on the priority areas of consolidating the transitions in eastern and central Europe and the process of NATO enlargement. Issues bearing on the future of Europe emanating from the south are often regarded as marginal and distracting. Considerations surrounding the articulation of a new strategic concept for the Alliance, and challenges in the Balkans and in and around Turkey, are weakening this tendency, but have not entirely reversed it.

At the same time, those responsible for policy towards the Middle East tend to regard Mediterranean initiatives as code for a greater European role in the Middle East peace process – a prospect few see as desirable. Mediterranean diplomacy appears as a complicating rather than complimentary factor, especially given current Arab-Israeli tensions and the stalemate in negotiations. More simply, the strict division along European and Middle Eastern lines, both inside the government and among non-government experts, leaves cross-cutting Mediterranean questions in a vacuum. Mediterranean approaches have few, if any, structural advocates in the formal foreign policy process.

American foreign policy over the last decade has come to focus heavily on functional rather than regional issues and objectives (for example, economic reform and 'democratic enlargement'). Some of the most prominent functional concerns, including proliferation of weapons of mass destruction, migration and refugees, the environment and transnational crime, and human rights, are also key issues for the Mediterranean region. This has had the effect of focusing additional attention on Turkey, the

Levant and North Africa. But the general tendency in American foreign policy circles has been to cast these functional concerns in global terms. Increased interest in the Mediterranean is simply a by-product.

Regional attitudes have also contributed to American ambivalence about a more explicit Mediterranean policy. Quite apart from the Gaullist and Non-Aligned legacies noted above, the Euro-Mediterranean partnership has never been presented as an initiative with a natural Transatlantic dimension. In security as well as economic terms, the Mediterranean has emerged as a theatre of special interest for EU and WEU activity, in part because these are the out-of-area roles NATO has left for European attention.[2] Even a symbolic US role as 'observer' in Barcelona was controversial and ultimately impossible to arrange. European attitudes were not uniform on this question, with, for example, greater interest in Spain than in France.

The absence of a US role in the Barcelona process was a result of both proximate and more fundamental realities. In proximate terms, US participation was doomed by the lack of strong advocates on the European side, together with Washington's own reluctance to express support for the initiative until the 'eleventh hour'. More fundamentally, real US involvement in Barcelona could only come about as a result of a broader Transatlantic bargain on mutual participation in regional initiatives, including US-led activities of concern to Europe, for example, in the Western Hemisphere or the Middle East peace process. No such bargain exists, and the desirability of developing one remains controversial on both sides of the Atlantic. Indeed, the entire question of political and economic relations in the Mediterranean, especially relations with North Africa, has come to be viewed by the US as a legitimate sphere for European leadership. Even in the security arena – where the US remains a preeminent actor – 'soft' security issues (such as, migration) continue to be seen as the natural preserve of the EU.

Strategic Stakes and the Prospects for a More Deliberate Approach

There is little in recent history to suggest the emergence of an explicit American policy towards the Mediterranean or a formal role for the US in existing Mediterranean initiatives outside the security sphere. This could change as a result of several factors, including the growth of US stakes in the region as a whole.

First, at a time of considerable interest in refashioning US engagement in Europe as a relevant, European power, Europe's own concerns about the 'South' take on new importance. To an extent, the Mediterranean matters to the US because it matters to Europe. If southern European countries are uneasy about the longer-term implications of migration, spill-overs of political instability and new energy dependencies for their prosperity and security, this is inevitably reflected in bilateral discussions. It has also had the effect of introducing a Mediterranean initiative in NATO. None of this can be ignored by the US, and has had an effect on Transatlantic agendas. To the extent that NATO enlargement proceeds smoothly, and the Alliance begins to take up a 'post-Madrid' agenda, Mediterranean issues will likely receive more attention. If five or six European allies press for greater attention to the Mediterranean, this has some significance. If this call is taken up by other leading, non-Mediterranean allies (Britain and Germany, for example) it will have far greater importance for Washington. Inclusion of France in this equation already gives Mediterranean questions far greater weight.

The crisis in Algeria provides an example. US interests in regional stability are influenced by the turmoil in Algeria, but the US stake in Algeria is indirect and far less pronounced than that of Europe. Notwithstanding enduring French suspicions about independent US motives in relation to Algeria, the primary and perhaps the only compelling aspect of the crisis for the US concerns its potential effect on Europe. For the US, Algeria is a Transatlantic rather than a regional issue. Washington has been as reluctant as the EU in contemplating any serious political intervention in Algeria. Yet Algeria has for some time been an important topic of discussion with France, Spain and Italy. If NATO and the EU move to strengthen transatlantic cooperation in the Mediterranean, the spectre of Algerian chaos will be a strong, contributing factor.

Second, the Mediterranean matters to the US because of its link to wider interests in the Middle East and Eurasia. In periods of success for the Middle East peace process, the Mediterranean dimension became important, not least because it allowed moderate actors such as Morocco and Tunisia to contribute. This activism of smaller Arab states in North Africa, as well as the Persian Gulf, was evident in the multilateral negotiations (as in ACRS and REDWG), and in the Casablanca economic conference.[3] There has been a persistent American interest in broadening as well as deepening the constituency for Arab-Israeli peace – to look beyond the disputes on Israel's borders – and this continues to include a Mediterranean dimension. The current period of stagnation in the peace process complicates the outlook for several Mediterranean initiatives, including NATO's efforts at cooperation with southern states. The burgeoning Turkish-Israeli cooperation introduces a new, Mediterranean factor, and suggests the possibility of wider Turkish-Israeli-Jordanian-US strategic cooperation.

Conceptualising Mediterranean Security: Three Models

During the Cold War, Transatlantic perspectives on the Mediterranean focused on the notion of NATO's 'Southern Region'; a concept that had less to do with objective security problems than with the political and geographic distinctiveness of NATO's five southern members. The sense of risk, including the risk of Soviet aggression, was low in relation to that in the centre of Europe. To the extent that NATO Europe worried about the problem of coupling security interests across the Atlantic, southern European countries had the additional concern of how to link their own more diffuse security concerns to wider Alliance strategy – a problem of double coupling. The risk of Soviet adventurism on NATO's southern periphery, and extensive bilateral cooperation with the US, provided the necessary basis for cohesion, but on the whole, NATO's southern region remained marginal in political and security terms..

It is a mark of the difficulty of portraying the Mediterranean as an area of strategic consequence in its own right that post-Cold War approaches also tend to couple the region to other facets of international security, both regional and functional. Three models for conceptualising the Mediterranean in security terms stand out in today's debate. First, the region is increasingly seen as 'Europe's near abroad'. Second, it can be described as an ante-room to more 'global' concerns in the Middle East, the Gulf and beyond. Finally, the Mediterranean is a prominent arena for North-South conflict and cooperation. Each model has something to contribute, and each plays a role in shaping regional intiatives. Significantly, these models also illustrate important differences in European, American and southern Mediterranean perceptions.

The Mediterranean as Europe's Near Abroad

Much as Russia has come to identify critical security interests on its immediate periphery, Western discussion of security in and around Europe is increasingly focused on challenges emanating from the south, both across the Mediterranean in North Africa and the Levant, and in the contiguous south, above all the Balkans. The crises in Bosnia, Albania and Kosovo have encouraged an expanded conception of the European security space. Although engagement in the Balkans remains out-of-area for NATO, it is arguable that the management of security problems in the Balkans is no longer really seen as out-of-area in all but a narrow, technical sense. Alliance policy toward Bosnia, and more recently Kosovo, has changed the way decision makers and publics perceive crises on the European periphery. The Western European Union has also come to focus on this near-abroad, including the Maghreb, as a natural sphere of activity, and initiatives such as EUROFOR and EUROMARFOR have had an implicit southern vocation. Indeed, many observers in the South express their concern that WEU efforts are oriented towards intervention across the Mediterranean.

The security problems of Europe's Mediterranean periphery are highly diverse, and fill a spectrum from intangible threats to identity and prosperity – above all, the highly politicised issue of economic migration and refugees – to more tangible concerns about internal security, including crime, drugs and spillovers of political violence from North Africa, the Middle East and the Balkans.[4] Much discussion about Mediterranean security rightly centres on so-called 'soft security', especially in relation to the western and central Mediterranean where social, political and economic challenges predominate. As the EU seeks greater competence in addressing 'Third Pillar' problems, additional attention will inevitably be focused on Europe's Mediterranean periphery where these challenges abound.

At the far end of this risk spectrum are concerns about the proliferation of weapons of mass destruction and the means for their delivery at ever increasing ranges.[5] The proliferation risk is especially meaningful for Europe because it implies a growing exposure to the consequences of conflicts beyond Europe but near enough to engage European interests. Ultimately, proliferation trends can imply an end to European sanctuary in relation to crises as far away as the Gulf, or as near as the Balkans.[6] This exposure also has the potential to complicate security cooperation between Washington and southern Europe.

Many regional risks are of a more traditional sort. Western and Central Europe now offer few serious examples of irredentism and territorial flux. But the Mediterranean near-abroad has a concentration of potential threats to borders. Europe and the United States will have a strong interest in assuring the territorial integrity of states on the periphery and a systemic interest in preventing the use of force to change established borders. This concern is an important part of the Western calculus in the Balkans in the wake of the Bosnian experience, as well as in the Caucasus. In North Africa, where internal security is a first-order concern, the conventional defence of borders is still an important factor. Potential conflicts between Morocco and Algeria, Libya and Tunisia, Libya and Egypt, Egypt and Sudan, all imply a likely Western concern about the security of borders as well as regimes.[7]

Energy security is emerging as another important issue shaping the security environment in Europe's Mediterranean near-abroad. This concern is, of course, long-standing and has waxed and waned with changes in the oil market and developments in the Persian Gulf. Most recently, it has become fashionable to speak of the Caspian as another Gulf, with all the economic and geopolitical significance this implies. The actual significance of the region in energy terms, and as a sphere of geopolitical competition, is still open to question.[8] Expanding European gas imports from North Africa may be a more important and direct concern. Southern Europe and Turkey are increasingly dependent on gas supplies from North Africa and Eurasia respectively. The capacity for the transport of gas across the Mediterranean has expanded significantly over the past few years, with increases in capacity of the Transmed pipeline and the opening of the trans-Maghreb line linking Algeria, Morocco and Spain. Russia has emerged as a Turkey's leading trade partner, largely on the basis of large-scale gas imports.

Unlike oil, the gas trade remains a regional rather than global market, and offers fewer opportunities for adjustment in the face of supply interruptions. Southern Europe's dependence on North African gas is therefore likely to be a 'permanently operating factor' in future Mediterranean geopolitics, and is already influencing security perceptions in diverse ways. In particular, concern over gas supply has played a role in French and southern European views of the crisis in Algeria.[9] At the same time, it is arguable that new, cross-border energy links across the Mediterranean and along the North African littoral, can foster economic interdependence and, perhaps, a shared stake in regional stability.

The 'near-abroad' model can be discerned in much of the current discussion about how the Mediterranean will be treated in future NATO strategy. There is probably a consensus within the Alliance on the need to adjust strategy and missions to meet more likely challenges on the periphery. Yet some states, notably France, will be reluctant to singularise the Mediterranean as an area of strategic concern, either because NATO is not seen as the appropriate vehicle, or for fear of provoking a negative reaction from the south A general tendency toward conservatism in Alliance behaviour suggests that the new NATO strategic concept will place additional focus on the Mediterranean, but will do so in functional terms. That is, rather than articulating a specific strategy for the Mediterranean *per se*, the strategic concept will likely highlight new functional missions for the Alliance such as countering terrorism and proliferation risks, and building the capacity for peacekeeping and crisis management. These missions are, however, most likely to be conducted on the Mediterranean periphery rather than in central and eastern Europe. The net result will almost certainly be a more southward-looking alliance.

In the eastern Mediterranean, the strategic environment is being shaped (distorted may be a more accurate term) by two persistent disputes with important implications for European security. First, the Greek-Turkish dispute is perhaps Europe's most dangerous flashpoint. There may be little strategic rationale for conflict in Athens or Ankara, but the complex of issues and the on-going military brinkmanship the risk of an accidental clash.[10] A serious military confrontation would imply enormous risks for both sides, and might well result in the permanent estrangement of Turkey from European and Atlantic institutions. The example of a conflict between two NATO allies would deal a blow to the processes of Alliance enlargement and adaptation, and could destabilise the larger southeastern periphery, from the Balkans to the Caucasus.

Beyond the problem of Greek-Turkish relations, security in the eastern Mediterranean will be strongly affected by the future character of the relationship between Turkey and the West. Turkey's role in relation to Europe is increasingly uncertain. Traditional notions of Ankara's position as a 'bridge' between Europe and the Middle East, or even a 'barrier' against instability on Europe's periphery, are being overtaken by Western perceptions of a troubled Turkey with a more assertive and independent foreign and security policy. The Luxembourg summit decisions regarding Turkey's bid for EU membership, and perhaps more significantly, the subsequent tone of the dialogue on all sides, has reinforced the idea of Turkish 'otherness' – part of the European system, but unlikely to become a formal member of Europe. Ankara can be a key actor in the Balkans, the Middle East, and the Caucasus-Central Asia. But the deterioration of the relationship with Europe has dimmed the prospects for a cooperative approach in these important areas of EU and Transatlantic interest.

The Arab-Israeli dispute is the second critical influence on security in the eastern Mediterranean, and to a important degree, across the Mediterranean periphery as a whole. Europe has become more actively engaged in the post-Oslo peace process, especially in the economic dimension. EU interests are now more closely bound up with the prospects for peace. In 'hard' security terms, Europe is exposed to potential spillovers from renewed Arab-Israeli confrontation, most obviously in relation to terrorism and proliferation risks. In diplomatic and economic terms, lack of progress in the peace process has had a variety of negative effects on initiatives important to Europe, and especially southern Europe, from the Euro-Mediterranean partnership to NATO's Mediterranean Initiative.[11] The gap between Europe's growing stake in Middle Eastern outcomes and its relatively limited role in the peace process is set to emerge as an even more contentious issue in Transatlantic relations. Washington's continuing discomfort with the notion of a more active European role in the process is inevitably a factor in the EU's own ambivalent attitude toward US involvement in its Mediterranean policies.

The Mediterranean as Strategic Waypoint

An alternative approach to the Mediterranean emphasises the region's importance as a waypoint to areas of perceived vital interest further afield.

This idea is not new, and is in fact a traditional way of describing the strategic significance of the Mediterranean in the West. Over the last century, the region, especially the eastern basin and its hinterlands, has been seen, variously, as a crucial link to the Persian Gulf and India, and as a means of outflanking dominant continental powers.[12]

Since 1945, and with even greater emphasis since 1990, the concept of the Mediterranean as a logistical ante-room to the Persian Gulf has been particularly prominent among American strategists and policymakers. The ability to project military power to the Gulf in a timely fashion depends critically on the lines of air and sea communication through the Mediterranean (lines that run from across the Atlantic, through the Azores and southern Europe to Suez, as well as Turkey in the north). Some 90 per cent of the troops and matériel sent to the Gulf during the Gulf War passed through or above the Mediterranean. Recent deployments to the Gulf have only underscored the importance of this link. As a result, the character of US political relationships around the Mediterranean exerts a strong influence on US freedom of action beyond the Mediterranean basin. If, for example, public opinion in Egypt compels Cairo to withhold transit for Western naval forces through the Suez Canal, this will have an immediate and costly effect on the ability to respond to crises in the Gulf or the Horn of Africa. Should Suez be unavailable to the West in a future Gulf crisis, the politically sensitive burden of access and overflight might fall even more heavily on NATO's southern members.

The notion of the Mediterranean as a strategic waypoint has been further reinforced by the issue of Caspian oil. Although the contribution of Caspian oil to world supply over the next decades may be modest in relation to Persian Gulf production, it has become fashionable among Western analysts to speculate about the new security demands arising from the Caucasus and Central Asia.[13] Much of the new Eurasian oil production will come to world markets via the Mediterranean, either through the Black Sea or by pipeline across Turkey (if the proposed Baku-Ceyhan route is built). This will augment the already important role of the Mediterranean as a terminus for Gulf and North African energy supplies, and it will likely bind together even more firmly the economic and security futures of areas adjacent to the Mediterranean. The West's ability to project power around the Caspian basin and the Caucasus in defence of energy security interests will turn on access to the Black Sea and cooperation with key regional states, most notably Turkey.

The Mediterranean-Eurasian link is not new, since much of the Mediterranean's Cold War importance flowed from its role as a theatre of East-West competition. The prospect of new overland and Black Sea routes for Caspian oil, and the revival of overland transport links from the Balkans to Central Asia and the Levant, suggests a growing economic, political and even security connection between these regions. Since 1945, few in the US or elsewhere have focused on the geopolitical implications of these links. Today, the growing attention to these issues is striking and reminiscent of strategic debates in the late nineteenth and early twentieth centuries.[14]

This aspect of the strategic evolution of the Mediterranean also raises the question of Russia's role and behaviour. Russia continues to have a strong economic stake in trade relationships and shipping routes through the Black Sea to the Mediterranean and Suez.[15] Russian political and security interests are engaged in the Balkans, the Caucasus and Levant. As a legacy of the Cold War era, Moscow retains close diplomatic relationships with key states in the region, and some of these ties (eg, with Serbia , Greece and Cyprus) have actually deepened in recent years. In military terms, Russia is no longer present in the Mediterranean in any meaningful way. There is no standing Russian naval presence in the Mediterranean, and Russia no longer shares a border with NATO in the Caucasus. But the post-Cold War environment presents new opportunities for conflict and cooperation with Russia on Europe's periphery.

Russia may share a basic interest in stability on its southern periphery, but its sensitivity to separatist tendencies may give rise to policies at variance with Western approaches, especially in the Caucasus (eg, Chechnya). In the Balkans, Orthodox affinities will be a motivating factor, as in the close relationship between Moscow, Belgrade and Athens. Elsewhere, in North Africa, the Levant and the Middle East, Moscow's arms and technology transfers, both conventional and unconventional, have emerged as a source of concern. These include sales to Iran, Syria and Libya. The transfer of SA-300 surface-to-air missiles to Cyprus has been particularly controversial. It remains unclear whether, as some observers assert, active Russian diplomacy and arms sales around the Mediterranean are evidence of a deliberate 'peripheral strategy' aimed at exerting influence in areas of concern to the West outside the centre of Europe.[16] In the worst case, an assertive, nationalist Russia might chose to confront the West through proxies in the Mediterranean and the Gulf. More realistically, Russian relations with the West across the region may be characterised by a mixture of conflict and cooperation based on perceptions of key interests in the Russian and European near-abroads.[17]

European observers and decision makers are, in broad terms, less comfortable than their American counterparts with a model of the Mediterranean as strategic waypoint, or with what is essentially a power-projection model for the Mediterranean. Southern Mediterranean opinion is even more strongly negative. As noted earlier, European forays in this area, such as those undertaken under WEU auspices, have been more narrowly drawn, and concerned with the ability to conduct limited humanitarian and crisis management operations on the European doorstep, in the Maghreb or the Balkans. Europe has a limited capacity for power projection, mostly French and British, and has displayed a selective willingness to participate in interventions beyond the continent. But Europe as a whole is reluctant to allow power-projection needs to drive strategy toward the Mediterranean, especially if these needs complicate political and economic relations with near neighbours in North Africa. To the extent that the American military presence in southern Europe and the Mediterranean becomes more heavily oriented towards power projection further afield, this tension in Transatlantic approaches to the region may deepen.

Finally, the Mediterranean has emerged as a political as well as logistical way point in the context of the debate over NATO adaptation and the future of Transatlantic cooperation. Those, mainly in the US, who argue for a more 'global' conception of Atlantic cooperation, with an expansive definition of alliance areas of responsibility, tend to view more active security engagement in the Mediterranean as a natural step toward globalisation. If Europe and the US can routinely cooperate in more than an ad hoc fashion to manage crises on Europe's southern periphery, the prospects for closer cooperation in areas further afield, in the Gulf and beyond, may be more promising.[18]

The Mediterranean as a North-South Arena

A third model for understanding the Mediterranean security environment emphasises the region's significance as a place where differing cultures, political systems and levels of economic development meet. This is largely, although not exclusively, a question of relations between north and south, between 'haves' and 'have nots', and between relatively secure societies and their relatively insecure counterparts across the Mediterranean. The question of whether the Mediterranean unites or divides, acts as a bridge or a barrier, is a perennial one, and has inspired sharply differing answers. The Braudelian tradition emphasises the historic unity of the Mediterranean in cultural, economic and geopolitical terms.[19] In this conception, the most significant divide – including in security terms – has been between the Mediterranean littoral and the hinterland. In an era of modern communications, including the global dissemination of information, it is doubtful that this distinction still holds. Indeed the process of 'globalisation' calls into question the entire notion of 'bridges' in international relations. If information, capital and people can move easily and rapidly with little reference to borders, and if ballistic missiles can reach across traditional theaters, the idea of geographical bridges loses much of its meaning. Yet a number of states around the Mediterranean continue to define their strategic significance in these terms. Morocco, Tunisia, Turkey, Greece and Cyprus are leading examples.

An alternative tradition treats the Mediterranean as a theater of civilisational conflict. Samuel Huntington's analysis of the 'clash of civilisations' and the prominent Mediterranean cleavage between Islam and the West illustrates this approach. Critics of his analysis often imply that it is a modern distortion in the same vein as Arnold Toynbee, but in reality the Huntingtonian thesis is part of a very old, even ancient tradition in which civilizations to the south (or the east) are seen as the 'other' and a source of insecurity in the Mediterranean world.[20] The mixed history of confrontation and coexistence across civilizational and geographic lines around the Mediterranean is suggested by the original use of the term 'cold war' to describe relations between Spain and the Ottoman Empire. Simple geopolitical divisions are unlikely to prove a useful guide to understanding the security environment, given the variety of cleavages along both the southern and eastern shores of the Mediterranean. The complexity of EU politics and the sharp differences between key states in the Muslim world on Europe's periphery illustrate this point.[21]

The potential for civilisational and developmental frictions in the contemporary Mediterranean to fuel security risks has been a leading force behind various regional initiatives and national policies. There has been a growing recognition, especially in the wake of the Gulf War, of security challenges along North-South lines. With few exceptions, these challenges are more accurately portrayed as the north-south spillovers of conflicts in the South.[22] Terrorist activity by Algerians in France or Kurdish separatists in Germany are examples. Similarly, the proliferation of weapons of mass destruction and ballistic missiles along the southern and eastern shores of the Mediterranean is, for the moment, driven mainly by the struggle for regional weight in the South. In both cases, Europe is exposed, but in a secondary fashion. Regime changes and the radicalisation of opinion in the south could alter this equation for the future. Europe and the US therefore face the difficult task of hedging against security risks in the south without provoking an aggressive response across the Mediterranean (that is, without encouraging new Libyas).

This tension between defence and dialogue is evident in NATO's evolving approach to the Mediterranean. The Alliance has developed a Mediterranean initiative aimed at promoting dialogue with selected non-member countries in the South – Mauritania, Morocco, Tunisia, Egypt, Israel and Jordan.[23] The addition of further states, such as Algeria, is possible, but highly controversial. The emphasis has been on information, education and North-South confidence building of a generalized sort. More significant contributions in the confidence-building area are constrained by the essentially bilateral, or more accurately, multi-bilateral nature of the Initiative. Arab-Israeli tensions make the development of a true multilateral process difficult, and prevent the Initiative from engaging in meaningful confidence-building activities along South-South lines. The 'political and security partnership' envisioned in the EU's Barcelona Declaration, as well as the WEU and OSCE dialogue efforts, face similar constraints in the confidence-building realm.[24]

At the same time, NATO and to a lesser extent the WEU are concerned with bolstering Western capabilities for defence against 'hard' security risks emanating from the south. Proliferation is the leading concern, and more active efforts to address ballistic missile and other threats along South-North lines can complicate North-South relations. Sensitivity here is evident, especially among some of the southern European states most directly exposed to proliferation risks. Spain and Greece, for example, are wary of 'counter-proliferation' strategies that envision preemptive action by the US or NATO against proliferators. Improved ballistic missile defences are less controversial, but imply daunting costs. There is also a presumption in some quarters that American systems will always be available for this purpose in the event of a crisis. In general, and with some exceptions (such as, Turkey), the European preference is for an emphasis on diplomatic approaches to limit southern capabilities, together with North-South dialogue to address the uncertainty of Southern intentions.

The northern and southern shores of the Mediterranean differ sharply in terms of the security institutions available to manage regional and trans-regional risks. The Euro-Atlantic area has a surfeit of architecture and institutions of varying competence to address security problems. The Middle East, including the southern Mediterranean, lacks any effective architecture for this purpose beyond informal alliances and external guarantees. In the absence of any real security architecture, even modest institutions for regional dialogue (such as, the Mediterranean Forum and EuroMesco have an important role to play in promoting transparency in security perceptions among societies with very different strategic cultures. Societies in the South are not only less secure, but also tend to define security in different terms, with a far greater emphasis on internal security. In Northern capitals, for example, the issue of Islamism is often seen in the context of human rights and political reform, whereas southern Mediterranean leaderships are inclined to view Islamic oppositions as a security threat.

Progress towards a comprehensive Arab-Israeli peace might facilitate the creation of security institutions for the South – whether Middle Eastern or Mediterranean in focus. In the absence of this, and with the erosion of

Cold War era alignments, states in the South may find it worthwhile to build closer relationships with capable European and Atlantic institutions, above all the EU and NATO – a tendency that might be described as 'borrowed' security.[25] At a minimum, regional states are seeking to vary the geometry of their foreign and security policies. The Turkish-Israeli strategic relationship provides a striking example, as do Israeli and Egyptian efforts to develop a more active political relationship with the European Union. A more developed NATO approach to the Mediterranean could provide another vehicle for diversifying southern security ties, although this will require considerable progress in reforming NATO's image among publics, and many elites, in the Arab world.[26]

Outside the narrow security realm, the EU's Barcelona Process has emerged as the leading instrument for engagement along north-south lines in the Mediterranean. In the broadest sense, European approaches to the Mediterranean are being shaped by the desire to promote economic development and stability on Europe's poor and increasingly populous periphery.[27] The Euro-Mediterranean Partnership Initiative is in large measure an attempt to 'subsidize' stability across the Mediterranean, or more realistically, to create the conditions for future investment and development.[28] The initiative recognises the reality that Europe will continue to be the critical economic partner, and a leading factor in development prospects, for states across the Mediterranean. The desire to foster prosperity and stability, and to limit migration pressure from the South, has obvious parallels in the US attitude towards Latin America and the Caribbean – Washington's own 'south', and a traditional area of policy regard.

The South also faces considerable challenges in the management of its relations with the North, and with Western institutions. A wider trade and investment relationship with Europe implies a need for economic reform, and very likely a degree of political reform, with implications for stability and the future of existing regimes. Growing European restrictions on migration threaten a long-standing economic and social safety-valve in North Africa, where regimes are already facing tremendous domestic challenges. Even if longer-term EU efforts to encourage prosperity in the South are successful, the political consequences are far from clear. As the Moroccan and Turkish cases suggest, higher growth rates are not necessarily a recipe for stability where income disparities are pronounced.

The societies on Europe's periphery are also increasingly aware of developments affecting the security of immigrants within Europe, as well as Muslim communities in the Balkans and elsewhere. Perceived Western indifference to the fate of Bosnia's Muslims has left a lasting impression in North Africa and the Middle East. Future Western policy on the Balkans, as well as towards the Arab-Israeli dispute and the Persian Gulf, will inevitably have an effect on Southern attitudes towards Euro-Atlantic institutions. The effect of public opinion along the Southern shores of the Mediterranean on the behaviour of leaderships during the Gulf War provides a potent illustration of the forces acting on regimes in the region.

Some of the most pressing hard and soft security challenges around the Mediterranean cut *across* North-South lines. Some risks, such as terrorism, international crime, refugee flows, and some forms of environmental degradation are inherently transnational, and may require a degree of North-South cooperation if they are to be effectively addressed. Other challenges, such as the relentless process of urbanisation on both sides of the Mediterranean – a significant factor in the political evolution of the region – are shared in character, if not necessarily in scale. Failure to cope with these challenges, and in the worst case the complete failure of states and a descent into anarchy on the Algerian model, could have profound implications for the entire Mediterranean.

Observations and Conclusions

The Mediterranean security environment is in flux, with important changes affecting the prospects for stability within societies, between states, and across regions. In the absence of a defining construct for understanding the strategic significance of the Mediterranean, differing intellectual and policy traditions are now shaping attitudes toward the Mediterranean in security terms. The Mediterranean has clearly become more prominent in the security debate on both sides of the Atlantic. This new-found attention is the product of compelling crises in Algeria, the southern Balkans, and the eastern Mediterranean. It is also the result of a more general recognition that the most pressing security challenges – of a political and economic as well as a military sort – are now along the European periphery. They are also at the intersection of traditionally distinct European, Middle Eastern and Eurasian theatres. Indeed, some of the most intensively debated contemporary security concerns, from proliferation to energy supply, are inherently trans-regional. The Mediterranean is at the centre of this cross-regional trend, and the Mediterranean security environment is increasingly defined by it.

The strategic significance of the Mediterranean emerges in somewhat different ways from the three models discussed in this analysis. Each has something to offer in understanding the current environment and possibilities for the future. These alternative approaches do, however, share a common feature – all three refer to interests beyond Mediterranean shores, whether in Europe, the Middle East or Eurasia – or view developments in the Mediterranean as a facet of wider transatlantic and north-south relations. In this sense, the Mediterranean security debate has moved quite far from the regionally-based approach typified by the notion of the 'Mediterranean for the Mediterraneans' or the CSCM idea. This may be one of the clearest indications that the period of Mediterranean marginalisation is drawing to a close.

NOTES

1. In the early 1990's, Spain and Italy led an active debate on the merits of a Conference on Security and Cooperation in the Mediterranean (CSCM).
2. For example, planning and exercises for EUROFOR and EUROMARFOR have focused heavily on Mediterranean, especially North African contingencies.
3. The Arms Control and Regional Security (ACRS) talks and the Regional Economic Development Working Group (REDWG).
4. See Politi, Alessandro, *European Security: The New Transnational Risks*, Chaillot Paper 29, Paris: WEU Institute for Security Studies, October 1997.
5. See Lesser, Ian and Tellis, Ashley (1996), *Strategic Exposure: Proliferation Around the Mediterranean*, Santa Monica, RAND.
6. Much attention has been focused on missile and WMD capabilities in North Africa and the Middle East, but it is also worth noting potential missile risks emanating from the Balkans. It is not beyond consideration that an isolated, aggressive regime in the Balkans could chose to respond to Western intervention in an 'asymmetric' fashion, for example, holding Rome at risk to deter attacks on Belgrade.
7. The Gafsa incident of 1980 illustrated the French, US and Italian commitment to the territorial integrity of Tunisia in the face of a small-scale Libyan incursion.
8. For example, unclassified CIA analyses suggests a significant but relatively modest role for Caspian production in world energy supply.
9. Early fears of energy supply interruptions have not materialized. Despite the crisis in Algeria, European and American firms continue to invest in new oil, gas and pipeline activities, and the country's energy infrastructure has been relatively untouched by the violence.
10. The Imia-Kardak crisis of 1995 illustrated the potential for conflict and escalation even in the absence of a deliberate, aggressive strategy. It is arguable that policymakers on both sides simply lost control of the situation in the face of assertive media and strong public opinion pressures.
11. On the Euro-Mediterranean implications, see Callaya, Stephen C. (1997), 'The Euro-Mediterranean Process After Malta: What Prospects?', in *Mediterranean Politics*, 2/2, Autumn.
12. See Black, Jeremy, (1998) *War and the World: Military Power and the Fate of Continents*, 1450–2000, New Haven, Yale University Press.
13. A conservative estimate suggests that Caspian oil will constitute perhaps six percent of total world supply by 2010. Less attention has been paid to the Caspian role in gas supply, where the regional contribution may be far higher.
14. See, for example, Kemp, Geoffrey and Harkevy, Robert E. (1997) *Strategic Geography and the Changing Middle East*, Washington: Carnegie Endowment. This and other recent analyses are very much in the tradition of writing surrounding the Berlin-Baghdad railway project prior to the First World War.
15. See Kovalsky, Nicolai A. (ed.) (1998) *Europe, the Mediterranean, Russia: Perception of Strategies*, Moscow, Russian Academy of Sciences/Interdialect.
16. This interpretation of Russian behavior is especially common among Turkish observers, who worry that Ankara will be left alone to face a more assertive Russian policy on NATO's flank.
17. An example would be the recent proposal to form a joint Russian-Turkish crisis response force for the Caucuses.

18. See Gompert, David C. and Larrabee, F. Stephen Larrabee (eds.) (1997), *America and Europe: A Partnership for a New Era,* Cambridge, Cambridge University Press/RAND.

19. Braudel, Fernand (1972 [1949]), *The Mediterranean and the Mediterranean World in the Age of Philip II,* New York, Harper and Row.

20. See the discussion of ancient Greek and later European thinking about the Orient in Hentsch, Thierry (1992), *Imagining the Middle East,* New York, Black Rose Books; and Lewis, Bernard (1982), *The Muslim Discovery of Europe,* New York: W.W. Norton.

21. See Lewis, Martin and Wigen, Karen (1997), *The Myth of Continents,* Berkeley, Univ. of California Press.

22. An exception is the potential for conflict between Spain and Morocco over the future of the enclaves of Ceuta and Melilla. If Turkish estrangement from Europe continues to deepen, Greco-Turkish friction may also acquire a more palpable north-south dimension.

23. *See* Larrabee, F. Stephen, Green, Jerrold, Lesser, Ian and Zanini, Michele (1997) *NATO's Mediterranean Initiative: Policy Issues and Dilemmas* (Santa Monica: RAND, 1998); and Pedro Moya, *NATO's Role in the Mediterranean,* Brussels: North Atlantic Assembly, Mediterranean Special Group Report.

24. See Spencer, Claire, (1997) 'Building Confidence in the Mediterranean', in *Mediterranean Politics,* 2/2, Autumn.

25. Some Israelis have long argued that their security interests are best served through alignment with existing Euro-Atlantic institutions rather than participation in new, regional security initiatives.

26. The severity of this perceptual problem is described in Larrabee *et al.* (note 23) see, in particular, chapter 4, 'Perspectives of the Dialogue Countries'.

27. See Oudenaren, John (ed.) (1996) *Employment, Economic Development and Migration in Southern Europe and the Maghreb,* Conference Proceedings, RAND/Luso-American Development Foundation/Fundacion BBV.

28. The funding goals are modest in relation to EU programs aimed at central and eastern Europe, and represent a small fraction of the EU's spending on cohesion programs for its own southern European members.

Framework Scenarios for the Mediterranean Region

OLIVER SPARROW

Issues of Development

The World Bank notes that the average inhabitant of sub-Saharan Africa has seen no significant change in per capita income since 1950. The difference between these states and the average in Asia has expanded, in constant money, from a few hundred dollars half a century ago to over $2,000 today. Modelling attributes this distinction to differences in institutions – such as the processes and probity of the law, macro-economics management and political representation – and to the capacity of the state to invest, or influence investment, in physical and human capital.

Development rests upon three pillars: on wealth generation (and the ability to attract resource), upon institutional stability and efficacy (and the ability to win confidence) and on the capacity of individuals to find ways to maximise their potential (and to feel that their efforts will be rewarded). These three factors are shown as potentially independent variables in Figure 1. It is clear, however, that all states – from the poorest at the threshold of development to the most complex and integrated of societies – have to operate within a circumscribed domain, in which these factors are kept in their proper relationship. It is the systems connections between these factors which police these domains and enforce their validity.

What is appropriate at the simplest level of these scales and at the most complex is, of course, different. This paper asserts that there is a continuum – shown as a cylinder – in which these successive states connect. Development, in this picture, is a gradual process of accommodation to complexity, and consists of balances struck between these three independent variables in ways which are appropriate to the circumstances of the state in question. The innate systems in human societies (and within international frameworks) enforce a quite narrow range of discretion, however, such that there is something of a blueprint available for what needs to be achieved at

Oliver Sparrow is Director of the Chatham House Forum.

each stage. Conversely, failure to achieve such balances (or attempts to strike balances outside of the systems limits) leads, in the medium term, to sharp realignments. It is beyond the scope of this paper, but the 1997-98 crisis in South East Asia can be attributed, at least in part, to exactly such imbalanced ambitions.

States have directly killed around 200 million people in the twentieth century, around 150 million in wars and the remaining 50 million through assault by the state upon its own citizens. Predatory government, corrupt officials and vested interests all thrive under conditions of unresolved conflict.

FIGURE 1
THREE 'THINGS TO BE GOT RIGHT' AT ALL STAGES OF DEVELOPMENT

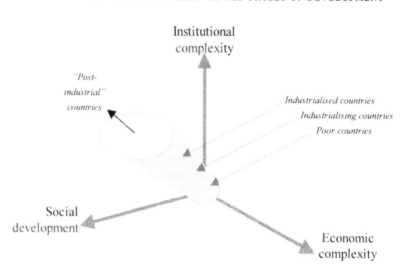

Corruption makes it impossible to rely upon agreements, and makes it certain that resources will be misallocated. It excludes most of the population from choice and prevents them from having confidence in their own society. Further, closed leadership and institutionalised privilege lead to populist leadership, seeking to substitute popular gestures and electoral bribes for real policies. The consequence may be that the state sector (or favoured industries) are protected from competition, propped up with public money when they make a loss and allowed to price their products in ways which bear no relation to their cost or to their utility to the public. Complex societies – such as those of the industrial nations – cannot be managed under such overheads. Figure 2 suggests the relationship whereby nations have to re-invent their institutions if they are to attain stable institutional complexity and with this, development.

Macroeconomic statistics are available for most countries, assessed from many perspectives and tested daily by capital and foreign exchange markets. Macroeconomic policy is open to relatively simple, central levers; and those trained to wield these have often received their training overseas and are keen to apply their skills. It is far from accidental that the model that we have of the appropriate paths to development began with macro-economics measures and has, gradually, grown outwards like ivy to embrace the other pillars of development. Briefly, the so-called Washington model of the early 1980s was focused on getting these balances right. Nations were to bring their state budgets into balance, chiefly by removing subsidies to loss making industries and by reforming their tax raising machinery. They were to control their money supply, chiefly through these measures. State-to-state lending was supplanted by private sector to industry transfers. As a subsidiary measure, exchange rates should be market-determined, capital should be freely transferable and trade subject to minimal tariffs and other controls.

FIGURE 2
ASSESSED LEVELS OF CORRUPTION AND INCOME PER CAPITA

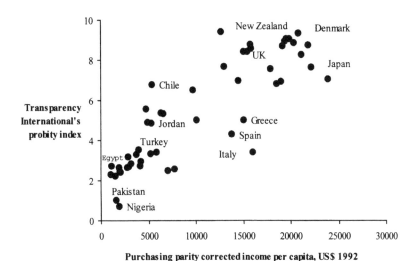

Purchasing parity corrected income per capita, US$ 1992

Source: Transparency International and World Bank

This recipe produced dramatic results, as is shown in the Latin American experience in the decade after 1987. It can have a devastating effect upon industries which do not meet international standards. It can – at least in the short run – have a sharply negative effect upon the conditions of the poor. Further, as rigid societies begin to churn into new configurations, vested interests are touched. Political alignments are weakened. The natural transition away from primary production, such as agriculture, is marked by rapid expansion of the informal sector, typically around the cities, typically associated with a complex pattern of transient migration to expanding slum areas around major cities. Crime increases, and radical ideas are carried into the countryside.

Criticism, much of it unfair, has been levelled at this immensely influential model. In recent years, it has been supplemented by attention to the second pillar of development: the development (and engagement) of human capital. The early Nineties saw emphasis shift to investment in people and particularly towards female education, which has knock-on effects on child care, family size and the like.

FIGURE 3
RATES OF RETURN TO INVESTMENT IN EDUCATION

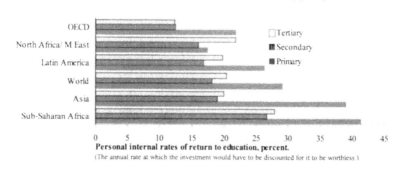

Source: G Psacharopolous in World Development 22/9, 1994.

The internal rate of return on investment in primary level education for women is estimated at over 70 per cent. In addition, stress was given to the creation of tangible infrastructure, such as transport, communications and energy, water and drainage, health care and housing. These, too, have been shown to have immensely powerful effects upon development.

In the past few years, however, the critical role of institutions has come to the fore: the third pillar of development. This may express itself in national governance, or in establishing the position of ordinary people within their society. Giving property rights to peasant farmers enables them to raise money and to invest. Thailand saw such investment grow by 30–66 per cent after taking such an essentially costless step on behalf of seven million peasants. Whilst there is no clear correlation between the constitutional form of government and subsequent economic performance, very strong relationships can be determined between economic growth and institutional probity. Countries in which the processes of policing and the law are uniform and predictable, where political decision-taking is transparent and open and in which access to influence is transparent, based upon the capacity to contribute and weighed upon its merits, are those which tend to grow rapidly. By contrast, politically appointed and underpaid civil servants are vulnerable to being suborned, networks of patronage exclude the majority and lead to distorted choice, and judges who are beholden to politicians (or to special interests) for their posts are prone to make decisions which erode popular consent. If citizens feel themselves as prey, entrepreneurialism will be muted, choices will be hard for the average individual to make and the future will be discounted. National life will lack vibrancy and will settle into the dull, sullen cart tracks of habit and passivity.

TABLE 1

Gross domestic investment as % of GDP		Law of contract	
		Unpredictable	Straightforward
Level of	Low	21.3%	28.5%
corruption	High	12.3%	19.5%

Source: World Bank 1997

Growth requires investment, typically funded from taxes, from domestic saving and from foreign direct investment. Effective state investment is critical to some activities – such as primary education – where the theoretical potential open to private investors is seldom, in practice, reaped. Unpredictable environments will deter investors, as the above table shows. Macroeconomic uncertainty can compound this effect. Uncertain or volatile labour supply, transient shortages of skills, failure of major infrastructure all add to the overheads associated with inward investment. Perhaps centrally, however, hypertrophied bureaucracies and byzantine procedures may waste significant amounts of management time. Until recently, winning a single export permit in Brazil required over 1,400 legal actions, involving over a hundred separate state departments.

More profound than this, however, is the deterrent effect of corruption, whereby regulation is applied capriciously, judgments are awarded unpredictably, agents of the state effectively claim protection money and managers are required to take a stance in respect of political divisions in the country, backing one side or the other. Deeper still, there are countries in which it is impossible to know with whom a deal may be struck, where rival elements of the state claim influence or where none do, where regulations

which can make or cripple a project exist at the stroke of a pen and can be
dispersed as easily. Here, firms invest only if they believe that they are so
valuable to the strongest powers in the regime that they can appeal to them,
over the heads of lesser predators.

Most of the Southern Mediterranean countries have some of these
problems, and a few have them in an acute form. It is, however, a reasonable
assertion that the main problems are institutional and social. People do not
see a way forward for themselves, socially sanctioned and practical; and the
institutions of state are often captured by habit and vested interest in ways
which amplify this. Also, for the most part, the region has high birth rates
and relatively slow economic growth. The upper part of the table includes
Turkey and Israel for reference.

With Turkey, Israel	1980	1995	2015, on extra-polation	Actual economic growth 1980–95	Implied economic growth 1995–2015
Population	144 mln	207	336	2.4%	Same
Nominal GNP	$02 bn	419	1107	5.0	Same
Nominal GNP/capita	$1403	2024	3297	2.5	Same
PPP GNP/capita	$4699	5946	7884	1.6	1.4
PPP corrected GNP	$677 bn	1231	2648	4.1	3.9
Without Turkey, Israel	1980	1995	2015	As above	As above
Population	96 mln	140	232	2.55%	Same
Nominal GNP	$111 bn	162	270	2.58	Same
Nominal GNP/capita	$1153	1158	1165	0.03	Same
PPP GNP/capita	$4115	4127	4144	0.02	0.02
PPP corrected GNP	$395 bn	578	960	2.57	2.57

Source: World Bank 1996. Purchasing Power Parity estimates for 2015 through regression.
Figures exclude Libya, for which there is no comparable data. Constant 1995 dollars.

The South Eastern Mediterranean region has shown annual per capita
increases in purchasing power of around 1.6 per cent per annum. This, due
to shifts in relative scale of the participants, would fall towards 2015 if
current trends continue. When Israel and Turkey are excluded, however,
there has been no growth whatever in individual incomes, a trend which
remains unchanged to 2015. Clearly some nations – such as Tunisia – have
done well, whilst others, such as Algeria, have not. On aggregate, however,
the region will have to shift radically if it is to avoid strife.

	Egypt	Morocco	Syria	Jordan	Algeria	Tunisia
Net-Present Value of external debt as % GNP	56	62	118	108	64	52
Gross Domestic Investment as % GNP	17	21	28	26	32	24
Growth in GDI, 1990–95	-1.5	-2.5	-7	6.5	-4.7	1.4
Net private capital flows as % GDP	0.6	1.8	0.3	-2.3	0.3	4.2
Export as % GDP	7	15	24	29	21	30
Agriculture as % GNP	20	14	16	8	13	12
Urbanisation, %	45	49	53	72	56	57
Water use, % fresh resource	97	36	9	32	30	80
Adult illiteracy	49	56		13	38	33
Infant mortality/100 live births	56	55	32	31	34	39

The table gives some pertinent World Bank figures for these countries. They are significantly indebted: the present value of their debt (principal and discounted interest) amounts to between half and the whole of a year's GNP. They invest quite strongly, but excepting Tunisia and Jordan, suffer net capital outflows which are a significant fraction of GDP. Excepting Egypt, they are strongly export oriented. Most are in the middle of their agricultural transition: roughly where Britain was just before World War One. They are already highly urbanised and are rapidly becoming more so. Excepting Syria, they are already using a significant fraction of their water resource. Adult illiteracy is high for middle income countries, excepting Jordan. Infant mortality is also high: the equivalent figure for Israel is eight deaths per 1,000 live births.

It is, of course, hard to assess whether a given value is an appropriate one for the country in its particular stage of development. The World Bank has, conveniently, calculated two indexes for a large number of countries. One index calculates the 'Human Development Index', a combination of values based upon educational attainment, economic performance, political involvement and similar factors. They have also assessed a 'Poverty Index' which is based on factors such as child and maternal mortality, access to schooling, personal security, sustainability and income.

The figure shows a strong trend, expressed in well over 100 nations, to diminish one index and to increase the other. Figure 5 shows what happens when these two trends are compared.

FIGURE 4
HUMAN DEVELOPMENT AND POVERTY MEASURES, PLOTTED AGAINST
INCOME PER CAPITA

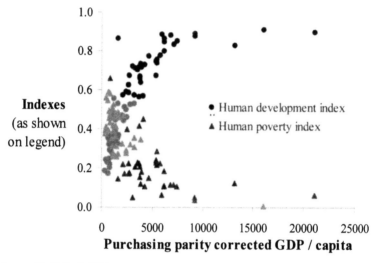

Source: World Bank, RIIA.

FIGURE 5
MIDDLE EASTERN AND SOUTH-EAST MEDITERRANEAN COUNTRIES TEND
TO LAG BEHIND THE TREND TO REDUCE POVERTY AND INCREASE HUMAN
CAPITAL IN PARALLEL WITH ECONOMIC DEVELOPMENT

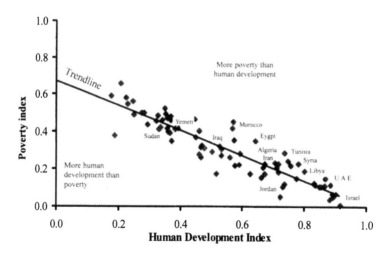

Source: World Bank, RIIA.

The indexes which are shown to change with the wealth of the country in Figure 4 are plotted against each other in Figure 5 with a trend line plotted through these points. Nations which lie above the trend line either develop their human capital more slowly or reduce their signs of poverty more slowly than the average developing and middle income nation. The nations of the region plotted on this chart except for Jordan, Israel and the Sudan, all lie in this unfortunate region of the chart. Although out of the region, it is worth noting that Iraq and Iran lie close to the average.

The shift out of primary production will continue. By 2015 cities will have grown considerably, not least as young people migrate and have children. Investment needs will be huge and the young population will be saving proportionately less than today. Consumption of natural resources – water, foods hitherto destined for export and energy – will have increased substantially, perhaps in line with or faster than GNP. The population will have access to the full power of twenty-first century information technology, networks, interactive entertainment media and education will be better informed, better able to communicate and more aware of alternative models of development. Unless economic growth picks up, however, and efforts are made both to invest in efficiency and institutional improvement, most of the people will be seeing the quality of their lives improving much more slowly than their aspirations will prompt.

This is, of course, a generic problem of nations in development. The Southern Mediterranean countries are, however, the only states of this nature with which Europe has a border, and it is natural for it to feel more concern about their capacity to grow in a socially and in other ways sustainable manner.

The World in 2015

World population in 1900 was around 1.5 billion, of whom 500 million lived in Europe and its offshoots. Their average age was lower than that of the rest of the world. The European populations faced a billion people whose most advanced technologies and capacity to manage were on parity with what Europe had been doing two centuries earlier. European and US populations were growing very rapidly, whilst births matched deaths in the rest of the world.

By contrast world population in 2015 will be somewhat over 6 billion, with a fraction over one billion of these living in the industrialised world. The population there is ageing: half of Germany will be retired, for example, and dependency rates will be high. Japan, currently supporting one dependent with around four workers, will have to meet extended aspirations with around 1.2 workers per dependent. Pension commitments cannot easily be met: US state debt would rise to several hundred per cent of GNP by 2020 if taxes were not raised, or taxes would have to rise to a mean of 70 per cent on income (versus 30 per cent today) to meet current commitment.

States are now spending around half of all of the value added in the industrialised world, excluding the US, which nevertheless spends something over a third, on a rising trend. Virtually all operate at a deficit. Transfers to persons makes up about a third of the flow of value added in these societies. Clearly, the trend that has taken spending from 28 per cent of GNP, on average, in 1970 to current levels cannot continue, yet the drivers of under-employment and ageing, expectations and the capacity of the elderly and the dependent to vote for entitlements will not go away.

In conjunction with this social fact, the societies of the industrialised world have been becoming less equal over the past two decades. This trend, most pronounced in the US, is the consequence of two sets of forces. One of these is the heightened competition that has resulted from coupling together hitherto isolated economic basins. The drive for efficiency that this has provoked has set up an endless race to cut costs. The second driver is that of the combination of IT and organisational technologies, such as re-engineering. It has become possible to substitute capital for labour in areas which were hitherto regarded as untouchable. Typically, it has been possible simply to design the need for modest skilled human labour out of the system.

Some of the effects of these forces have been offset by the expansion in the scale and scope of the economies of the West. Firms need more expert assistance than hitherto, and have created a plethora of service industries in order to deliver this. Wealth has created mass demand for products which were hitherto restricted to elites. Technology has created new products. The capable have been absorbed by this, but the less capable have not. Unemployment in the OECD has risen from 10 million in the 1960–70 period to around 45 million today, but under-employment under other names (such as the expansion of disability allowances) suggest that underlying unemployment may be as high as 25 per cent of the work force in the EU. In the US more people work, but real terms median wages have been static since the 1970s and the income of the lowest few per cent in society has halved. The corresponding income of the elite few per cent has, however, doubled since 1980.

There are a number of possible outcomes to this.[1] We might run faster and faster to stay in the same place. We might slip into populist, bitter politics, leading to irrational policies such as protectionism. Equally, however, regenerated commerce (and reconsidered institutions and the renewed ability to manage individual lives) could provide the wealth needed to overcome the worst of these difficulties. Clearly, there are more extreme situations that can be considered, but these central cases will suffice for current purposes. The developing world would confront three very different faces in each of these scenarios, and the dispersion of views upon (and fears about, aspirations for) the Southern Mediterranean would be the more extreme.

It is in the interest of Europe (in those instances in which this administrative convenience can be said to have a coherent interest) that the Southern Mediterranean states grow rapidly and grow well. It is in the specific interest of the Mediterranean facing states of Europe that they do so. The chief sources of revenue in the Union, however, either are facing more acute issues in the geographically contiguous states of the East, or have Atlantic interests at heart.

The changing nature of the European voter and of the European state purse both suggest that the chief interaction which the two regions have will be circumscribed. Major transfers of funds may well occur, but this will comprise direct commercial investment by outsiders (some of them European) rather than state aid. Where aid is to be paid, such as the Ecu 4.7 billion committed under the Euro-Mediterranean Partnership Initiative, this would best be directed to those projects (such as primary education) where experience suggests that FDI flows with greatest difficulty, but which also have the greatest potential for the nation in question. Achieving such hypothecation of aid is always difficult, but five decades of experience amongst donors suggests that the finer the targeting, the more acute the response. Certainly, aid delivered to cover 'transitional pain' during liberalisation almost invariably vanishes in an inflationary smog of consumption.

Framework Scenarios

We are concerned with the possible evolution of the interactions between the EU (and its most affected constituent nations) and the Southern Mediterranean states, their internal sources of agency and their cultural and economic affiliates. These two loosely coupled sets of players define much of the dynamics but we do need to consider the broader context in which these interactions may be taking place.

The European Union is an entity of sufficient scale that the fate of all of these nations jointly sets much of the tone of the global context. That is to say, up to at least 2020, if the industrialised nations prosper and demonstrate a viable path forward, then the rest of the world will follow in their train. They will converge economically upon global best practice where individual conditions permit this to occur, as has already been discussed.

FIGURE 6
THE INTERSECTION OF THE MAJOR AGENCIES

The global context:
• Relations between wealthy and poor populations
• Leadership or mixed signals from the industrialised world

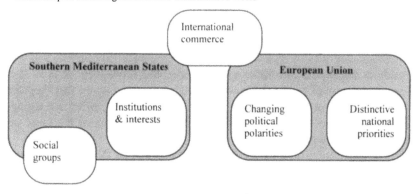

Implicitly or explicitly, they will also accept a process of more or less gradual cultural and institutional convergence.

If, by contrast, the industrial world shows signs of chronic internal difficulties – and if its economies slow or become protectionist – then it is far less likely that this convergence of interest and practice will occur. The poor and poorly managed nations will be far more prone to spiral into difficulties, which their growing populations and scarified environments will make it hard to reverse. The nations which have grasped their opportunities will tend to look more to their peers than to the West for their principles of organisation, and distinctive styles of operation – some authoritarian, some highly introverted – will develop around the major attractors of shared culture and common economic and security interests, and around the facts of geography and wealth.

The rhetoric of partnership and the humanitarian impulse conceal the goals which the European Union might have for the Southern Mediterranean region. The chief aim has to be that the region should become, in one way or another, integrated into the global economy in such a way that each nation is capable of satisfying the reasonable aspirations of its citizens. Healthy, wealthy and wise, they will then make good neighbours and the source of profitable trade and investment. Elderly Europeans may retire to the warm fringe, in which labour costs are low, communications excellent, health care at world standards and EU pensions paid on time in stable currency. From this, everyone wins. At issue is how this is to be achieved.

FIGURE 7
THE FRAMEWORK IN WHICH THE RELATIONSHIP WILL WORK ITSELF OUT

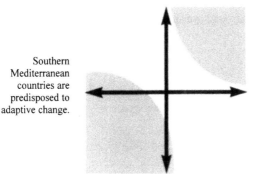

Europe is seen as a helpful partner. The
region moves to join the global economy.

Southern
Mediterranean
countries are
predisposed to
adaptive change.

S. Mediterranean
countries feel themselves
under seige. Change is
blocked, politics become
populist, authoritarian;
nations look East for
their social & economic
models.

Europe is seen as an invasive, predatory and a
threat. European citizens tend to see the region
as a source of problems.

We have noted the constraints on the wealthy nations, and the distinctive
global environments that this may create. We have also noted the issues of
development, many of which are particularly poignant in the region. As we
noted in the introductory section, therefore, there are two key dimensions
along which uncertainty can be arrayed. In the first place, either the bulk of
the nations fringing the Southern Mediterranean will adopt policies which
promote social and institutional change – and as a result, achieve the means
by which to develop economically – or they will not do this. Far from
independently of this, the European Union may be seen as a helpful partner
in this process of change, or it may be seen as a major player in a world
economy turned invasive, predatory and threatening.

The figure shows these axes, shading areas which appear to be unstable.
Thus it is signally improbable that the Southern Mediterranean countries
would, simultaneously, feel that the European Union was a helpful partner
(particularly if its partnership was, as we have observed, focused upon their
internal change) and, at the same time, feel themselves under siege from the
international forces of change. Similar thoughts influence the positioning
and shape of the shading on the lower left of the figure. Readers may alter
these to taste: they are indicative guides, based solely upon the internal
dynamics of the model that we have posed.

It is also helpful to graduate these dimensions, asking ourselves what is
entailed in moving a given distance on them. A useful benchmark is the

point at which the elastic in the system declares itself fully stretched. Thus a full blooded, Singaporean determination to change every aspect of society may well be beyond the grasp of all of the nations of the region for at least a generation. Equally, an Iranian type retreat to xenophobia may be provoked only in a few of these often relatively cosmopolitan societies. We signify these limits with two vertical dotted lines on the figure, as reproduced in Figure 8.

FIGURE 8
THE NATURAL BOUNDS TO THIS SPACE

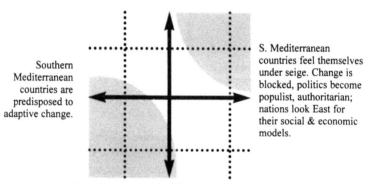

Europe is seen as a helpful partner. The region moves to join the global economy.

Southern Mediterranean countries are predisposed to adaptive change.

S. Mediterranean countries feel themselves under seige. Change is blocked, politics become populist, authoritarian; nations look East for their social & economic models.

Europe is seen as an invasive, predatory and a threat. European citizens tend to see the region as a source of problems.

We can perform a similar task on the 'European' axis. Full partnership, in which all aspects of society happily grasp the cultural norms and economic paradigms of the grey, pluralist, technophile West may characterise central European integration, but not the majority of the nations of this region.

The equivalent lower line is harder to establish, however, as economic interest battles with potential mutual xenophobia in the more extreme conditions that could prevail in 2015. Two horizontal dotted lines mark these bounds.

These operations give us a certain grasp of the space in which the future relations between the various agencies that are involved may work themselves out. Figure 9 represents the familiar axes, embellished with where we may now find ourselves (1998) and with three possible cases. These are expanded as crude, generic scenarios in the paragraphs which follow but it should be emphasised that these are framework scenarios, offering a structure against which more complex development could be

FIGURE 9
FRAMEWORK SCENARIOS

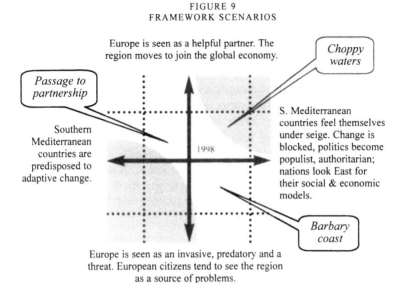

Europe is seen as a helpful partner. The region moves to join the global economy.

Choppy waters

Passage to partnership

Southern Mediterranean countries are predisposed to adaptive change.

1998

S. Mediterranean countries feel themselves under seige. Change is blocked, politics become populist, authoritarian; nations look East for their social & economic models.

Barbary coast

Europe is seen as an invasive, predatory and a threat. European citizens tend to see the region as a source of problems.

worked out. It would, for example, be necessary to test the numerical implications of each, and define credible political pathways by which the nations in question could migrate to the new locus.

Passage to Partnership

Global economic growth maintains its historical patterns of around three per cent per annum, and the industrial nations make their way forward by exploiting new technologies. Significant aspects of the manufacturing and service value chain are subject to international trade, constrained by the capacities of information networks and trade to handle real-time scheduled processes. Trust in the ability of medium income nations to deliver subcontracts reliably has, however, improved markedly in the preceding ten years, not least as institutional modernisation and economic management have made many of these nations attractive and predictable places in which to set up industry. Such nations have experienced massive injections of capital and expertise, and they are, on average, growing at twice the international average. Two thirds of the Southern Mediterranean countries have achieved this status, supplying European nations with manufactured intermediates, short run assembly and services.

The transformation of these countries began slowly, with intensive interaction between decision-takers, generating both recognition of the need to change and a clear, mutual view of the paths that would lead to sustainable change. Whilst Europe had much to tell the nations in question, the Union itself had to change. The Common Agricultural Policy had to be altered, for example, to cease dumping food internationally – thereby reducing the income of peasant farmers the world over by anything up to a third – and to concentrate on funding a bio-diverse countryside that offered healthy food, energy crops and other useful public goods. Security policies needed intensive review in order to offer the region the advantages of mutual assurance. European social attitudes to transient workers (and to displacement of low skilled jobs in Europe through outsourcing to the region and to Eastern Europe) had to be handled with political sensitivity. These tasks took the best part of five years to specify to the satisfaction of all, but by 2010, the positive rewards that flowed from them were clearly evident.

Choppy Waters

European growth continued to lag behind the USA, and its burden of the jobless and the retired remained a heavy one. Political attention tended to focus internally throughout the first decade of the new millennium, with only broad brush attention being given even to Eastern European integration. Popular opinion in the Union was equivocal about such integration, and in individual sectors, such as agriculture and mass assembly, directly hostile. Indeed, the enterprise of the Union itself was under some internal stress.

The Southern Mediterranean countries present a heterogeneous picture by 2015. Some have changed, often more to an American model than a European one, and all are significantly more adept in macro-economics management. Their growth averages around four per cent per annum and their populations are, for the most part, less equal than they are now, better educated on average and – with significant national and class differences – far more focused on the outside world than was the case two decades earlier. Internal markets have grown, as has intra-regional trade. The European Union is seen as a honey pot, well guarded by rules and regulations, tariffs and patrol boats. The xenophobia of the retired communities that ring the Northern Mediterranean is legendary and remittance workers tell tales of a tired and irritable society which 'takes it out on the poor dog of the Mahgrib' when they have had a bad day. Unless supported by large sums of money, European attempts to influence political and social change in the region are brusquely rejected.

Barbary Coast

The industrial world is finding the passage through the age bulge of its demographic profile to be a painful and drawn out struggle. Its commerce is subject to very fast change, but the capacity to find projects that generate lasting returns is difficult in the face of intense competition. Global growth slows to two per cent and global savings are soaked up by state borrowing in order to pay subsidies. Capital is expensive and attractive projects are scant. The poor nations, in particular, find this a terrifying period, and a variety of political-religious 'explanations' of what is happening to them fan out and spread around the globe. The tendency to believe that 'they' have got us into this mess and that 'they' are continuing to exploit the poor is widespread. The wealthy, elderly nations fear the actual or latent turmoil in the poor countries, whilst the middle income nations grope for alternative policies which will avoid the apparent failure of the Western paradigms. There is a widespread tendency to manage the extent of trade in order to preserve jobs in otherwise uncompetitive industries is widespread. The alternative – to drive these industries to achieve competitiveness – is deflected both by costly capital and by social reaction to high unemployment.

This is a world that is governed by attitudes rather than economic realities. People sense that their societies are fragile, and they themselves feel exposed and frail in their turn. The large number of elderly people in the wealthy world enhances this. In the middle income nations, however, this insecurity expresses itself as a distrust of outside influence, in an unwillingness to change what has worked for what might (or might not) work. There is a widespread sense that all that can be achieved is to hold back the barriers for another few years.

The Southern Mediterranean undergoes considerable change in such a world. Europe is seen as a heavy thundercloud, which is as likely to offer floods as welcome rain. In the individual nations, the much enlarged urban proletariat finds its progress blocked. Their attempts to lodge able youngsters amongst the middle classes for the most part fail, and the sense of progress that keeps the *forces vives* content is markedly absent. At the same time, persuasive ideologies are easily accessible through the new telecommunications media. Populist, often rejectionist politicians attempt to grasp the diverse opportunities which this represents. For the first time, such movements may become significant and integrated transnationally, often around ethnic and other cultural linkages that exist within the region. The sources of traditional power in the region will, with greater or lesser success, resist these forces. The European Union may be forced to take sides, facing the dilemma that confronted the US in South America during the Cold War. Indeed, the region has much of the flavour of 1970s Central

America as 2015 approaches. Popular attitudes to the Union (and the tendency of local powers to play its influence as a trump card whilst managing disruption) make it as popular as the US was during those turbulent years.

NOTES

1. The Royal Institute of International Affairs has been conducting an enquiry around these issues for three years. In 1996, it published *Unsettled Times, Three Stony Paths to 2015*, in which these scenarios are explored in depth. In 1997, it published *Navigating Uncharted Waters*, which explores what is entailed in grasping the opportunities that will lead us to the positive case.

The Euro-Mediteranean Partnership Initiative: Problems and Prospects

GEORGE JOFFÉ

The EMPI cannot be properly evaluated in isolation. It forms part of a more general statement about the process of economic development inside developing countries and is both a reflection of European ambivalence about the policies Europe wishes to adopt towards its periphery and a reflection of the geo-economic reordering of the international arena. It also reflects a new approach to the issues of co-operation in the social, cultural and security spheres, although the details of the ways forward here are, perhaps, less clear precisely because the concepts involved are so novel. Some of these issues are primarily political or strategic in nature and will be discussed later. However, the fundamental assumptions that govern the economic philosophy behind the Initiative also deserve attention because they will have the most immediate impact on the outcome of the process itself.

The economic objectives of the Barcelona process are clearly delineated in the Barcelona Declaration. They are:

- accelerated sustainable socio-economic development,
- improved living conditions, increased employment levels and a reduced Mediterranean development gap, and
- and the encouragement of regional cooperation and integration.

The means to achieve these objectives are equally clearly stated. They are defined as:

- the progressive establishment of a free trade area,
- appropriate economic cooperation, and
- substantial increase in European Union financial aid.

This is to be achieved by the creation of bilateral free trade areas (FTAs) in

George Joffé is the director of studies at the Royal Institute of International Affairs and co-editor of the *Journal of North African Studies*. He was also the senior research of the project on the Euro-Mediterranean Partnership which generated the papers published in this book.

industrial goods and services by the year 2010 between the European Union (EU) and the individual states of the southern Mediterranean rim. These new FTAs differ from past bilateral agreements with such states which provided for unrestricted access to the European market for industrial goods. Instead, the onus for adjustment is now placed on the Mediterranean non-member countries of the European Union (MNMCs). Industrial services are not yet included in the FTA agreements although there is no reason why they could not be in the future.

In addition, between 1996 and the year 2000, European Union aid (through the MEDA programme) is to be ECU4.685 billion. Similar amounts are to be made available on soft loan terms from the European Development Bank – a 25 per cent increase in direct aid over the previous Five Year Financial Protocol, although the amounts under the protocols themselves have been doubled. The MEDA programme – the acronym merely means *mesures d'ajustement* – itself is to be directed towards support of the private sector with 20 per cent of its funding committed for that purpose. Although the aid is allocated on a country basis, within each country it will be issued on a first-come-first-served basis, thus avoiding problems of uptake and implementation in the past and ensuring that inefficient and ineffective public sector support should cease.

The Underlying Purpose

This programme of economic partnership has clear links with the EU's antecedent policies towards the southern rim of the Mediterranean basin, particularly as far as the Maghrib countries are concerned – and they are the primary focus of this paper. It derives from the long tradition of economic interaction stretching back to 1957 and the Treaty of Rome which reflected former colonial ties. It mirrors, in many respects, the provisions of the old Cooperation and Association Agreements and, in particular, the policy initiatives undertaken by Brussels at the start of the 1990s in the atmosphere engendered by the end of the Cold War. It essentially reflects European anxiety over the security implications of economic failure amongst the southern rim MNMCs, particularly in North Africa.

Neo-Liberalism, the Washington Consensus and the WTO

The programme must also be seen, however, in the context of the radical change in economic development theory that became economic orthodoxy during the 1980s. It is essentially neo-classical and neo-liberal in its inspiration. It thus assumes that the unhampered operation of the market – national or global – will ensure efficient allocation of resources and that the state must not interfere in this process, either by controlling resource allocation or by artificially stimulating resource accumulation. It also assumes that liberalisation of external regimes – in terms of currency, capital movement and trade – rather than any kind of domestic protectionism, is the best and only means by which additional resources can be accumulated.

To a considerable degree, the EMPI is, therefore, closely linked to the Washington Consensus articulated during the 1980s by the World Bank and the International Monetary Fund (IMF). As with the Consensus, it is the *commonality* of the economic problems facing MNMCs, not the *specificity* of national economic difficulties which is to be addressed by the EMPI. Furthermore, it sees that these should be addressed by endogenous reform, not by exogenous adjustment. It also implicitly supports more recent calls for domestic liberalisation, particularly the privatisation of state assets and state-controlled activities, as part of the process of forcing the state to withdraw from the economy. This raises a primary, albeit theoretical, consideration: are the economic assumptions on which the Barcelona process is based correct? And to what extent does or should the EMPI implicitly support the more radical liberalising trend within contemporary economic theory?

Free Trade and Economic Development

There are additional considerations, however. The EMPI does not provide a global process by which, even under neo-liberal principles, economic development can be achieved in the southern Mediterranean rim states. It is only concerned with the external macro-economic arena for it is formally limited to the creation of a series of bilateral free trade areas across the region by 2010, in effect, the removal of tariff barriers across the Mediterranean. Although agriculture is excluded, to that extent the EMPI anticipates the requirements of the Uruguay Round of the GATT and the regulations of the World Trade Organisation (WTO) – under which the Maghrib is one of the few regions which, it is admitted, will be in net deficit within the global economy!

The exclusion of agriculture, which remains subject to controls to preserve the Common Agricultural Policy (CAP), is significant, although it will be reviewed. Even in the case of Israel, to which special conditions apply, agricultural exports are limited by quota, although they bear no tariff. As a result, the EMPI does not create a free trade area as defined under the GATT but merely provides a degree of free access for agricultural goods. The effective exclusion of agriculture, mainly because of intra-European anxieties to preserve the CAP, means that the MNMCs have lost one important area of comparative advantage. South Mediterranean agriculture, since it is labour intensive, would also have provided a means of limiting urban drift, had it been included in the free trade area provisions, and thus been able to exploit its competitive edge. This might also have had knock-on effects in modernising agricultural technological expertise. This would have been particularly important in the area of water use, since the South Mediterranean region faces the threat of water shortages and needs the stimulus of competing demand to modernise its water pricing structures.

Furthermore, the EMPI does not extend the wider integrative principles of the European Common Economic Space (ECES) enjoyed by EFTA countries or of the customs union agreed with Turkey to these MNMCs. These include mutual recognition agreements over domestic standards and consultation over such technical matters. They also imply the removal of non-tariff barriers in addition to the tariffication of non-tariff barriers required by the WTO. At present MNMCs do not even have rights of consultation of the kind enjoyed by central European states through the Central European Free Trade Area (CEFTA), which is merely a preliminary step towards EU membership. The MNMCs are therefore not in a position to influence the subsequent decision-making process in Brussels, even though they will be affected by it.

Admittedly, the institutional difficulties in creating an ECES including the South Mediterranean states would have been so great that the European Commission did not consider this possibility. At the same time, the inability of the MNMCs to influence EU policy – even to the extent enjoyed by Switzerland which has consultative, if not deliberative, rights with the union – place them in a highly dependent position and one which emphasises their hub-spoke dependency on Europe. This, in turn, will make South-South economic integration, which is expected in the post-2000 period, more difficult to achieve. Yet, with a little encouragement of the type implied by the EU-CEFTA consultation process, even the Arab Maghrib Union might have been preserved as a forum to encourage future South-South interaction. There is no doubt that such a process must take place and it is already worth noting that, given the virtual collapse of the Arab Maghrib Union, Tunisia and Morocco are already discussing with Egypt the possibilities and modalities of economic integration. It is legitimate, therefore, to pose the question if tariff-free trade alone will be a sufficient factor to dynamise domestic synergies in economic development? Or should full EEA status be implemented by instituting the removal of European non-tariff barriers and the provision of mutual standards recognition?

Economic Issues

Quite apart from these underlying issues of principle, there are detailed economic issues associated with the Barcelona process that should be questioned. Some of these arise directly from the underlying issues and some arise from the specific nature of the process itself. One of the most important – and one which is linked to basic considerations over approaches to economic development – is the way in which such benefit is to be diffused.

The Issue of 'Trickle-Down'

The original neo-liberal agenda anticipated that the removal of barriers to trade would liberalise the price of capital and labour through competition and thus stimulate domestic employment. Under late capitalism this has been re-interpreted to mean that export-oriented trade would stimulate domestic entrepreneurs, provided that the domestic economy was also liberalised by the removal of the public sector and government from direct involvement in the economic process. The state would be there merely to provide public goods that the private sector would not generate – physical and human infrastructure, for example – and to provide a light regulating and guiding hand. It would become a facilitator, not a regulator, for the private sector. This situation, in turn, would generate savings as domestic surplus for investment and, together with foreign investment (primarily in the form of direct private foreign investment but also as portfolio equity investment), the process would force economic development.

The EMPI does not directly impinge on any of these domestic considerations, either at the macro- or the micro-economic level, except insofar as it generates aid through the MEDA programme for the private sector. Unless it indirectly stimulates foreign investment, it cannot, therefore, influence the nature or size of the domestic entrepreneurial group which is key to economic development, nor can it directly affect the nature of the domestic market. There are, no doubt, good political and diplomatic reasons why it cannot do this but, insofar as the Barcelona process falls within the scope of the Washington Consensus, the domestic effects of the integrative trade policies it proposes must form part of its agenda of concerns. Since the ultimate purpose of economic development is not merely to correct macro-economic distortions but to contribute to overall individual welfare – as stated in the Barcelona Declaration, it is reasonable to ask how the Barcelona process will in practice achieve such objectives?

The basic mechanism implicit in the EMPI is the process of trickle-down whereby economic benefit at the macro-level is diffused throughout society by increased employment and improved wage levels. State-directed redistributive mechanisms are prohibited because they would interfere with the 'hidden hand' of the market process. There are various problems with this, not least the fact that, in the past fifty years at least, 'trickle-down' has proved to be a very unreliable means of diffusing economic benefit and some kind of redistributive mechanism has always proved necessary. The experience of multinational corporations in the developing world underlines this quite clearly.

Furthermore, since the concept of export-oriented growth depends on the allied concept of comparative advantage – often in terms of unit labour costs – increases in wage levels towards those typical of Europe destroy the very process whereby comparative advantage was originally established. In addition, the means by which this can be countered – technology transfer, so that the labour content of production costs is reduced – is rarely achieved through the simple and single process of free trade. Instead, technology transfer has usually been restricted by the objectives set by foreign investors who are more concerned with out-sourcing to benefit from reduced labour costs than with establishing effectively autonomous industrial operations. It seems reasonable, therefore, to question whether a process limited solely to the external economic arena can create the necessary and sufficient conditions to materially facilitate significant economic development in North Africa?

Problems of Trade

Furthermore, the way in which free trade is to be stimulated – on a bilateral basis – also raises considerable anxieties over the static and dynamic effects on trade in the MNMCs concerned. European industry will compete both with domestic industries and with third country exports to these MNMCs. If products from domestic industries are replaced, so that *trade creation* will have occurred, questions may reasonably be asked as to how this can benefit the domestic economies involved, in the short-term. Ideally, in the longer term, those previously employed in what were, in effect, import substitution industries can be re-employed in export-oriented industries. Here, however, there is a further problem because the EMPI cannot offer significant opportunities for increased export earnings within the European market. If imports from third country producers are replaced by European products – *trade diversion* – this may create problems between those countries, the importing economy and the EU, although it would not necessarily adversely affect the domestic economy in the short-term. It would, however, hinder domestic productive growth because of the tariff preferences and the foreign exchange costs involved.

Trade creation involves employment losses in the recipient economy and this, of course, is inevitable as far as import substitution industries are concerned unless they can compete effectively with their European counterparts. In principle, this is unlikely and it has been estimated that one third of Tunisian industry, together with 60 per cent of Moroccan industry, will disappear. A further third of the industrial base in Tunisia will be threatened with bankruptcy. Although significant programmes of industrial restructuring (*mise à niveau*) costing $2.2 billion in the case of Tunisia and $5.4 billion in the case of Morocco – most of the funding being raised on the international financial markets – have been put in place, it is not clear that the industrial sectors in either country will eventually be able to compete sufficiently effectively to counter the adverse effects of trade creation, even though the FTA agreements provide for lengthy transition periods.

It has to be admitted that, since there is little overlap between European industrial exports and Maghribi industrial production, trade creation effects are likely to be small. The same may not be the case as far as trade diversion is concerned and, unless tariff barriers between Maghribi states and their other major industrial suppliers – Japan and the USA – are reduced, difficulties might well develop in the economic relationships with both third country suppliers. As far as the Mashriq is concerned, such concerns are far more immediate and significant because of the greater role of the USA in trade in industrial goods. The EU should, therefore, consider whether or not it should facilitate such relationships by encouraging global tariff reductions for Maghribi states.

Trade creation, of course, operates in both directions and, if the Maghribi economies successfully adjust to the tariff reductions they have undertaken, then there is considerable scope for trade growth through exports to the European market. However, the range of products to which this would apply is very limited – textiles and leather products in the main and greater diversification will require both direct private foreign investment and improved terms of trade. One of the major factors here is a dynamic, rather than a static, trade effect. This is the issue of encouraging economies of scale in the Maghrib so as to reduce unit labour costs and thus increase competitivity. Almost certainly this will require the culmination of rules of origin so as to increase the geographical spread of any manufacturing base and to encourage intra-industry trade within the South Mediterranean region. The EU might, therefore, consider how it could aid in this process through, for example, a know-how fund arrangement, particularly since cumulation of rules of origin has been agreed for Maghribi states since 1976, if not for the Mashriq.

At the same time, other dynamic trade effects may run counter to these objectives, particularly if they involve 'tariff-jumping investment'. Here investment in made in southern Europe in order to penetrate MNMC markets which are more accessible from Europe because of the reverse tariff preferences offered to them under the EMPI. The process is similar to the static effect of *trade deflection* where producers take advantage of tariff differences between FTA member states and could be a real danger between Maghrib and Mashriq countries in future. This would, in effect, add to the static negative trade creation effects noted above.

Of course, the negative aspects of these processes will be countered if, as the World Bank argues and is implicit in the Barcelona process, exposure to unrestricted European industrial competition generates genuine modernisation and expansion of the Maghribi industrial sector. Such modernisation and expansion, however, must feed into the expansion of trade across and within the Mediterranean, otherwise it may merely distort national economies. It is not clear that genuine economic growth will be the actual outcome, however, and, as a result, the actual economic effects of the Barcelona process should be more carefully monitored.

Exclusions from the EMPI

In two respects, the EMPI cannot not even be considered to have created a full free trade area, for crucial aspects of such an arrangement have been omitted. There is no concomitant free flow of services with rights of establishment – although this will eventually be required under WTO regulations. Nor are there arrangements for protection of intellectual property rights – again something which will eventually be required under WTO regulations. Much more significant are the omissions of free movement in agricultural goods and free movement of people – migration.

At present, agricultural imports into the EU are regulated by the regime established after Spanish and Portuguese entry into the Union in 1986, modified for Tunisia and Morocco by the terms negotiated in 1995. In effect, these simply modified some of the provisions of the earlier agreement. In essence, there are quotas, buttressed by tariffs, established for specific classes of agricultural goods outside certain specified periods when European producers are not producing the goods in question. Modifications have been obtained for Tunisian olive oil and for Moroccan tomatoes and cut flowers.

The importance of agricultural exports to Europe is underlined by the fact that Egypt's FTA agreement with the EU is being held up precisely over this point. Morocco, too, is likely to impose additional pressure for further concessions, once the current fishing agreement with Spain comes up for re-negotiation. The main reason for MNMC concern is that agricultural exports could be major stimulants for employment and would certainly contribute towards resource generation for other purposes if agricultural free trade were established.

The Union has, however, made it clear that it will not even discuss this issue seriously until five years after the bilateral agreement enters into force in each case. Furthermore, with negotiations for the accession of central European states to the EU about to begin, it is unlikely that the issue will be given much serious attention even then. Serious problems are already anticipated with the Common Agricultural Policy (CAP), both because of the Blair House agreement within the Uruguay Round of the GATT which has forced subsidy reductions on agricultural exports and because of further anticipated subsidy cuts as part of the Central European accession process. It is unlikely, therefore, that the MNMCs will receive much attention in this respect. Nevertheless, if the EMPI is to work effectively before 2010, serious thought must be given to the inclusion of agriculture within the FTAs, despite the problems that might cause for southern European states and their agricultural producers.

Migration is a far more complex issue since one of the reasons why such emphasis has been placed on economic development within the EMPI has been the desire by European states – particularly France and Germany – to end labour migration into Europe. Muslims from North Africa make up 2.3 million of the 10 million foreign workers in the EU, quite apart from the official figure of 1.56 million Turkish *Gastarbeitern* in Germany. True levels of Muslim migrants in Europe – including dependents and illegal migrants – are certainly far higher. The search for common immigrant visa regimes through the Schengen agreement has been the legal counterpart of the EU-inspired promotion of indigenous economic development within the MNMCs so as to render economic emigration unnecessary.

The evidence is, however, that this will prove to be a forlorn attempt, even if the MEPI is successful at promoting economic development. Not only will demographic pressure in North Africa continue, since employment creation – at the moment officially running at about half the demand for employment – will continue to lag behind demand. European labour demand will also grow since, by the year 2035, it is anticipated that there will be up to 56 million unfilled semi-skilled and unskilled jobs in Europe itself. Admittedly, part of this demand for labour may be satisfied by central and eastern European labour and part of the rest might well have been out-sourced to the southern Mediterranean rim. Nonetheless, there will still be an unsatisfied demand for migrant labour. This implies that Europe should address the issue of relations between economic immigrant host and supplier countries on a more permanent basis, as suggested by Tunisia and Morocco. This is a matter which should be brought under the rubric of the Barcelona process. Due weight should be given in this process to issues of xenophobia and social integration into Europe, even though the acceptance of labour migration as a permanent phenomenon runs counter to the implicit objectives of the EMPI.

Social Goods and Fiscal Regimes

Even if the above factors prove to be positive, rather than negative, in the short-to-medium term, so that there is a significant increase in GDP growth rates, attention needs to be given to the domestic consequences that the

EMPI process may have. Amongst the most important of these are the consequences for state budgets. Trade has, in the past, been an important source of government income, both through tariffs levied on imports and through export levies. Tariff regimes before liberalisation often ranged towards the 100 per cent mark. Today, in the Maghrib at least, they range between 23 and 25 per cent, generating 25 per cent of government revenues in Morocco and 40 per cent in Tunisia, and being equivalent to five per cent of GDP in Morocco and eight per cent in Tunisia. Of course, the challenge of the loss of concomitant fiscal revenues is part of the intended catalytic effect of the EMPI. This is designed to force change in MNMC economies but its short-term effects should not be underestimated.

Removal of tariff barriers, therefore, will severely affect government revenues and alternative fiscal sources will have to be found. The obvious candidate will be the taxation of domestic consumption through increases – either in the spread or in the rate – in value added tax. This indirect taxation system has been introduced or is being introduced in all southern Mediterranean rim countries as a result of IMF and World Bank pressures. Although it provides a very effective method of tax collection, it is retrogressive and does not contribute towards wealth distribution. It thus acts as a counterpart to consumer subsidies which have been largely removed under similar pressures, in increasing the tendency towards wealth inequality. The EU should, therefore, provide detailed advice on ways in which potentially retrogressive consequences of changes in fiscal regimes attendant upon the introduction of the EMPI can be ameliorated.

A further important consideration is the effect of the Barcelona process on GDP growth rates. In the final analysis, of course, this will be one of the most important factors in determining whether or not the process has been successful in economic terms. It is generally considered that growth rates at South East Asia levels (before July 1997, at least) will be necessary for real economic take-off to occur. More realistically, a doubling or trebling of the average growth rate during the 1980s – between 1.5 and two per cent per annum for the Maghrib and Mashriq combined – is anticipated, together with the replacement of the violent swings of the past for a steady progression, otherwise the EMPI will have failed to achieve one of its primary objectives.

This improvement in GDP growth rates will be necessary because one of the consequences of past economic restructuring has been to reduce government expenditure on social infrastructure – health, housing, education and social security. Yet given the great demographic pressures experienced by all the economies concerned, it is precisely in these areas that the pressure for expenditure is the greatest. Even though population growth rates have declined in the past ten years from 2.3 to 2.1 per cent per year for the Maghrib, unemployment levels – officially 16-17 per cent in Morocco and Tunisia but more realistically 25-30 per cent – remain high and educational levels amongst school-leavers are inappropriate for the types of economic activity now being encouraged.

Indeed, in Morocco in 1996, two reports – one commissioned by the government from the World Bank and the other made by the government itself – suggested that GDP growth rate would have to average 6-7 per cent per annum if social and employment conditions were not to worsen. The situation is better but not much different in Tunisia and is certainly worse in Egypt and Algeria. This increased GDP growth rate, it should be emphasised, is necessary merely to generate the necessary fiscal revenues for social expenditure, quite apart from any intensification in domestic savings or investment.

To date, export-led policies, which have been in force in Morocco since 1983 and in Tunisia since 1987, have improved GDP growth slightly but have done little to overcome both the fluctuations in GDP growth or the overall trend in growth rates. Yet these policies, as precursors to the Barcelona process, should have demonstrated the real potential of export-led growth through liberalised external regimes to stimulate economic development. It can be argued that none of them implied the stimulus that unrestricted competition with European industry should provide. This is true, yet there should have been perceptible and enduring improvements in the pattern of GPD growth, if the assumptions behind the structural adjustment process were correct. The EU should consider ways in which social expenditure can be stimulated, given the fiscal difficulties created by the FTA agreements. It should evaluate the relative effectiveness of the public and private sectors in making such provision.

Most importantly, the fluctuating pattern of GDP growth, due mainly to GDP dependence on the domestic agricultural sector and hence on climatic conditions, should have begun to disappear if trade liberalisation had provided the spur to export-oriented industry that had been anticipated. The fact that this has not occurred reinforces the argument that agricultural exports should be brought into the FTA agreements because of the stimulus they would provide to employment and to GDP growth. This is particularly important for non-traditional exports, such as horticultural and exotic agricultural products – although the environmental consequences of such activities need to be very carefully monitored. The EU should encourage diversification in agriculture and associated agro-industrial activities, as well as the transfer of agricultural technology, with a view to bringing related exports within the FTA framework earlier than planned. Advice and monitoring of the environmental consequences of such diversification should be provided under the MEDA programme.

Conditions for Foreign Investment

In North Africa, at least (although the same is substantially true for the Mashriqi non-oil economies except Israel and Turkey), the other component of economic growth under conditions of exogenous liberalisation – foreign investment – has proved difficult to attract, partly because comparative advantages are small and domestic political conditions are unattractive to investors. Quite apart from political uncertainties, legal structures for investment in the region are inadequate both in terms of the general legal systems and in terms of specific conditions for foreign investors. There is also the fact that North Africa suffers adversely from competition for private foreign investment from central and eastern Europe, particularly now that EU membership is being offered to three of the key economies there.

An additional reason for this is that there are few facilities for effective portfolio equity investment, although embryonic stock exchange facilities exist in all countries and are under rapid development in Egypt, Tunisia and Morocco. Even then, their major function is to aid the privatisation process under way in most countries as governments reduce the role of the public sector in their economies. As a one-time process, this will eventually do little to foster an active and permanent financial market. The result is that, until 1996, receipts of direct private investment have been running at about half predicted levels. It is unlikely that any of these factors can be countered without specific European intervention – as occurred in South East Asia originally through Japanese investment, although the trend in foreign inward investment underwent an up-turn in 1997 in Morocco. Attempts should be made to encourage domestic institutional change to render the southern Mediterranean rim more attractive to foreign investors. One factor here would be to encourage the application of culminated rules of origin. Another would be to revise legal systems and investment provisions. A third would be to intervene to aid the development of physical infrastructure, where necessary, to create the conditions which will attract foreign investment.

Regional Integration and the Leopard-Spot Economy

The ultimate purpose of economic development, as emphasised above, is to generate generalised improvement in the macro- and micro-economy, together with improved living-standards for the population-at-large. This implies that a domestic economy, either alone or in co-operation with neighbouring economies, creates conditions for self-sustaining development. Under the assumptions of the EMPI, this requires private sector investment, export-led industrialisation and service creation and, as a concomitant, technology transfer to help create conditions for sustained growth.

The problem is that there are few examples – outside the original industrialisation revolution in Britain – that demonstrate the validity of this model, not least because the requisite long-term investment is difficult to attract from foreign investors who have little inherent commitment to a particular country. There are also acutely important issues of governance that affect investment perceptions and these need to be advanced in all MNMC if long-term investment is to be attracted. Endogenously-generated growth is extremely difficult to achieve and, where it has been achieved, as in Latin America and more recently in parts of South East Asia, has often resulted in economic distortions and developmental crises. Indeed, the social implications of investment in environmental and human rights terms require special attention. The encouragement of foreign investment, particularly in the form of equity investment or through debt instruments, has tended to introduce financial instability and crisis – as with Mexico in 1995 and Korea in 1997.

Quite apart from the issue of international financial behaviour or failures of domestic economic management, the neo-liberal development process has often failed to provide the essential component of technology transfer that would allow a developing economy to move towards sustained development. Even direct private foreign investment has rarely produced such benefits, except in a few specialist sectors such as the oil industry, largely because out-sourced industries of the kind that it usually produces, particularly in North Africa, frequently depend on imported inputs. Ironically enough, in effect they differ little from the universally derided experience of import-substitution industries, except where their produce is primarily directed towards foreign – European – markets.

One consequence of this kind of development will be to create leopard-spot economies in North Africa. Economic growth will occur in sectors which have a direct benefit to European producers through exploitation of comparative advantage. Thus North African economies will increasingly become *satellite producers* for European consumers as a result of out-sourcing. Such sectors, however, are unlikely to have much impact on the development of fully differentiated national economies in the MNMCs and the wider national economies, therefore, will continue to operate at lower levels of economic efficiency with little synergy from these export-oriented sectors which will be effectively enclaves within them. The situation, in short, will be similar to the *maquilladora* system that has developed along the US-Mexican border region in which foreign investment exploits cheap Mexican labour to service the American economy. This is indeed what occurred with German outward investment in Tunisia in the 1960s and 1970s and in Malta under the Mintoff government – although here specific political considerations entered the picture.

Of course, this development need not necessarily be disadvantageous in the medium-to-long-term, for provided that there is a sufficient degree of technology transfer, the enclaves could become increasingly self-sufficient in terms of inputs and research-and-development or become part of autonomous transnational intra-industry chains of suppliers and consumers, so that their profits are not simply repatriated. In short, if they become parts of trans-national commercial operations, rather than simply multinational outsourcing, then genuine and lasting benefits in terms of economic growth will occur for the national economy itself. Similarly, integration into intra-industry trade – the fastest-growing sector of international trade as far as the Triad states are concerned – is also likely to have useful backwash effects on the national economies themselves.

It should also be borne in mind that such disadvantageous developments can also be prevented if the hierarchical hub-spoke North-South economic relationship implied by the FTA agreements can be overcome. It is for this reason that eventual South-South economic integration is so important. However, the way in which this is achieved is also crucial since immediate regional integration in the South will be difficult to achieve – as the Arab Maghrib Union made clear. Thus a multi-bilateral approach to the problem of integration is indicated, as is currently being explored by Morocco, Tunisia and Egypt.

At the same time, however, the problem of inequalities is distribution and diffusion of such economic benefits remains very worrying. The political implications of this are bound in the short-term to increase levels of social discontent and thus threaten the abilities of governments to sustain support for such policies. In some respects, the *distribution* of economic benefit is more important that its *generation*, at least in terms of political perceptions, and governments cannot remain indefinitely indifferent to this consideration. There is, therefore, an interest in engaging in the investment and development process – as, indeed, occurred in South-East Asia – in order to support development which maximises employment and stimulates training as well as creating mature economic structures. The EU should consider combining with MNMC governments to create a system of 'orientation planning', as was done in France in the 1960s and 1970s and in South-East Asia in the 1970s. This would seek to mitigate the effects of 'leopard-spot' economic growth.

Of course, one solution to this problem would be to create an integrated economic area which would permit self-sustained economic growth. Indeed, this is one of the ultimate objectives of the Barcelona process. However, it is not due to occur until after 2010, whereas it could be argued that it should occur before since it becomes an essential condition for the economic aspect of the process to succeed. The danger is that, if the process of South-South regional economic integration is not accelerated, the 'leopard-spot' economic patterns that will develop – which emphasise North-South trade links – will become the permanent pattern of economic interaction for the future.

It has to be recognised, in this context, that South-South economic interactions in the past have been minimal – at between one and two per cent of total trade, except in the case of Tunisia, where it reached seven per cent, largely because of border trade with Libya. Attempts have been made to counter this in the past, most notably with the Arab Maghrib Union (UMA). The UMA experiment foundered, however, on the rocks of political tensions, although there were also apprehensions over its economic plans. The Middle East peace process, too, generated a complex economic integration process, based on the REDWG group and the MENA economic summit process. Quite apart from a significant degree of economic incoherence, the political motivations of this initiative have proved its undoing and it is unlikely, in its current form, to offer a means of genuine economic development.

This does not mean, however, that attempts of this kind should be abandoned. Indeed, recent economic agreements between Israel and Turkey indicate that there is an awareness of the need for such integration. There have been similar moves between Syria, Egypt and the Gulf Co-operation Council states – although the political motivation of this initiative will probably condemn it to ineffectiveness. There is every reason, therefore, to encourage the revival of a regional framework as a vehicle primarily for encouraging economic integration, rather than for regional security.

The Political Issues

Economic issues in themselves are only part of the Barcelona process, although far less attention was devoted to the political/security and cultural/social baskets of the process in the original Declaration. In part this reflects the relative ineffectiveness of the EU's common foreign and security policy (CFSP) and the unwillingness of EU member-states to engage in initiatives which are fraught with diplomatic difficulties. It also, however, reflects the strange ambivalence towards a redefinition of the international arena that characterises international relations today. Although old assumptions about state sovereignty still dominate the diplomatic scene, there are increasingly fewer such inhibitions about the global economic process.

One reason for this is that economic theorists have increasingly strayed into the cultural and political domain. Rational choice theory and the economic theory of politics are increasingly used to justify political and cultural behaviour, to the detriment of more traditional explanations. Indeed, such views have achieved mantra-like status in some arenas so that the scepticism that should be innate in any objective enquiry has been abandoned in favour of the new market-directed revelation. Application of such concepts to the political and cultural situation in North Africa should, however, be avoided, for the current crises there demonstrate their irrelevance.

Europe and its Periphery

In part, also, this attitude reflects the growing acceptance of the identity between a global economy and 'globalisation' – although there is a very important cultural component to this concept. It is also worth considering the extent to which globalisation is a genuinely new phenomenon – at least in its economic context for, in cultural terms, there are more substantial arguments in favour of such a view – or even relevant to what is actually happening today. As other papers in this collection make clear, it may well be that the genuinely new development is not 'globalisation' but 'regionalisation' and that it is for this reason, rather than because of genuine concerns over security issues. On this reading, then, the Barcelona process is merely the consequence of European attention being directed towards its geographic and cultural periphery.

This is not an insignificant issue. If, in reality, Europe's claimed anxieties over regional security are exaggerated, then the assumptions behind its periphery policies can be re-examined. One of these reflects relations with the United States – partly because of the Middle East peace process and partly because of European defence anxieties. At present, despite claims about issues of Mediterranean collective security, the reality of EU defence policy is closely tied to its attitude towards NATO and the WEU – and, behind these, stands the knotty question of European links with the United States. Similarly, it is primarily consideration of EU-US links that inhibits new approaches over the question of peace in the Middle East and continued formal support for the MENA economic summit process, despite the implicit contradiction that exists with the Barcelona process itself. The EU should reconsider its strategic concerns in the Mediterranean and the assumptions that guide its approach towards relations with the region and third party actors. This should be a priority since it is crucial to any proper development of the non-economic components of the Barcelona process.

Transparency and Rent-Seeking

One aspect of the economic process that does have very acute political implications is the question of the transparency of the indigenous economic process in MNMCs. This is related to the Barcelona process – as it is to the

Washington Consensus – through the process of foreign investment. Foreign investors require transparency both over the issue of evaluating an investment and for corporate reasons in terms of accountancy. As a result, although it is not directly part of the FTA agreements, southern Mediterranean rim states will increasingly have to adopt European accountancy and reporting procedures. This, of course, is not a process limited to the Mediterranean but is one of the genuinely global developments in the modern world.

Its political relevance in North Africa – and, by extension, in the Middle East – is that such transparency attacks the autonomy of established private sector elites. These elites, whose economic power is often the result of political patronage, are often profoundly anti-competitive in their attitude towards the economic process. Their benefits have often been derived from rent-seeking, rather than market-oriented economic activities, and their retention of economic position owes much to their role within the political structure of the countries concerned. It remains to be seen to what degree the EMPI, by virtue of the economic assumptions built into it, will be able to end such behaviour. Certainly the 1996 *Campagne d'Assainissement* in Morocco and the commitments of the new government there suggest this may happen.

As a result such groups, whilst welcoming the potential access to the European market, are unwilling to abandon their entrenched political advantages and thus resist genuine economic transparency. By doing so, they lend to the Barcelona process a political dimension that was never anticipated. This elite resistance to economic transparency is articulated in both economic and political terms in that, provided that it can continue to dominate the political process, it can avoid economic threat. The coalition between the economic elite and the Ben Ali regime in Tunisia or Driss Basri, the Minister of the Interior in Morocco, for example, is most instructive! The EU should engage in support for restructuring of legal regimes to introduce appropriate accountancy and disclosure standards. It should also encourage competitivity policies designed to counter entrenched economic privilege.

The occultation of political and economic transparency in this way, however, also vitiates measures taken to counter corruption or the illegal sectors of the formal economy. In the case of Morocco, for example, drug exports – worth $1.8-$2 bn annually – have been estimated to earn close to half as much again as the total visible export account. Although these funds do not figure in the official balance of payments, they certainly contribute to the balance on the external account! However, the process by which they enter the domestic economy has serious implications for administration and the political process.

At the same time, the wider informal economy is a vital component within southern Mediterranean rim economies. It is conventionally estimated to be equivalent to 40 per cent of the formal economy in Morocco and of comparable size in Egypt, although somewhat smaller in Tunisia. It is often associated with other foreign currency-earning activities such as tourism but, because of its informal nature, it makes no contribution to government finances. It would be of considerable significance if it could be integrated into the formal economy, for it would ease issues of social discontent over the inequalities created by economic restructuring and liberalisation whilst, at the same time, improving fiscal regimes and public financial structures. The EU should seek to aid attempts to integrate informal sector economic activity into the formal economy in MNMCs in order to improve economic performance evaluation and fiscal standards.

Culture, Democracy and Development

It is a moot point as to whether the democratic process is essential to economic development – although effective systems of governance certainly are. Insofar as investors, both domestic and foreign, are primarily concerned with political stability and reproducible investment conditions, it is not self-evident that these can only be provided by a democratic political system. Furthermore, since the FTA process inherent in the EMPI is likely, in the short-term at least, to intensify social discontent, it is likely that repressive political policies will be inevitable. There thus appears to be a certain discordance between the call for democratic government in the Barcelona Declaration and the emphasis on economic development along neo-liberal lines. Consent, in short, is not a necessary concomitant of free trade, particularly when economic inequalities are likely to be intensified.

At the same time, it is also clear that repressive, unrepresentative government is a further factor of social discontent and political instability. Consent, in short, at some level is an essential part of the economic development process. There is an additional problem, too. This is that allowing the factors of production, particularly labour, to compete in the marketplace without regulation – whilst desirable from an economic point of view – is undesirable from a political point of view because it, too, will stimulate political instability. Governments, to achieve consent, must demonstrate a degree of social justice in the ways in which they organise or monitor economic affairs; yet this may run counter to the interests of investors.

One solution to this has been the corporatist model used in Singapore and another has been the repressive policies followed in South Korea in the 1970s and 1980s. The Singaporean model succeeded in terms of its results; it did provide general economic benefit. The South Korean model eventually had to cede a degree of accountability, although that is once again under threat. In North Africa, elite interest has combined with regime preference in Tunisia to produce a quite unnecessary degree of repression, whilst a similar but much more extreme process has produced catastrophe in Algeria. In Morocco, a degree of accountability has been permitted, but at the cost of an 'adjusted' political process that has sought to reassure elites that their interests would not be threatened.

In the final analysis, however, popular consent and government accountability cannot be avoided, if the economic reform process is to succeed. This requires establishment of genuinely independent rules of law and the provision of social justice. It also requires some system of popular participation in the decision-making process, although the forms by which that should be done have to respond to indigenous preferences. This aspect of the Barcelona process cannot, therefore, be ignored – in the interests of accelerating the process of economic restructuring – although the means by which it is encouraged by the EU require far greater attention than accorded in the past.

Foreign investors, too, need to recognise that the means by which they participate in the productive process in North Africa cannot be governed simply by their experiences elsewhere. The process of management, like the political process, must respond to indigenous cultural imperatives. This is, indeed, a microcosm of the process by which essential popular consent for the process of economic restructuring can be achieved and by which appropriate levels of economic efficiency can be maintained.

Conclusions

The EMPI falls within the neo-liberal framework of the Washington Consensus and cannot, in effect, deliver its promise of economic development without the concomitant measures proposed for North African economic restructuring by the World Bank and the IMF. At the same time, it is the only effective panacea on offer to the Mediterranean basin as far as economic development is concerned. However, as it stands, it is unlikely to achieve its economic objectives.

Specific steps need to be taken to ensure its success, mainly by the European Union – although, admittedly, EU member-states will generally be reluctant to engage in any revision which is both far-reaching and potentially involves increased cost. The most important of these steps are probably the following:

- accelerate plans for the expansion of the Barcelona process to include agricultural goods within the FTA arrangement,

- facilitate expenditure on social and physical infrastructure and on appropriate training,
- encourage domestic reforms designed to stimulate economic transparency and independent judicial systems,
- encourage review and expansion of domestic fiscal systems to compensate for tariff losses,
- consider measures to minimise disincentives such as trade creation, diversion and deflection,
- consider means to stimulate foreign investment, including expansions to the MEDA programme,
- encourage political transparency, accountability, good governance and the growth of civil society, and
- promote South-South regional economic integration as a priority.

Behind many of these proposals is a further implicit requirement that the fundamental economic and political principles on which the Barcelona process is based should be reviewed. It would be advisable, for example, to reconsider the assumptions of neo-classical and neo-liberal economic theory because of the potential danger of prescriptive failure. It would also be wise to reconsider the assumptions about international relations in the Mediterranean, for these will, in the medium-term, have a profound influence on the outcome of the process. Even though Europe's 'southern flank' may be far less significant today than its interests in 'eastward expansion', the innate problems of the South Mediterranean region and their influence on future European energy provision mean that they cannot be marginalised in the context of the European, let alone the Maghribi and Mashriqi, future.

References

Mediterranean Politics (Spring 1996), 1/1; (Summer 1997). 2/1.

'Estabilidad y Conflictos en el Mediterráneo'. (September 1997), *Revista Cidob d'Afers*, 37.

'European Foreign Policy' in *Cambridge Review of International Affairs*, X, 2 (Winter/Spring 1997).

Bensidoun, I and Chevallier, A. (1996), *Europe-Méditerranée: le pari de l'ouverture*, Paris, Economica.

Sid Ahmed, A. (1995), *Un projet pour l'Algérie: eléments pour un réel Partenariat Euro-Méditerranéen*, Paris, Editions Publisud.

Ouallalou, F. (1996), *Après Barcelone...le Maghreb est nécessaire*, Casablanca, Les Editions Toukbal; Paris, L'Harmattan.

Toye, J. (1993), *Dilemmas of Development*, Oxford, Blackwell.

Brohman, J. (1996), *Popular Development: Rethinking the Theory and Practice of Development*, Oxford, Blackwell.

Article Abstracts

Euro-Med Free Trade Area For 2010: Whom Will it Benefit
Eberhard Rhein

In Barcelona in November 1995, the declaration signed by the Foreign Ministers of the 15 EU countries and their counterparts from 12 Mediterranean countries agreed on the progressive establishment of a vast Euro-Mediterranean free trade area, to be completed by 2010. Essentially, this initiative was inspired by the 1993 Oslo agreement and by positive developments in Eastern Europe which suggested that regional stability could be encouraged by economic co-operation through the back-door of free trade. The concept of Euro-Mediterranean free trade, far from being a purely mercantile vision, is therefore part of a more comprehensive strategy aiming, in time, to transform the Mediterranean into an area of peace and prosperity. The Euro-Mediterranean Partnership Initiative (EMPI) design defies all historical references in scope and complexity with no previous free trade agreements (EU, EU-EFTA, EU-Israel, EFTA, CEFTA, NAFTA, LAFTA, MERCOSUR, ASEAN, GCC) able to constitute a truly valid reference.

Development Economics, the Washington Consensus and the Euro-Mediterranean Partnership Initiative
Diana Hunt

In 1995, the European Union (EU) and the states of North Africa agreed to embark on a process designed to redefine their economic relations. This paper seeks to contextualise these changes from the perspective of development theory. It explores the relationship between the Euro-Mediterranean Partnership Initiative (or EMPI) and the 'Washington Consensus' and, in doing so, reviews some of the key aspects of the underlying theoretical debate in contemporary development economics.

Global Euro-Mediterranean Partnership
Nadia Salah

The purpose of this analysis is not just to describe Moroccan-European relations, nor even to separate the good from the bad aspects of the agreement signed in Barcelona in November 1995. Instead it seeks to anticipate the changes that could result from the agreement in a country as complicated as Morocco. It is possible that the agreement with the European Union will serve as a point of reference, or even as a catalyst, for these changes in which–and this is a new phenomenon–the actors are no longer the ministers or senior officials who served as negotiators, but the simple mass of people for whom Europe is, in the common parlance, 'Rropa'.

The European Challenge to North African Economies: The Downside to the Euro-Med Policy
Jon Marks

This paper seeks to situate the Euro-Mediterranean Partnership Initiative (EMPI) in the context of wider European Union policy and to outline the opportunities and dangers confronting the Barcelona Declaration's southern Mediterranean signatories. It focuses on the three Maghrib states which are embarking on the new EU Association Agreements: Tunisia, Morocco and Algeria, highlighting the potential negative aspects in order to provoke debate on the Euro-Med policy. The writer is convinced that understanding the downside to the Euro-Med policy is essential if efforts by Europe and other Western powers to improve the economic and political conditions of North African countries are not to have unduly negative consequences for those they are trying to help.

Globalisation versus Regionalisation?
Grahame Thompson

Although globalisation and regionalisation are often thought to be contradictory processes, the argument posited here is that this is not necessarily the case. Whilst not contradictory they are argued to be *alternative* trajectories for the international economy. Furthermore, it is the relationship between multilateralism and regionalism that is the key one although the discussion begins by differentiating between globalisation and regionalisation since this is the main distinction made in popular accounts. Since globalisation has become a central concept in current analyses of the international system a number of definitions are first provided. This is followed by an exploration of the idea of regionalisation and its associated term of regionalism. The character and nature of the contemporary international economy is then considered and, in conclusion, some relatively unsystematic comments made about where Europe fits into the overall picture.

Regionalisation and the Mediterranean
Alfred Tovias

This paper deals with the systemic implications of one of the central aspects of the Euro-Mediterranean Partnership Initiative, namely the creation of industrial Free Trade Areas between the EU and all Mediterranean Non Member Countries (MNMCs) by the year 2010, as well a proposal for concluding the same kind of agreements among MNMCs themselves. This specific subject has not yet been treated by the literature dealing with the economic effects of the Euro-Mediterranean Partnerships and a number of related questions present themselves which this paper will attempt to explore, and to critically assess.

Free Trade Agreements in the Mediterranean: A Regional Path Towards Liberalisation
Bernard Hoekman

A major policy issue facing many of the countries in the Mediterranean region is to achieve and sustain levels of economic growth high enough to raise real per capita incomes of the population. The need for reform has been recognised by many governments in the region and significant efforts have been made to liberalise trade, facilitate investment and reduce transactions costs for the private sector. This paper discusses one dimension of these efforts: the Euro-Mediterranean Partnership Initiative (EMPI) that most Mediterranean governments have, or are seeking to negotiate, with the European Union (EU). These agreements commit governments to free trade with the EU over a 12 year transition period and key questions that arise in this connection are the likely economic consequences of implementation of these agreements and whether these regional initiatives will create incentives to pursue the more general liberalisation that is required if MENA countries are to become more integrated into the world economy.

Globalisation, Culture and Management Systems
Riadh Zghal

For the past twenty years, researchers and managers have questioned the universality of concepts of management, on the one hand, and the pertinence of contingent factors linked to the environment in determining different managerial models and styles in organisations, on the other. It seems that there are as many arguments to justify the universality of effective management criteria as there are to account for local variables in the explanation or the prescription of effective management methods. This paper examines these two different trends of management theory by examining a number of developed and developing countries and making particular reference to the new context of globalisation.

Social Feasibility and Costs of the Free Trade Zone
Azzam Mahjoub

Since the middle of the 1980s, Tunisia has been operating a programme of adjustment and economic liberalisation designed to establish market mechanisms, liberalised external trade, stimulus to the private sector and the privatisation of the state sector, effectively making progressive integration with the world economy irreversible. Tunisia's adoption of a free trade area with the European Union thus forms part of the logic of structural adjustment to generate growth and greater economic efficiency. At the same time, however, the free trade area with the European Union should introduce significant deregulation within the system created by government as part of the liberalisation process. In short, even if Tunisia's choice of openness towards the world economy is strategically irreversible, it must also be marked by practical realism reflecting the means employed to achieve this objective. The free trade area could significantly accelerate this process without identifying and subsequently mobilising the means required to manage a transition which itself will brutally and definitively influence the major parameters of the economy. It is these aspects of Tunisia's engagement with the European Union and the wider international context that this paper will address.

The Uses and Misuses of 'Culture' – A Comment
Kevin Dwyer

This paper explores notions of culture and the relationship between culture and other spheres of human activity. It takes as its starting point recent discussion concerning how notions of culture are being used to foster hostility and aggression and to defend new forms of exclusion, and argues that these belligerent uses are in part a result of 'billiard-ball' views of culture: that cultures are self-contained and relatively stable entities. To counter this, the author argues that 'cultures' should be seen as 'constructed', elaborated in particular situations from particular perspectives, with an inherently self-reflexive and self-critical component. This helps us see 'culture' as a dynamic arena where meanings are in competition and are negotiated through controversy and struggle, and encourages us to question the positions from which constructions of 'culture' are made, as well as the programs these constructions imply. This also enables us to avoid essentialist and determinist views – that culture, simplistically characterised, makes development and change difficult or perhaps impossible. The paper uses these arguments to comment on one of the preceding papers in this workshop which addressed the relationship between culture and economic activity and its application to the case of management in Tunisia.

Latin America's Path From Backwardness to Development
Joseph L. Love

Because of the enormous scope of the period and region under discussion, this examination of the economic development of Latin America is confined to Brazil, Mexico, and Argentina, plus Chile, which together were the most industrialised nations by the early twentieth century, and remained so later. The extent to which Latin America's relative backwardness can be explained by the colonial experience, the nature of the nineteenth-century export-oriented experience, and the way various countries tried to catch up with the West by industrialising will form a major part of the assessment. Furthermore, an attempt will also be made to determine the extent to which this condition was externally imposed, i.e., determined by foreign investment patterns and inducements to engage in certain types of trade, and to what extent the backwardness was due to internal socio-economic factors.

The Lessons of South East Asia's Miraculous Growth and Fall From Growth
Jonathan Rigg

Until 1997 the growth economies of Southeast and East Asia represented, in the view of the World Bank and many governments and mainstream economists, paragons of development and exemplars of 'best practice'. As such they also appeared to offer lessons for the rest of the developing world. This view begs a number of important questions, of which three in particular will be addressed here. First, what contributed to this so-styled 'miracle'? It is one thing to observe that there 'must be something' that we can learn; quite another to identify what that 'something' is. Second, to what degree can the miracle thesis be refuted? And third, what specific lessons, if any, does the Asian miracle hold for other countries of the developing world? In other words, how far is the miracle (or elements of it) replicable. Since 1997 economic wisdom has, apparently, been turned on its head as many of these former fast-growth economies have entered a period of economic crisis and contraction. The paper also addresses, therefore, the implications of the crisis on our understanding of Asian growth and whether the 'lessons' to be learned have, in the process, changed.

Lessons to be Learned by the Mediterranean: Jordanian Development, the MENA Process, Water and Value Systems
John Roberts

This paper examines the problems of trying to secure sustainable economic development in a generally hostile political climate and makes some suggestions as to how Middle Eastern and North African states might begin to address some of these problems. In relation to this, an assessment is given of the Middle East and North Africa Summit (MENA) process and the reasons behind its eventual collapse. To highlight the need for substantial investment in utilities and how this can prompt the steady privatisation of utilities in most partner countries, the example of Jordan's experience with water reforms is looked at in some detail. Finally, the paper raises the question of culture and value systems and using comparisons with Asian economies asks to what extent a societies breakthrough to long-term economic development can be attributed to a unique nature.

Security Implications of the EMPI for Europe
Claire Spencer

The Euro-Mediterranean Partnership Initiative (EMPI) marks a new departure for the European Union (EU) in the sphere of European security co-operation with adjacent regions. The three chapters of the Barcelona Declaration of November 1995 indicate that for the first time, non-military (or 'soft') aspects of security have received as much attention as more traditional military-based (or 'hard') approaches to security in European policy towards the Mediterranean. It is this recognition of the importance of integrating conventional security approaches with policies to redress the root causes of social, political and economic instability in the region which marks the real novelty of the security provisions of the EMPI. The inclusion of measures within the EMPI for restricting arms proliferation in the Mediterranean region, however, does not shield the fact that the EU's strength and main focus still lies in its ability to channel and promote economic and financial assistance. This paper will examine the implications for the EU of attempts to diversify its security agenda in ways which complement existing initiatives in the security field.

The Changing Mediterranean Security Environment: A Trans-Atlantic Perspective
Ian O. Lesser

The Mediterranean is set to become more important to the United States as well as Europe, and more central to transatlantic relations. But many political and intellectual obstacles will need to be overcome for a more concerted approach to Mediterranean security. The essence of the transatlantic interest in addressing the region's problems will be the wider interest of relatively secure, wealthy societies in managing relations with far less secure, less developed societies on their periphery. At the same time, states along the southern shores of the Mediterranean will seek means of addressing their own security challenges, both internal and external. Their success or failure will have increasingly direct meaning for European security and the nature of the US engagement in and around the Mediterranean.

Framework Scenarios for the Mediterranean Region
Oliver Sparrow

Europe looks to the entities which lie on its borders and, for the most part, feels unsure of their prospects and propensities. Some of these entities can be best thought of as regions, and some as commercial, cultural and historical networks of interaction. Still others have to be viewed in terms of their special properties or strikingly distinctive characteristics: Israel, for example, or Libya. Complex neighbours, such as the United States, require scrutiny at all of these levels. The aim of the scenario-generator is to find the right level of abstraction to provide insight into the key issues, without undermining the special cases, and the goal of this text is to establish the bare bones of such a model. It will take two key variables: the first is concerned with adaptive responses which the Southern Mediterranean region may make to the challenges innate in their individual paths to economic development. The second is related to the efficacy and ambition of Europe's efforts – and the efforts of other forces at large in the world–to modify these responses. In order to explore this, it is first necessary to sketch out the implications of achieving the conditions necessary for a radical change in the pace of development and, secondly, we need some insight into the shape of the world (and of Europe within it) in the 2015 period Finally, the key variables can be brought together to define a broad framework within which these complex issues can intersect.

The Euro-Mediteranean Partnership Initiative: Problems and Prospects
George Joffé

The Euro-Mediterranean Partnership Initiative (EMPI) is now just over three years old – since its formal proclamation at the Barcelona Conference in November 1995 – and this is, perhaps, an appropriate moment to review its problems and prospects. As enunciated in Barcelona, the process was designed to create a zone of peace and prosperity in the Mediterranean basin. Its inspiration was clearly derived from the Helsinki Conference of 1975 which ultimately led to the end of the Cold War, but which was also mediated through the CSCM (Conference on Security and Cooperation in the Mediterranean) proposal made in 1990 by Spain and Italy. Its objectives were expressed through three baskets of measures – on political change and collective security; social and cultural issues; and economic development – The economic dimension was the most detailed, largely because of the European Union's own pre-occupations and its belief that increased prosperity in the Southern Mediterranean was the best way of resolving the multi-faceted crisis there. This paper is intended to set the scene for such a discussion of progress to date and will focus primarily on the economic aspects of the Barcelona process, since this was the primary focus of the original declaration, although it will inevitably stray into the security-political and social-cultural aspects of the process because they are often intimately linked to the underlying concern of economic restructuring, liberalisation and development.

Index

www.ingramcontent.com/pod-product-compliance
Ingram Content Group UK Ltd.
Pitfield, Milton Keynes, MK11 3LW, UK
UKHW020433010325
455677UK00029B/1130